I0165513

On the Rim of the Sea

Mike Robbins

**THIRD
RAIL**

On the Rim of the Sea

THE MORAL RIGHT OF THE AUTHOR HAS BEEN ASSERTED

NO PART OF THIS BOOK MAY BE USED OR REPRODUCED
IN ANY MANNER WHATSOEVER WITHOUT WRITTEN PER-
MISSION FROM THE PUBLISHER EXCEPT IN THE CASE OF
BRIEF QUOTATIONS EMBODIED IN CRITICAL ARTICLES OR
REVIEWS.

© Mike Robbins 2022
ISBN: 978-0-9914374-8-1

Cover picture:
Ivan Konstantinovich Aivazovsky (1817-1900),
The Wave (1889)

**THIRD
RAIL**

Third Rail Books
thirdrailbooks@gmail.com

Acknowledgements

I would like to thank Samuel Astbury, Patric Devitt, Neil Monk and Kevin Wilson for their comments on the manuscript, which were very helpful. I would also like to thank Neil for his suggestions with regard to the chapter on detective fiction, which was completed after the rest of the book. Thanks are also due to Roger Hall for valuable advice as the project neared completion.

About the author

Mike Robbins is a journalist turned development worker. He is the author of *Even the Dead are Coming* (2009), a memoir of Sudan; *Crops and Carbon* (2011), on agriculture and climate change; and *The Nine Horizons* (2014), a pen-portrait of some of the countries in which he has worked and travelled since 1987. He has also written three works of fiction, *The Lost Baggage of Silvia Guzmán* (2014), *Three Seasons* (2014), and *Dog!* (2015).

Foreword

For some years now, I have been writing pieces about books. I generally select two or more books that cover a related subject or period, so that they can be looked at in a single piece that forms a cohesive whole.

I'm not sure to what extent one chooses the books one reads; maybe they choose you. But at some point I realised that the books I had been reading were a picture of the last century. So I have gathered them together for that purpose. I hope that they'll give a slightly quirky view of the last 110-odd years. General history books don't always say much about (for example) the last sailing ships, Chinese labourers on the Western Front, the boom in detective fiction or Yehudi Menuhin on TV. This book does, and I hope it will inspire some to read the authors for themselves.

The collection was too eclectic, and some of my favourite pieces have had to go. Even so, what's left is a little lopsided. I'm all too aware that this book is biased towards the first half of the 20th century; there is nothing in here about the Cold War period, for instance – a point raised by a friend who reviewed the manuscript; like me he grew up in that era. Maybe that is something for a later edition.

These pieces may seem rather random. However, they have one thing in common; they use one or more books (or in one case, TV programmes) to give a picture of a given time or incident. If a further thread does tie these pieces together, it is that most of the books show us the last 100 years of history through the eyes of individuals that lived it. After all, history isn't a collective experience; it's what happened to us and those close to us.

The book's title, *On the Rim of the Sea*, was inspired by a passage in the splendid *Instead of a Letter*, by the late Diana Athill. In it she describes how, as a child, she shocked her grandmother by talking of life as being in a bowl, floating on the sea; provided one stayed at the bottom of the bowl, one might be serene – but every now and then the motion of the sea flung one up the side and forced one to a view of "dangerous, cold grey water" that would be unbearable. That, she said, was the origin of madness.

Is it? The years covered in this book (roughly, 1912 to the present) certainly showed us more of the sea than we should have liked. As I write (March 2022), the cold grey water is back with a vengeance. But it has not always been that way. This book has its darker bits, but there were lighter times and I hope the reader will find a few of them in the pages that follow.

Besides, we're masters of our own destiny, aren't we? If it was a harsh time, that was the century we made; what we do with the next one is a matter for us.

New York City
March 2022

Contents

The Last Days of Sail

On March 17 1894, *Scientific American* had its usual varied diet for the curious and intelligent. There was a report on a cablecar service over the Tennessee River in Knoxville. Figurines in Oriental dress had been unearthed in Mexico's Oaxaca state. The number of immigrants landing in New York had been down in 1893 (the largest group was Italian, at nearly 70,000).

Tucked away in an inside page, however, was a story that was bigger than it seemed. The Arthur Sewell & Co. yard at Bath, Maine, had launched the *Dirigo* – the first steel sailing ship to be built in the USA. The article reported that she was 330ft overall, of 45ft beam, and was to carry 4,500 dwt in cargo. "The vessel is rigged as a four-masted ship ... and will spread about 13,000 yards of canvas," the *Scientific American* reported. "In the early spring she will be fitted for sea and will load at pier 19, East River, New York, for San Francisco, Cal."

Westward round the Horn, then, against the prevailing wind; a baptism of fire. But this was an important ship. Eugene Chamberlain, the USA's Commissioner of Navigation, clearly thought so. Patricia M. Higgins, in her *Hidden History of Midcoast Maine*, quotes him as saying that the *Dirigo's* construction represented "the beginning of a new industry in this country. The ship of the future is to be of steel, and the introduction of that material is necessary to the maintenance of, for foreign trade, a fleet of large sailing vessels."

But neither the *Scientific American* nor, probably, Chamberlain fully grasped that the iron or steel-hulled sailing ship, or windjammer, was not a new era for sail. It was its brilliant apotheosis.

The windjammer's time was brief. Today we celebrate them as "tall ships", and those still at sea are usually training vessels. In their heyday, they were hard ships on which to work. Usually four-masted barques with steel hulls, their era started sometime in the late 19th century. They are not to be confused with the clippers, which were smaller but carried far bigger crews, enabling them to be driven hard in poor weather, and were therefore much faster; their time was already really over when the *Dirigo* was launched. The windjammer's purpose was not to fly to Tilbury with the first of the year's tea. It was to carry non-perishable bulk cargo such as coal, grain and nitrates at lower cost than the new steamships, by using the prevailing winds, and taking as long as they needed on the journey. When the windjammer era began, this made sense; steamers still needed frequent stops for water and bunkering, and were often quite slow.

By the 1920s, much had changed – and in time the motorship appeared, cleaner, more economical and easier to run. The wind-jammers fought harder and harder to compete; costs were slashed, crews were small – sometimes almost too small to work the vessel – and the conditions on board were basic. Yet they represented the last flowering of a technology that had evolved from the time humans had gone to sea. They were also romantic; and they have left their mark on literature as no container ship will ever do.

*

The *Dirigo* played its part in this. In March 1911 writer Jack London and his second wife, Charmian Kittredge London, boarded her in Baltimore, bound westward round the Horn to Seattle. The voyage would provide the backdrop for one of London's last novels. *The Mutiny of the Elsinore*. Written and edited with help from Kittredge, it was published in 1914, only two years before his death. It isn't one of his most famous books, but it may deserve to be; it is memorable.

The book's plot (without spoilers) is as follows: It is March 1913 and a successful but world-weary young playwright, John Pathurst, seeks refreshment and inspiration by going round the Horn as a passenger on a windjammer from Baltimore to Seattle. He knows the *Elsinore* may take months over the voyage, but that's fine. He has paid highly for his passage, and is accompanied by his manservant; he intends to be comfortable. But the rounding of the Horn is drawn-out and dangerous, and the ship is nearly lost. Moreover the regime aboard the *Elsinore* is harsh, and the crew are a bunch of no-good lowlifes who will eventually mutiny against it. Pathurst's luxury passage will turn into a nightmare.

The long voyage south-east towards West Africa and then south-west to the Horn is used to build up character and tension, so that by the time the *Elsinore* gets stuck in westerlies off the Horn, you know there's a disaster waiting to happen. It helps that London does a fair job of evoking what life in a windjammer must have been like. He can do this because this book was drawn, at least in part, from life. London and Kittredge boarded in Baltimore very much as Pathurst does in the book, and Kittredge later described the voyage in *Book of Jack London*, a memoir of her husband that she published a few years after his death. The *Elsinore* is clearly the *Dirigo* and the novel includes a number of incidents that that are in Kittredge's account. Most are trivial (London/Pathurst's fox terrier, Possum; an attack of hives; the chickens in the hut amidships). One or two are major. For example, in the novel, the captain dies on passage off the Horn. On the Londons' real voyage he did fall sick there, and died shortly after the ship reached Seattle. The captain and mate in the book also seem to match those of the *Dirigo*. The captain, according to Kitteredge, was: "The fast disappearing type of lean New England aristocrat, who always presented himself on deck immaculately attired... The calm kingliness of his character was in cool contrast to that of the Mate, Fred Mortimer, hot-hearted, determined ... driver of a crew that was composed ...of landlubbers and weaklings."

London takes these two officers and exaggerates their characteristics, and those of the crew too. As the latter board in Baltimore: " ...I encountered a few laggards who had not yet gone into the forecastle. These were the worse for liquor, and a more wretched, miserable, disgusting group of men I had never seen in any slum. Their clothes were rags. Their faces were bloated, bloody, and dirty. I won't say they were villainous. They were merely filthy and vile. They were vile of appearance, of speech, and action." And later: "I ...wondered where such a mass of human wreckage could have been obtained. There was something wrong with all of them. Their bodies were twisted, their faces distorted, and almost without exception they were under-sized."

Long before the mutiny of the title, life on the *Elsinore* becomes a struggle of two worlds – the gracious, comfortable world of the officers and crew in the poop, dining pleasantly every night, the Mate, Pike, playing classical gramophone records with enthusiasm; and the forecastle, full of degenerate wretches that Pike controls with an iron fist and great savagery. Bit by bit the *Elsinore* seems to appear a microcosm of a divided, unfair society. Is this what Jack London was trying to say in this book? Or is there something more sinister being said? Pathurst is the narrator, and his sense of superiority expresses itself in a belief that the Captain and the Mate are superior beings, and the crew scum. His class is thus destined to dominate.

Meanwhile a number of the crew meet with nasty ends even before the mutiny. During it, two die quite horribly, torn apart by giant albatrosses: "A great screeching and squawking arose from the winged things of prey as they strove for the living meat. And yet, somehow, I was not very profoundly shocked. These were the men whom I had seen eviscerate [a] shark and toss it overboard, and shout with joy as they watched it devoured alive by its brethren. They had played a violent, cruel game with the things of life, and the things of life now played upon them the same violent, cruel game."

Oh dear. Men born to rule over their inferiors, and nature red in tooth and claw. It's the narrator's voice, but London seems to use it with great enthusiasm (with references to the captain as a Samurai warrior, and occasional references to Nietzsche). It's just a little too genuine, and Pathurst's views are not discredited by the way the book ends. Jack London was a socialist all his life, but was there also a whiff of fascism about him?

George Orwell thought so. Writing about an earlier London book, *The Iron Heel*, he commented that London was "temperamentally ...very different from the majority of Marxists. With his love of violence and physical strength, his belief in 'natural aristocracy', his animal-worship and exaltation of the primitive, he had in him what one might fairly call a Fascist strain" (*Prophecies of Fascism*, 1940). In *The Mutiny of the Elsinore*, we see this; it's also evident in his earlier and greater book, *The Sea Wolf*. However, Orwell didn't say London actually *was* a fascist. Rather, he thought these traits made London better able to understand the nature of the ruling class, and that far from espousing fascism, he understood its dangers before it existed (*The Iron Heel*, published in 1908, describes a fascistic dystopia). It is more likely that London is using Pathurst to warn how the ruling class really think. Still, the earliest Nazis appealed to a certain type on the left as well as the right. Reading *The Mutiny of the Elsinore*, you do wonder whether, had London lived into the Fascist era, he might have been swept up in it all.

That apart, *The Mutiny of the Elsinore* is quite a read. The description of the ship as it fights to round the Horn is excellent, bringing forth a picture of a great steel ship, its sides streaked with rust, burdened by a cargo of thousands of tons of coal, wallowing in the huge seas as the sun comes and goes behind fast-moving, hostile clouds. The crew are also well-drawn. Now and then they do get close to caricature, but most work well. In particular, there is a frail man with a twisted spine who radiates malevolence; he is also very well-read, and it is easy to see where his hatred comes from as he compares Pathurst's luck with his own. Several of the crew are clearly "bad lots" and there is a reign of terror in the forecastle, from which the officers mostly dissociate themselves. By the time the ship reaches the Le Maire (or Lemaire) Strait at the southern extremity of Argentina, several of the crew have gone mad, or killed themselves or someone else.

Perhaps London exaggerates somewhat (he's writing a novel, after all). But life on a windjammer was indeed hard. To compete with steam, they sailed on small margins; the crew were paid little, the food was bad and the ships were sometimes worked with too few men. London does not exaggerate the difficulty of rounding the Horn from the Atlantic side, either. Now and then a skipper just gave up, turned round and sailed east around the world instead. *The Mutiny of the Elsinore* is a striking account of how it must have been. Maybe it says how London saw his fellow-man. Maybe it doesn't. In any case, London is not the only person whose attitudes now look suspect because of events they pre-dated, and would not have condoned. *The Mutiny of the Elsinore* might not be the greatest book that London wrote, but it is enthralling nonetheless. It is also a vibrant picture of a world that has passed.

*

That world would endure a little longer. On January 19 1928, 17 years after London's voyage, two four-masted barques loaded with grain left Port Lincoln in South Australia, bound for Falmouth. One was the *Beatrice*, an elderly 2,000-ton iron ship built on the Clyde in 1881, and now owned in Sweden. The other was the steel barque *Herzogin* [Duchess] *Cecilie*, built in Germany in 1902, and now Finnish-owned – by the world's largest remaining sail-ship operator, Gustaf Erikson of Mariehamn in the Åland Islands. The two skippers knew each other, and both intended to reach Falmouth first. There they would await orders as to where they would discharge their cargoes.

On board the Finnish ship was the Australian writer and seaman, Alan Villiers. At the time he was only 24 (though he had already written two books). He had shipped on the *Herzogin Cecilie* as an able seaman, but it was understood that he would write of the voyage. *Falmouth for Orders*, his account of that voyage, was the result. It is an odd book, part travelogue, partly an account of the then state of sail.

The post-war slump of 1921 had caused freight rates to collapse. By 1927, according to Villiers, there were about 30 such ships remaining, of which perhaps 15 were actively trading. Those that were, were mostly either German vessels carrying nitrates around the Horn from Chile to Germany, or they were Erikson's, working the grain trade. The latter would sail, usually in ballast, from Europe around the Cape of Good Hope and across the Indian Ocean, load in South Australia and return either the same way or eastward round the Horn. The skipper might not decide which way round to go until he was at sea.

Villiers describes the trade, and the fates of individual ships, in great detail. It is all a bit geeky, and the book would have been the better with less of it. When he writes of the voyage itself, he is more interesting. There's a charming glimpse of life in Port Lincoln, where both ships host parties for the locals on board: "The [*Herzogin Cecilie's*] own orchestra, in the shape of four of her boys supplied the music, and ...a real Scandinavian supper was provided. ...The presence of two uninvited guests, in the shape of two rats who made their presence known in the middle of a waltz, added considerably both to the noise and the excitement." No-one seems to take much notice of a young woman who visits the ships in port, and keeps stating her determination to sail in a ship like this. On the second day out she appears on the *Herzogin Cecilie's* deck, dressed as a boy, having got a fisherman to bring her to the ship by pretending to be a seaman who's been on a bender. She hides in the hold and emerges only when she thinks the ship will no longer want to put about. "It was Petrén who saw her first," writes Villiers. "He got such a shock that he nearly fell out of the jigger rigging." The woman was not welcome on board, but became more so as the voyage progressed, making herself useful and minding her behaviour. Villiers does not give her name, at least in this book, but it seems to have been Jeanne Day or Jennie Day (another source says Jean Jeinnie). She was 23 and from Adelaide, where she had apparently been a teacher in the Methodist Ladies' College. She stayed with the ship to England, where she is said to have died only a few years ago.

The captain, reconciled to his stowaway, decides on an eastward passage; he will go round the Horn. The *Beatrice* fades from sight (in fact, she has gone via the Cape). The *Cecilie's* progress is slow at first; some blame this on the presence of a woman on board. But eventually they pass south of New Zealand, and the pace picks up.

The same is true of the story, but only up to a point. Villiers diverts too often into discussions of the dying industry, and there are long lists of ships and their voyages. His description of the passage across the Southern Ocean, one of the most challenging places on earth, is not really resonant, although the ship has gone a very long way south and there is a smell of ice in the air. Rounding the Horn seems easy enough, though it can never really have been (it is true that westbound ships had it much worse).

The later chapters are better. The ship is caught in the Doldrums and does not move for days. Villiers and others take the opportunity to circle the ship in a launch, and he is struck by its beauty; he takes a photograph, which shows the *Herzogin Cecilie* perfectly reflected in the flat calm. Later, a mystery ship is spotted that could be the *Beatrice*; overhauled, she turns out to be the Swedish-owned *C.B. Pedersen*, built in Italy in 1891. They exchange visits, complete with bands and feasting, and a good time is had by all. The meeting is a major event for the crew of both ships, for it is not unusual for a windjammer to sail from South Australia to Falmouth or Queenstown without seeing another ship, or land; on this voyage the *Cecilie* has sighted land just once, a brief glimpse of Isla de los Estados off the southernmost tip of Argentina.

Then on towards England, and one morning in the early hours the *Cecilie* runs into a bad North Atlantic storm: "With appalling suddenness the sky seemed to burst into a sheet of flame that lit up the whole ocean ...there was a roar as if all the stars ..had been throwing gelignite at each other ... Queer blue lights danced about the steel rigging and on all the steel yardarms. ...And we had to lay aloft and set the royals fast in the midst of those blue lights." But the *Herzogin Cecilie* makes Falmouth in 96 days – a fast voyage even for her. She has beaten the *Beatrice*, which has had a dreadful voyage, by many days.

It's an evocative book, but is also flawed. There is a slight *Boy's Own* air to some of the writing; it is all just a little too jolly given that conditions on these ships were hard, and could also be very dangerous. Still, Villiers was well aware of the danger; at one point he lists some of the accidents and deaths that have occurred off the Horn. He was to become a distinguished figure, and would go on writing about the sea for another half-century. I remember being enthralled, as a young boy, by his *Battle of Trafalgar*. He also wrote much more about the last days of sail, and took wonderful photographs of this voyage and others (many now held by the National Maritime Museum, which has exhibited them). *Falmouth for Orders* is probably not his best book. But for those who love ships and the sea, there is much to enjoy.

*

The *Herzogin Cecilie* continued to trade. In April 1936, after an even faster passage, she again arrived off Falmouth, and was ordered to Ipswich. On her way she ran aground off South Devon; despite attempts to salvage her, she eventually sank off the mouth of the Kingsbridge Estuary. She lay in shallow water and one could (and still can) swim over and view the wreck. Two years later 18-year-old Eric Newby did just that.

In 1938 he was a bored 18-year-old working in a London advertising agency. When it lost an account, many of his colleagues were sacked. To his disgust, he wasn't. Apparently he was not important enough to sack. After the holiday on which he swam over the *Cecilie*, he left the agency anyway and signed on as an apprentice on the windjammer *Moshulu* for a round-the-world voyage. *The Last Grain Race* is the story of that voyage. Published nearly 20 years later, it was the first book from one of the best-loved of British

THE LAST DAYS OF SAIL

travel writers.

In 1935, the year before the *Herzogin Cecilie* ran aground, her owner, Gustaf Erikson, had bought the 30-year-old *Moshulu*, one of the largest and best windjammers left afloat. He paid just $12,000. It was not much. But freight rates were still collapsing, especially in the grain trade, for there was a slump in wheat prices in the 1930s. Erikson must have thought hard about this, even at the price. But he was probably not the sort of man who leaves a record of his thoughts. In any case, Newby joined her at Belfast in September 1938. As usual, she would sail in ballast via the Cape of Good Hope and the Indian Ocean to South Australia, where she would load several thousand tons of grain; then she would return via the Southern Ocean and around the Horn. The journey would take from September until the following summer. Moreover Newby was indentured; his father had paid £50, no small sum in 1938, and would forfeit it if Newby failed to discharge the terms of his apprenticeship. If he was killed, his father would of course get it back. This would look likely on several occasions.

Boarding at Belfast (with a Louis Vuitton trunk), Newby is sent straight up the rigging, in unsuitable shoes. It is a good move because he does not seem to have felt such terror again. He will have more trouble in the forecastle, where he is the only Englishman in a bunch of hard-boiled Scandinavians. He is not popular. Eventually he finds a turd in his cigarette-tin. He takes on the perpetrator in a fist-fight; it is a close contest but Newby prevails, hurting his opponent badly, only to be told later that the turd has actually been left by someone else. But that isn't the point.

Life in the forecastle would be rough anyway. In bad weather the water sloshes around inside and nothing is ever dry. Work is hard, a constant battle against changing winds, decaying ropes and rust. In the high (e.g. low) latitudes of the Southern Ocean, bound

19

for the Horn, they are thrust into a force 10 gale that lasts for days. On one occasion Newby is thrown from the rigging and is lucky to be caught in a cradle of ropes some five feet down. Yet throughout this he never loses his sense of adventure, or his eye for the beauty. *The Last Grain Race* is an achievement, and is a reminder that the greatest travel books transport us across more than one dimension. To read this book is to go right to the middle of a world that is gone forever.

It would vanish sooner than Newby imagined. Soon after the *Moshulu* returned to Belfast, the war broke out and the windjammer grain trade – the last in which they were profitable – came to an end. It never really re-started after the war, and Erikson himself died in 1947. The ships too have gone. The *Herzogin Cecilie's* fate we know. *Dirigo* is not far from her; she was stopped by a German submarine in 1917 while on passage from New York to Le Havre, and sunk with explosives six miles south-west of the Eddystone Rock lighthouse (the position of the wreck is known). The *Beatrice* was broken up in Stavanger in 1932, not long after her hard-lost race with the *Cecilie*.

The *C.B. Pedersen*, the ship Villiers encountered in mid-Atlantic, survived until April 1937. In that month, about 600 miles south-west of the Azores, she collided with a Scottish steamer, the *Chagres*. Everyone aboard the *C.B. Pedersen* was saved, though the skipper of the *Chagres* died of a heart attack. The *Sydney Morning Herald* for April 27 reported her loss and recalled that on her last voyage to Australia, she had been unable to find a cargo; she had loaded passengers instead and made for Europe via the Torres Strait, a difficult passage for a windjammer. The voyage, says the *Herald*, had been "enlivened by several exciting incidents. Three days after the vessel put to sea a girl stowaway was found on board, and later, one of the apprentices in the crew deserted by fitting an outrigger to the captain's wooden bath, and sailing it to an island – a voyage which occupied six days." Further details are lacking.

Newby's ship, however, has survived. The *Moshulu* was dismasted during the war and spent most of the next 30 years as a floating grain store. Yet for her, at least, it was not the end. Fitted with dummy masts and rigging, she was brought to Philadelphia, where today she is a floating restaurant. The owners clearly respect the ship's history, which is recounted in some detail on the restaurant's website.

The food seems to have improved. That served in the forecastle, according to Newby, was terrible. Early in the voyage they are served something very pungent that Newby thinks is fried herring. "Ees not fish," says Newby's enemy, Sedelquist. "Ees bacon, smelly like English girl." It is, says Newby, "ghastly and apparently putrefying". He throws it overboard. Later he learns never to waste even the worst food and to eat what he can get. Were he to visit the *Moshulu* today, he would be offered "Herb-rubbed Italian-style pork sandwich, Ciabatta Roll, Provolone, Pickled Eggplant & Hot Pepper Relish; House Cut Fries". One wonders what Newby (or Sedelquist) would have thought of *that*.

But if dining on the *Moshulu* is a little different now, the books, at least, give a flavour of the past. The *Elsinore* (or *Dirigo*) fighting for her life off the Horn. Sunsets of bright yellow as the light slants under dark grey clouds across a rough sea; great albatrosses swooping around the ship; the warmth as she turns north after rounding the Horn. Seas of blue, green and white washing across the deck of a rolling ship, smashing men sideways and into the scuppers or, if they are unlucky, over the side. A thunderstorm, with electric light flashing across the yards. Or a near-flat calm, the ship rolling a little on a slight oily swell, its silhouette perfectly mirrored in the surface of the sea.

Before Yossarian

I met B. when I was 12. He had retired, but at 70 still did a little tutoring, and came to the school two or three days a week to help the weaker candidates for public-school entry. In the autumn of 1969 he started to teach myself and another boy Latin and French. For several periods a week the two of us left our class to join our tutor, who struggled to interest us in French pronouns. It was a moist, clammy winter. This was during a period when, as an experiment, the clocks were not put forward. In December, one went to school in near-darkness and watched the dawn through cracks in the dirty-grey clouds.

I was a dreadful pupil (I would leave school at 17), but B. lost his temper with me just once and I am grateful for his forbearance. Still, he was a strict man and said little that was not business. He was short and pugnacious with a round form and a partridge face with a sharp nose and eyes that bored straight into you. He always seemed grave; but looking back across the years I am sure there was a ghost of a smile that never quite went away.

One French lesson towards the end of that winter he was talking, for some reason, of the Seine. "I travelled all the way up the river by boat once," he recalled. "When I was 15." I asked if he had been on holiday, assuming he was with his parents.

"No," he said. "I was going to the Western Front."

"Oh, were you in that, sir?" I asked.

Quite suddenly, his eyes glistened and rivulets of tears appeared on his cheeks. "Punishment for my sins," he said. "Punishment for all my sins." He repeated this phrase over and over again. We sat, embarrassed, for several minutes. At length he recovered himself and placed his glasses on his nose.

"Irregular pronouns," he said. He was quite restored, and

never mentioned the matter again.

The school was and is well-known, and he taught there for many years, so I hoped I might find some reference to B. on the internet – at least a brief obituary, which would tell me when he died. But I can't find much. There are just two references that I am almost sure are to him. One, from before the First World War, is in the journal of a small preparatory school in Pangbourne. It is, as school magazines always have been, mildly bonkers, and is full of trivia. The Hon Charles Rothschild visits the school with his father, who turns out to be an enthusiastic butterfly-hunter and captures a Purple Hairstreak on the school grounds. Lord Baden Powell also visits, and there is a flurry of excitement in the spring of 1912 when an aeroplane flies over: "It was clearly visible a long way off... and looked, as everybody remarked, like a large dragon-fly."

It is also recorded that Earl Roberts kindly offered to present a copy of his book, *Forty-One Years in India*, to the boy who had done best all round at the school. Our man was the recipient. If it was him, he was twelve years old; the same age as the century. He would journey up the Seine just three years later, one of many who lied about their age to flock to the colours. I can find no further reference to B., save for an online cricket archive that lists a man of his name and initials as having played for Dorset between 1927 and 1934. There is almost nothing else; he must have died before the internet arrived, so does not exist.

*

At about the same time I was taught by B., I read a magazine interview with the writer Compton Mackenzie, then very old; he was confined to a four-poster in at his home in Edinburgh, where he would die a year or two later. In the interview, he said: "I have sat

24

upon the knee of a veteran of Waterloo." Mackenzie was born in 1883, so I suppose it is just possible that he had. As I grow older I am sure people find it extraordinary that I was taught by a survivor of the Great War. I suppose the day will come when that war will be very remote, and may not influence our thinking, and our self-image, any more than Wellington's campaigns do today.

That is a pity, because it should do, especially in Britain, where we will be asked to remember it in the way that those in authority over us think we should. I wrote the first version of this chapter in 2014, the centenary year. At one point while writing, I had open a web page from the UK's Department for Culture, Media and Sport (DCMS). The headlines on the DCMS page included the following: "Prime Minister urges public to plant poppies for First World War commemorations", and "Pickles [Eric Pickles, a UK Government minister] backs campaign to restore Victoria Cross hero graves". No coincidence perhaps that the DCMS's policy statement included the following: "We believe that people can come together in strong, united communities if we encourage and support them to have shared aspirations, values and experiences". For which the war centenary must have looked jolly useful.

Most British people would want to commemorate 1914-1918, and I am no exception; in fact it would be disgraceful if we didn't. But I am not sure if politicians are the right people to do it. What I did do, in that anniversary year, was read about the War. Was it a story of "shared aspirations, values and experiences"? Or was it all a bit messier than that?

*

The British literature of the First World War has an identity of its own as a body of work – something that from the second war lacks.

25

It's no mystery why. Most of those who fought for Britain did so on the Western Front; this gives the war literature a certain cohesion, as does the fact that many of the authors were from highly literate and privileged backgrounds, or were men of letters, or both. Edmund Blunden, Robert Graves, Frederic Manning, Richard Aldington and Ford Madox Ford all fit into these categories. Posh non-literary figures also got in on the act (Anthony Eden, for example, whose *Another World* is rather good). Yet not all of this cohesive body of work speaks to us directly now; sometimes the language can seem archaic and mannered. J.B. Priestley's autobiographical fragment *Carry on! Curry On!*, in his *Margin Released*, is an exception (it was written much later). But much Great War writing, superb though it is, seems increasingly of its time.

I picked out three books. It's an eclectic selection. Two do indeed feel of their time, but are good enough to transcend it. This third was written so long after the war that it reads more like a product of our own era, and has a startling immediacy. But all three have two things in common: the absurdity of conflict; and a vivid picture of a class-ridden society at war.

The first book is by Rebecca West. Like many people, I knew of West as a writer but only through her famous book on Yugoslavia, *Black Lamb and Grey Falcon*. Born in London in 1892, she had little formal education, her family being in genteel poverty. She trained as an actress, but seems to have acted little, becoming a sufragette and then the lover of H.G. Wells. She then turned to writing and had a distinguished career in serious journalism. She also wrote a number of novels, but it seems unlikely that most are widely read now. *The Return of the Soldier*, however, has never quite been forgotten and was filmed, with a stellar cast, in 1982. Her first book, it was published in 1918.

The plot may be summarised as follows. Two women are in a

country house just outside London on a bright day in the early spring of 1916. They are well-to-do; Kitty is the attractive wife of Baldry, the master of the house, and Jenny, less pretty, is his cousin. The latter has started to worry that they have heard nothing of Baldry, a serving soldier, for several weeks. Kitty assures her that the War Office would have informed her if there were anything amiss. They are interrupted by the arrival of Margaret, a dowdy woman of limited means from a bleak suburb nearby. She informs them that Baldry is, in fact, in hospital in Boulogne, that he has lost his memory after an explosion, and that he has regressed some 15 years to the time when, as a young man, he loved her. That is why the War Office has not been in touch; it is Margaret to whom Baldry has written, and it is her that he wishes to see.

Baldry is brought home, and is indifferent to his wife; a little less so to his cousin, who he does remember, albeit as a young woman – but he spends his time with Margaret, and is unconcerned that she is now a middle-aged, married, suburban dowd. It becomes clear that he still loves her. Kitty, the spurned wife, calls in a series of doctors to try to bring back his memory and restore him to normal. If she succeeds, he will of course return to the front. Cousin Jenny understands this, and feels growing sympathy for Margaret: "While her spell endured, they could not send him back into the hell of war," she says (she is the book's narrator). "This wonderful, kind woman held his body as safely as she held his soul." It slowly becomes clear that, by trying to restore him to "normal" and send him back to war, Kitty is being monstrously selfish. The lover is right; the wife is wrong; restoration to "normal" means death. This was a brave message for 1918.

Not everyone has read the book this way. Some have seen it as a clinical description of combat trauma. Others will see a feminist message here – that the dependence of women on men distorts the behaviour of both, and is even a driver for war. There is plenty of evidence in the book for this interpretation and besides, West was indeed a strong proponent of women's rights. But perhaps we shouldn't apply modern labels to people who pre-date them. In any case, the book does not have the feel of one with an agenda; it is driven by its characters, and they are well-drawn.

Moreover there is an understated lyricism in West's writing that makes the book poignant and vivid. The sequences in which Baldry remembers his early courtship of Margaret 15 years earlier are set on Monkey Island at Bray, in a curve of the Thames, where Margaret's father is landlord of the Monkey Island Inn. The place was real enough, and still is. Today it is an hotel and conference centre just a mile or so from the M4 motorway that runs from London to Bristol and thence into Wales. West and Wells frequented it immediately before the war, but one suspects it was already rather posher than it is in the book, in which it is a quiet country pub catering to the odd passing boatman. The young Baldry describes how it was reached, via a ferry to "a bright lawn set with many walnut-trees and a few great chestnuts, well lighted with their candles... presently Margaret in a white dress would come out of the porch and would walk to the stone steps down to the river. Invariably, as she passed the walnut-tree that overhung the path, she would pick a leaf, crush it, and sniff the sweet scent..." To anyone who knows the countryside in the south of England, this is evocative. In April, May and June the sky turns a deeper blue and the trees and hedgerows come alive; the white and pink chestnut candles are a delight, as are the white patches of hawthorn.

There are other key elements in *The Return of the Soldier*, and they link it to the two other books I have chosen. But first, to the second of these two books.

*

Frederic Manning is an oddly elusive figure. Born in Australia in 1882, he migrated to England as a teenager. A friend, at various times, of Ezra Pound, Richard Aldington, T.S. Eliot, W.B. Yeats and T. E. Lawrence, he was regarded by many contemporaries as a fine writer; but he was affected throughout his life by the weak chest that eventually killed him. He also drank. When he died in 1935 at the age of 52, he was really only known for one book, and little else that he left behind is widely read today.

That one masterwork was published in 1929 under the title *The Middle Parts of Fortune*; soon afterwards, an expurgated version was brought out as *Her Privates We*. Today it can be found as either. Both titles are taken from the same dialogue in *Hamlet*:

Guildenstern: *On Fortune's cap we are not the very button.*
Hamlet: *Nor the soles of her shoe?*
Rosencrantz: *Neither, my lord.*
Hamlet: *Then you live about her waist, or in the middle of her favours?*
Guildenstern: *Faith, her privates we.*
Hamlet: *In the secret parts of fortune? O, most true; she is a strumpet.*

The book concerns Bourne, a private soldier; although not in the first person, it is written from his point of view, and we mostly see no other. It is set late in 1916, after the Somme offensive. The book opens with Bourne groping his way, dugout by duckboard, away from the trenches as his unit is withdrawn; it finishes with their return. In between, the unit is marched from one place to another behind the lines, supposedly resting.

The book is packed with petty incidents in the life of a soldier. It is punctuated with darker events: a deserter is returned, perhaps to be shot; a popular officer dies on a work detail; a pointless parade leads to the death of several men when it is shelled. In between the men pick the lice off their bellies, avoid guard duty, and try to have "a *bon* time" at *estaminets* where the beer is poor. There is detail here that never made the history books. Planes communicate with troops on the ground using klaxons. Bourne's boot is split at the heel by a cart he is towing, and he is lucky to be issued with boots that are of a higher grade, being for officers. In the *estaminets*, the best booze is labelled "For Officers Only". When the weather turns cold the men are issued with fleece-lined leather jerkins and, as a result, the lice multiply. As Orwell wrote in *Homage to Catalonia*: "In war all soldieries are lousy, at the least when it is warm enough. The men that fought at Verdun, at Waterloo, at Flodden, at Senlac, at Thermopylae - every one of them had lice crawling over his testicles."

Bourne, the lead character, is a little different from the others; he is better educated, there is a hint that he is not 100% English, and he is under pressure to try for a commission, having turned down one on enlisting. This matches Manning's own life – up to a point. Already 32 in 1914 and in poorish health, he made several attempts to enlist before finally being accepted as a footsoldier in the King's Shropshire Regiment. In *Her Privates We*, Bourne maintains to a superior that he turned down a commission on enlisting as he felt he did not know enough of men to command them.

In real life, Manning, an aesthete, may indeed not have been a natural leader of working men. However, he did not turn down a commission. John Francis Swain, who included a concise and informative biography of Manning in a 2001 doctoral thesis, reports that he was accepted for officer training but was caught drunk and was returned to his regiment. He joined it on the Somme in August 1916. He had missed the bloody start to the battle but he did fight.

At the end of 1916 he was again sent for officer training and this time was commissioned into the Royal Irish Regiment. However, he did not settle to life as an officer, and took again to drink. Early in 1918, he was allowed to resign his commission on health grounds. *Her Privates We* is based, then, on just three or four months in France. Moreover some of its early passages are wordy and philosophical. But at its best, it is a vivid portrayal of a soldier's life.

*

These are two very different books, and see the war from distinct viewpoints. However, they have important threads in common. First, they say nothing explicit about the war in general; they are about individuals, and we see the war through their eyes, not from on high. Both avoid the puddingstone hell of the didactic novel.

The second thread that binds them together is class. In *Her Privates We*, the soldiers are reminded constantly that they are inferior. Towards the end of the book, Bourne and his fellows come across a Forces canteen with "hams, cheeses, bottled fruits, olives, sardines, everything to make the place a paradisal vision for hungry men." Entering, he is refused service by a man who "turned away superciliously, saying that they only served officers." Another attendant is friendlier and tells him he can get cocoa and biscuits at a shed in the yard. Bourne is incensed, knowing that the goods in the shop have been paid for by public subscription and were intended for them all.

But the class distinctions have more subtle dangers. Bourne is pressed to apply for a commission, because it is obvious that he is not from the same background as the others. Reluctantly, he does.

31

Meanwhile, in the trenches, thinking he has seen a sniper, he reports to an officer. The meeting is a tense one, for they are of different rank but the same class, and the officer feels unable to place him; he therefore treats him coldly. Anyone brought up in the multi-layered jungle of the British class system will recognise this. The tension between them ends with Bourne being sent on the patrol that ends the book.

Class is if anything a more explicit theme of *The Return of the Soldier*. Margaret, the woman to whose affections Baldry has regressed, is a woman of a lower station. Jenny and Kitty meet Margaret for the first time, when she first calls at the Baldry house· ("The sticky straw hat had only lately been renovated by something out of a little bottle bought at the chemist's...") Margaret starts to explain that Baldry is wounded, in Boulogne, and that it seems they do not know. Her words are not taken at face value; they assume Margaret is a fraud. "Presently she would say that she had gone to some expense to come here with her news and that she was poor..."

These class tensions have not been excised from British life. Anyone who thinks they have, should look at the treatment being meted out to benefits claimants over the last few years – especially those claiming sickness benefit. This wretched hatred and suspicion of the poor is as alive as it was in 1916.

*

Which brings us to the third book. Like Manning, its author served in the ranks. Unlike Manning, he was a working man so was meant to. And unlike both Manning and West, he was writing nearly 60 years after the war ended. Eric Hiscock's *The Bells of Hell Go Ting-A-Ling-Ling* thus has a life and freshness that you won't find in the classic memoirs.

The Bells of Hell has not had the impact of either of the other two books. But because it was written far more recently, its language is much easier for the modern reader than (say) Edmund Blunden, who is a wonderful writer but can feel very old-fashioned. To read Hiscock, by contrast, is like hearing about the war from a gifted raconteur in the pub. The gap in years means he can also look at the war with modern eyes, and can be quite brutally frank.

Hiscock was born in 1900 and brought up in Oxford. His parents had met when both in service to an aristocrat, Lord Lane-Fox, and his father had later become a "scout" – a member of domestic staff – in one of the Oxford colleges. Hiscock's home was not a wealthy one, but seems to have been secure and cheerful. As the book begins, however, Hiscock joins the army at the age of just 15. The army clearly knows he is underage, and he spends the next two years in Britain. (In this he is luckier than B., to be sure.)

The young Hiscock is shipped off to Edinburgh, where he makes the acquaintance of one Sergeant-Major Priestman. The latter is a regular who "had had a testicle shot off in the Mons retreat", and who "bullied from Reveille at six in the morning ...to Lights Out at night, spitting venom. But at week's-end, he was not averse to accepting hard cash for a forty-eight hour pass." It reminds one of the famous wartime song (which Hiscock quotes):

When the bloody war is over,
O how happy I shall be...
No more crying out for furlough,
No more bribing for a pass,
You can tell the Sergeant-Major
To stick his passes up his arse.

In other words, never mind the mud and the lice of Flanders; you were bullied on a massive scale long before you got there. That's something you won't find so much in Edmund Blunden or Robert Graves (though Frederick Manning, who spent time in the ranks, hints at it more).

Hiscock does get to the front, in early 1918 when he is still some months underage. As he and his companions file into the trench for the first time, a sniper kills the sergeant (not Priestman) a few feet from him. "Possibly somebody did something about him as his lifeless body fell to the sodden duckboards ...but I think we just left him there. As [we] scrambled into the shelter my steel helmet caught a protuberance in the muddied roof. It was the knee of a khaki-clad corpse." There is plenty more like this. One of the most evocative passages in the book, for me, is Hiscock's description of repeated night journeys up to the trenches, on duckboards across the mud; it is a treacherous passage and it is not unusual for an overladen man to simply lose his footing and fall into the mud or a flooded crater below, never to be seen again.

Yet some at least of this can be found in many books (though perhaps not quite so vividly). What marks this book out, besides its contemporary feel, is its frankness. Hiscock doesn't bother with the King and Country nonsense. Instead we hear how months of bully-beef wrecks his digestion so that he will be seriously ill in later years. We hear how he gets his penis bitten by a vengeful French girl after he decides, as the last minute, not to have intercourse with her (she was, "it turned out, a diseased nymphomaniac"). It's played for laughs but then he quietly tells us, at the end of that passage, how a fellow-soldier later catches a dose at the end of the war and shoots himself rather than go home to his family.

But perhaps the most extraordinary part of this book is

Hiscock's own court-martial for cowardice. As he recounts it, he injures himself accidentally while cleaning his rifle, and is accused of doing it deliberately to get himself repatriated. The accuser, a Lieutenant Clarke, is (according to Hiscock) a homosexual jealous of Hiscock's friendship with another man. It is impossible to know if this account is correct; one could, I suppose, find the transcripts of the court-martial if they exist, but they might not settle the case. For what it is worth, Hiscock is acquitted and returns to combat – incredibly, he is returned to the same unit, which must be dangerous for Clarke – and serves until his discharge in 1919. This does not suggest cowardice. Yet a quite startling number of men were convicted; most were not actually shot, but over 300 were, and Hiscock would have been well aware he was on trial for his life. If one does take Hiscock's account at face value, it demonstrates that this war put ordinary men at the mercy not just of the enemy, but of the very worst of their own people.

Hiscock survives the war and goes on to take part in the post-war occupation of Germany – itself fascinating, as there are few enough accounts of the post-WWII occupation, let alone of this one. The book ends back in Oxford as he picks up the thread of his life.

In these last parts he describes friendships with two intellectual homosexuals in some detail. In the book he also talks about feelings of love for other soldiers. Hiscock does not appear to be especially prejudiced against homosexuality, and his attitudes seem fairly liberal for 1976, let alone 1918. I have heard it suggested that Hiscock himself had repressed feelings for men, not uncommon at that time. But I do not see why his sensitivity towards others' sexuality should be ascribed to that. It may be that, having spent much time at close quarters with other men in his youth, he was forced acknowledge the existence of diverse sexuality; after all, he was also (if the Clarke story is true) nearly killed by its consequences.

There is much that in *The Bells of Hell* that is grim but in the end, oddly, the book itself isn't. Hiscock writes warmly of his parents, of his life in Oxford and of (for example) fishing for Sunday breakfast with his father at Godstow. He seems to have been aware of his luck in surviving the war. The book is also peppered with character sketches, often wry and funny (I loved the forger and general spiv, Vanner). And the various fumbling sexual adventures show a keen sense of the ridiculous.

I first read this book in 1991 and never forgot it, to the extent that I decided to track it down 25 years later. I found it as startling and vivid as I did before, and wondered why it has not had the impact of other books about the first war. Hiscock went on to a successful career in advertising and Fleet Street, and married Romilly Cavan, a novelist and playwright who also wrote some early TV scripts. *The Bells of Hell* was published by Desmond Elliott's Arlington Books, a small company but a distinguished one. It did also get a brief release as a paperback. But its impact seems to have been small. Hiscock was not of the officer class that still dominated publishing and criticism in the 1970s, and maybe you still had to be an Oxbridge poet, or at least of the slaughtering classes, before you were really allowed to write about the Great War. If so, that is our loss, because there are things that those classes would not have questioned, or seen in quite the same way. Wars are not just about what a country does to its enemies; they are about what it does to its own people in the process, and the way in which men like Clarke, or people of a certain class, can suddenly wield huge authority over those of another. That is something we could perhaps remember in our own times, when some would have us believe that it's only foreigners who are our enemies.

*

Besides the use of individual viewpoints, and the perspectives on class, there is a third strand that binds these books. They make a point that is made much more explicitly, and in my view less well, by a more famous book, Heller's *Catch-22*. That is the whole question of the logic of war.

Almost nowhere in *Her Privates We* does anyone express support for the war; they just accept it as a fact. They are angry with a deserter, because he left them to fight without him; his betrayal of the Crown as such concerns them little. More important are the commonplace stupidities of authority. A major training exercise, planned to perfection, is brought to a halt by the fury of a peasant woman because the troops are trampling her clover, and she will have no feed for the winter. On another occasion the unit is sent up the line as a work detail, but because someone has recorded their fighting strength as their pay strength, everyone must go, including the cooks, and there is nothing to eat in the morning. War and authority are quite random:

"There's a man dead outside, sergeant," he said, dully.
"Are you sure he's dead?"
"Yes, sergeant; most of the head's gone."

Meanwhile Hiscock's world is one of VD and bad digestion, petty crooks, troops rioting on the night of the armistice and bribing the sergeant to get a leave pass. There's no glory here, just a sort of quotidian surrealism and discomfort.

But West goes farther than either Manning or Hiscock. Read their books and you will sense the absurdity of war. But you will not find it its logic explicitly challenged. In West's, you will.

Towards the end of *The Return of the Soldier*, an expensive specialist has arrived to "cure" Baldry – that is to say, restore his memory. Margaret, the dowd that he loves, protests to the doctor that he cannot cure him, in the sense of making him happy; he can only make him ordinary. Yes, says the doctor; that is all he does do. "It's my profession to bring people... to the normal," he explains. "There seems to be a general feeling it's the place where they ought to be. Sometimes I don't see the urgency myself."

In *Catch-22*, the American airman, Yossarian, finds that there is a twisted logic: if you request relief from combat duty on the grounds of insanity, you must be wrong, because to do so is sane. West is subtler but the message is the same; by being "cured", Baldry will be made to go back to the front, which is mad. Being restored to sanity makes Baldry do something insane.

If you have seen an old man's tears on a winter's day, then commemorations like 2014's do strike a false note. Perhaps that's no-one's fault. It does not mean the dead of the First World War should not be remembered. But one does wonder whose business remembrance should be, and whether it should be handed down from above. In any case, all these books should give the politicians pause. In *Her Privates We*, stupidity and class conflict get Bourne killed. In *The Bells of Hell*, they damn near land Hiscock in front of a firing squad. And in *The Return of the Soldier*, conformity to society and authority is inherently insane. There are some deeply subversive messages here. If I were a British government minister, I'd stay a million miles away from the First World War, lest people start thinking too hard about it and, in so doing, question the very nature and legitimacy of the authority of one human over another.

The Chinese on the Western Front

Towards the end of 1917, a junior officer in the British army, Daryl Klein, arrived in Qingdao in China's Shandong Province. He had come to take up a posting as a Second Lieutenant in the Chinese Labour Corps (CLC), which between 1916 and 1918 recruited nearly 100,000 Chinese labourers to do war work, including the digging of trenches on the Western Front. In so doing it freed up huge numbers of Allied troops to take a more direct part in the fighting. The French also recruited Chinese labour on a large scale. Not all returned to China safely.

Although little-known in Britain, the CLC's story has never been a secret. I first read of it back in the 1970s, when the *Sunday Times Magazine* ran a series called *The Unofficial History of the 20th Century*. It mentioned the CLC, and referred in passing to a book by one of its officers, Daryl Klein, "with the nonchalant title *With the Chinks*." The title stuck in my mind but it was only recently that I was able to confirm that the book existed; it was rediscovered and republished by Naval & Military Press in 2009 and is now available as a download as well as a paperback.

Klein's book is based on his diary from December 1917 to May 1918, and covers the training of the labourers at their camp in Shantung (as it was then called), their transport across the Pacific to British Columbia and their stay there, and their onward passage towards France as far as New York. It ends there, and does not cover the labourers' service on the Western Front. Nonetheless it is fascinating, the more so because it was published in 1919 and is thus a very contemporary account. It is also shocking, confronting the reader with a stunning level of casual prejudice.

The CLC's story has slowly been uncovered and there are now

several books about it. For the casual reader, it is set out in a short but very well-written and well-researched book, Mark O'Neill's *The Chinese Labour Corps* (2014), one of a series called China Penguin Specials. O'Neill has a family connection; his grandfather was a Presbyterian minister in China and accompanied the CLC to France.

O'Neill explains that the roots of the CLC lay in China's weak international position and its wish to use the war as a way to improve it. In 1914 China, although an independent state, was firmly under the thumb of the Western colonial powers and Japan. It was saddled with a huge indemnity for its supposed crimes during the Boxer Rebellion at the turn of the century, when nationalist Chinese rose against the imperial powers and their "concessions" in China. The latter were extraterritorial enclaves where the foreign powers had special privileges; the most famous was Shanghai, but in 1914 there were actually 27 concessions, according to O'Neill. (If you broaden the definition to include all foreign enclaves, there were more.)

In particular, the Chinese would have liked to regain control of Shandong, where the German concessions had been seized by the Japanese in November 1914. Japan was an ally of Britain and France, and China also hoped that taking a pro-Allied line would earn it their help in dealing with its neighbour. Thus in 1915 the Chinese offered to send a total of 300,000 workers to Britain and France. In the event, Britain would recruit just over 94,000 and the French a further 40,000; of these 135,000-odd men, about 10,000 would later be "lent" to the US when it entered the war. About 80,000 of the CLC were from Shandong, and were from a predominantly agricultural background; it was felt they would deal better with the hard work, and the North European winters, than the Cantonese from further south.

The CLC was not to bear arms or be exposed to combat. Inevitably, however, some did come to harm; O'Neill says that about 3,000 died from bombing and shelling, accidents while clearing munitions (which was clearly dangerous work), and illnesses such as tuberculosis and 'flu (a number would perish in the Spanish Influenza epidemic at the end of the war). Modern Chinese researchers have claimed that the losses were higher. Moreover China would reap few diplomatic rewards in return for their sacrifice.

*

To read O'Neill's account in conjunction with Klein's is to be hit hard by the changes in the way we think about the world. For a start, one is taken aback by the title *With the Chinks*. In fact, "Chink" was then American slang, not British. Klein barely uses it in the book. Instead he calls the men "coolies", a word that has mostly vanished now but was still used when I was a child 50 years ago for a Chinese or Indian worker. But these days it would be mostly regarded as offensive, and "chink" would now be taken as a racial slur. These are not words I would use out of context today.

Although coolie was sometimes used simply for Chinese manual workers, strictly speaking it meant an indentured labourer – that is, one who works to pay off a debt, and is effectively unfree. The history of empire includes the most awful abuses of such men, mostly Chinese and Indian, who were transported across the world, worked in many cases to death and, if they survived, left to rot rather than brought home. The worst abuses had been brought to an end in the late 19th century, but in 1918 they were well within living memory. One wonders to what extent Klein knew of them.

The CLC men were not indentured as such, but they were under contract and could not leave. Early in the book, Klein states that

41

they were free men and could do so, were they able to produce a good enough reason. But the fact is that they were effectively prisoners, and at several points Klein describes incidents in which they "escaped" and were forcibly brought back to Qingdao. Klein expresses no great surprise at this.

Moreover his attitude to the men was completely paternalistic. He describes the induction process at the camp as the "sausage machine", in which a man has his hair cut, is washed and is taught to drill: "A process which turns an ordinary uninviting workaday coolie into a clean, well-clothed and smartly active human being. An astonishing process which is doing a great good for a corner of China." When a man tries unsuccessfully to escape, Klein is simply puzzled:

Questioned why, at a court of inquiry held this morning, he was desirous of so impolitely leaving his comrades, a dry warm wooden bed, no end of rice, and the interesting prospect of seeing France at war, he said that he wanted to give up all for his wife and follow her.

In Klein's view the men are not much troubled about their destination provided they are not going into combat. It does not occur to him that they *should* worry about this point. He describes how a mutiny broke out at sea in one of the first drafts because an "absurd rumour" had spread that they were going into a "death trap". But as stated above, some 3,000 men of the Chinese Labour Corps and its French equivalent would indeed die in France. As Klein's book was published in 1919, he should by then have known that, and his insouciance seems inexcusable.

Moreover he makes light of the danger from the journey itself. Thus in January 1918 there is a mass break-out from the camp: "A malicious report has lately gained credence among them that the last two transports were either torpedoed, or captured by the Germans; a story, needless to say, entirely baseless." But it wasn't. In February 1917 the French troopship *Athos*, carrying Chinese labourers to France, had been torpedoed in the Mediterranean. "The incident resulted in the loss of 754 lives," says Mark O'Neill, "including 543 Chinese men who were destined to never set foot on European soil, and who would be the first Chinese casualties of the Great War." In the Atlantic, 1917 had been the worst year for submarine warfare, and later in his own book Klein will describe disciplining labourers who light cigarettes on deck, lest they attract submarines. Klein's paternalism had blinded him to the fact that these men were not imagining things; that their concerns were, in fact, real.

And yet Klein clearly liked "his" Chinese. The book is peppered with references to their strength and to their solidity of character, and he was especially impressed by their kindness to each other:

They showed the sort of spirit which makes one positively love the Chinese—the Chinese of Shantung at any rate. They are wonderfully good to one another in adversity. They have warm hearts and willing hands. There was something so eternally and touchingly human about this business that whatever vestige remained in me of the conventional conception of the coolie quite disappeared.

*

Klein's narrative takes us across the Pacific to British Columbia, where the labourers were kept in camps until transport was available to take them onwards. Although Klein does not say so, the camps were secret – initially to protect Chinese neutrality (though by now China was in the war) but also so as not to inflame anti-immigrant sentiment in Canada. The men were then usually taken across the country in sealed trains and embarked for France in, one assumes, Montreal or Halifax. Klein's draft, however, were unusual, being taken instead on the *Empress of Asia*, through the Panama Canal and on to France via New York. It is, Klein tells us, a constant battle to make the men understand the danger from submarines. (Oddly, the ship would survive the First World War but be sunk in the second.)

The journey through the Canal and the Caribbean gives Klein further occasion to shock the modern reader, with descriptions of n*****s and c**ns. ("Coolie" and "chink" I can manage, but only given the context; and I cannot bring myself to type those.) The narrative ends in New York, a fact that disappointed the reviewer for *Punch* when it was published the following year. The review also criticised the book for failing to show why the men had joined up, but conceded that: "For the conscientious historian it will have a certain unique value. And in fairness it must be added that in the latter half there are touches of humour and humanity which make the reading easy and pleasant." This was not entirely wrong. Klein was clearly not a bad man and for all his youthful paternalism, his regard for the Chinese was real. Yet there is little evidence of him talking to, or trying to understand, them, or to see them as individuals.

Or is there? Some way through the book Klein introduces his friend Julius East, or Jule, who has, he says, given up a good career in banking to join the CLC. On the three-week voyage across the Pacific it occurs to East to find out more about his charges: "The second day out in the Pacific it came to Jule that it would be interesting to know what was passing in the minds of his coolies. So, picking out the most intelligent of the interpreters, he descended

44

to the 'tween decks and closeted himself with his two sergeants." The ensuing conversation is described in some detail. Jule appears to have learned little of the two men's thoughts and interrogates a third, a "six-foot-two, magnificently built, open-mouthed hayseed, one Lun Zun Chong ...Jule asked many straight questions, but never a satisfactory answer did he receive." Klein concludes that "the moral to be drawn from Jule's interview with three members of his company is that nothing passes in the mind of a coolie ...Nothing, that is, of a philosophic nature." Jule is disappointed. "He expected whimsical points of view, quaint definitions, intellectual oddities." He still maintains that he can uncover them, but not through an interpreter, and decides he will learn Chinese.

We don't learn whether he does, but we do encounter Jule again, and hear of his thoughts and actions in surprising detail. Finally, in New York, he has dinner with his sister – who lives there – and her friends. The coolies, he assures them, will not be allowed to fight in France even if they want to (and as we have seen, they didn't). But Jule makes the following observation:

At all events, if they don't get a Tommy's chance in this war, they will get it sooner or later in their own country. It will be a war of their own – a civil war ...clean, clear open minds against the dirt and truck and turgidness of centuries. When these men go back to China they won't be satisfied with the old life...

Was that Jule's opinion? Or was he an imaginary cypher for Klein himself?

I think the latter. A search of the website of Britain's National Archives turned up his full name, and his middle names were Julius Ernest. Julius East? It may be that Klein wrote the racist hogwash he thought was expected of him, but used the Jule device to express his genuine interest in the Chinese themselves – an interest that might then have been seen as a little odd and even unsettling in some circles, including those in which Klein knew he would have to return to work as a civilian. It may be that the book does reflect Klein's own attitudes. But it could also be that this whole book is subversive.

Of the man himself, I can find out very little. He was a British officer, but his name sounds more American – and as we have seen, if he *was* Jule, his sister lived in New York. His use of the word 'hayseed' also suggests he was American. But he could also have been Canadian or Australian; many Empire subjects would have been thought of as British then. The fact that the National Archives had his full name meant I could establish from other sources that he served from 1914 to 1920, and was gazetted temporary 2nd Lieutenant with effect from December 31 1917. I also found reference to an American with a Russian-born father and English-born mother who may have been our Klein; if that is our man, he was probably born in 1895. The answers will be buried in the War Office files, for those with the time and skills to find them.

*

Whatever Klein really thought, I found parts of his book hard to read, and if I were Chinese I would have been climbing the walls somewhere around page three or four. Behind the paternalism was the historical suffering of indentured labourers alluded to earlier, and while the CLC men did not suffer as badly as that, their conditions in France were hard. Neither was this the case only for those employed by the British. Mark O'Neill states that those employed by the French fared better, but his own account does not always seem to bear this out; Chinese workers did die in the French factories, he says due to accidents and disputes, or untreated ill-nesses. Moreover they sometimes found themselves in dispute with either the French or other groups who were working for them. "In January 1917, in a gunpowder factory in Bassens, a brawl with Arab workers left two Chinese dead," O'Neill records. "A few days later, at a gunpowder factory in Bergerac, 500 Chinese attacked 250 Algerians; one Chinese was killed and sixty people were injured."

Meanwhile the British organized a well-equipped hospital in the base area that had 1,500 beds and Chinese-speaking doctors and dressers, and the workers received the same care and attention as the British soldiers. "To give a flavour of home," writes O'Neill, "each ward had a canary and a model pagoda several metres high stood near the main entrance, with a gong that struck the hours of the day."

On the other hand, O'Neill also reports that the British-built hospital had "a large compound for the treatment of those who had lost their mind under the stress of war." He also records that quite a number of workers died in bombing raids on their camps and elsewhere. Moreover O'Neill does recount incidents in which British officers mistreated Chinese workers, saying that when they presented a complaint and their officers could not understand them, it was not unknown to simply open fire; in one such case, four workers were killed. Neither was this the worst incident; in October 1917, five men were killed and 14 wounded after a dispute over discipline, while two months later there was a mutiny because of bullying by British NCOs. This resulted in the deaths of four Chinese workers and a Canadian soldier.

Klein records no such incidents. Still, reading *With the Chinks*, it is not hard to see how they happened. He himself, though of his time, was clearly decent enough but his fellow-officers seem to have been a rum lot. One, for example, is a Russian officer from a crack cavalry regiment (or so Klein assures us) who has been stranded by the Revolution and has left all his baggage "in the Carpathians". He misses the sophisticated company he had when he served in the London and Washington embassies before the war, and finds his brother-officers a poor substitute. The other officers seem to have been a mixed bag of missionaries and other China hands. One advocates converting all the labourers to his muscular brand of Christianity. This idea is wisely quashed by the others, but most are not above a little casual violence: "There is rivalry among the officers in regard to the number of canes broken on the backs, legs and shins, not to speak of the heads of defaulters," reports Klein. "The supply of canes ran short in Tsingtau some time ago." He quotes a brother-officer as saying that "nothing... knocks anything into a coolie so well as a nose-bleed." The officer concerned is, says Klein, "well practised at drawing a coolie's blood at first slap," and assures everyone that "they soon get over it and bear you no malice, either."

Klein recalls an officer called Harris, "who has an excellent digestion and the temperament of a lamb," admitting that he was "growing astonishingly callous in his treatment of the coolies." He tells Klein and the others that "'the smallest breach of discipline drives me into a fury ... I don't know what has come over me. Time was ...I could initiate a coolie into the knowledge of left and right without loss of temper. To-day I cane him into this knowledge ...' In Harris' heart is a great fear of becoming like a Prussian officer. 'What if I should become like that which we are seeking to destroy?'"

Herein lies what for me is the key message, albeit unintentional, of *With the Chinks*: that the power of one group over another is as bad for the first as it is for the second. I'm reminded of what the playwright and MP Benn Levy said in a 1946 Commons debate on the occupation of Germany (which was not going well). "It is not good for a nation to be conquered," he told the House. "But it is also not good for people to be conquerors." I may remember Daryl Klein the next time I hear someone praising the achievements of colonialism. In fact *With the Chinks* is an example of why we should not censor or bowdlerise the past. Let it speak for itself, and it may tell you more than it meant to.

The Monkey's Benison

One day in the mid-1920s, in the cool season, a British shooting-party went to hunt in the country outside Delhi. They left at dawn, killed things, then lunched with the ladies, who had driven out from Delhi to meet them. The ladies dressed well. One, in her late teens, wore "a pale pink dress and a hat to match that I thought pretty, white, straw-brimmed with a chiffon crown patterned in pale colours." They ate curry puffs and game pie. As they did so, monkeys "peered down at us from the branches. Suddenly, one of them let fall a stream of shit on my precious hat." Now she would be lucky all her life, a friend told her.

It is not clear why the friend thought being shat on by a monkey would mean luck, good or bad; but in fact her life would bring her plenty of both, as she would recall over 60 years later: "As if the monkey had given me a benison, I have had extraordinarily good luck and extraordinarily bad ... in my case bringing ups and downs so unusual it has often been difficult to believe they were happening."

Rumer Godden would indeed have both good luck and bad, and would have trouble in her personal life, with an unsatisfactory marriage, a child who died in infancy, a miscarriage, and wartime destitution. And yet she would also become one of the most successful novelists of her lifetime, and her books would be filmed by, among others, Powell and Pressburger, and Jean Renoir. But it is her life in India, and her recounting of it, that has drawn me.

*

Rumer Godden was born in December 1907; as it happens in Eastbourne, but her family was in India, where her sister had been born a year or so earlier. Her parents were part of that large long-gone white tribe of India that ran what we now call the Raj, although they would not have called it that; they would have called it the Indian Empire. (They would not have called it British India, either, as that then meant the two-thirds or so that was under direct British rule, as opposed to the Princely States.) This white tribe was not homogenous. At its apex was the Indian Civil Service – the so-called "heaven-born". The military came second. Those engaged in business or industry, known as the "box-wallahs", came next. In fact, one wonders if this caste system afforded the Indians a little ironic amusement.

Godden's father was a box-wallah, but one of some importance, managing the river steamer services. He was stationed in Assam at the time of Godden's birth but moved when she was still a child to the Bengali town of Narayangunj (Godden's spelling; it is now known as Narayanganj). The city lies on the Shitalakshaya River, which is part of the same river system as the Brahmaputra; it is only a few miles from Dacca. Today the district has a population of about three million. A century ago it would have been a sleepier place. But then, as now, it was an important centre for jute.

But when the family moved from Assam to Bengal, neither Rumer nor her older sister Jon went with them. In 1913 both had been exiled to England, at age six and seven respectively. It was then the custom to send the children "home", to a country that often felt like anything but home. The two girls found themselves in a large gloomy aunt-filled house in Maida Vale. In 1966, in a memoir written jointly with Jon, *Two Under the Indian Sun*, Godden would write that, in India, "children are largely left to grow ...we had not really been "brought up" before. It was a painful process, for us and the Aunts. ...The Aunts were so truly noble and good, ...but never, in all that tall dark house, was there a gleam of laughter or enterprise or fun..."

Rescue came in the unlikely form of the First World War. The Goddens, afraid that their daughters would be at risk from Zeppelin raids, decided to recall them to India, and their paternal aunt Mary arrived to take them there on the P&O liner *Persia*. In retrospect it seems an odd decision. Although air raids did kill about 1,400 civilians in Britain, largely in London, the U-boats were a much bigger menace. Maybe that was not yet clear. The Goddens do not mention that the *Persia* herself would be sent to the bottom with great loss of life while sailing the same route a year later.

For the young Goddens, the voyage was a liberation. Their Aunt Mary took one look at their heavy, unattractive clothes and as the ship began to move, she snatched the ugly straw hats from their heads and tossed them through the porthole. The young Goddens watched them sink slowly amongst the bits of box and orange-peel as the *Persia* was swung out into the Thames. "They were the last sight we had of England," they later recalled. "We were reprieved – for five years."

*

Rumer Godden's sister Jon was also a successful novelist, though never as well-known or as prolific as her sister. *Two Under the Indian Sun* was a collaboration. How much of each woman is in the book is hard to tell, but the writing style does feel similar to Rumer's own later memoirs. In the second volume of her autobiography, *A House With Four Rooms*, she mentions the book but says little about its creation. *Two Under the Indian Sun* is now out of print in both the UK and the US, but like Godden's other autobiographical works it has been reissued by an enterprising Indian publisher, Speaking Tiger.

The book is one of the best memoirs of childhood I have ever read. Thanks to the Zeppelins, it records a childhood in India with the family instead of exile in a draughty English boarding school smelling vaguely of cabbage, being bullied for one's accent and wearing a prickly, uncomfortable uniform while dreaming of one's parents and the warm, bright colours of India. Arriving at Narayanganj, the girls are startled by the profusion of flowers in the garden – roses, sweet peas, hibiscus, oleander and more. "Here was a new world of scent and colour, warm in the sunlight … 'Is this our garden?' asked Jon, dazzled."

It was not just a garden. The household was a huge establishment of gardeners, grooms, dining-room attendants, sweeps, bearers and more. According to the Goddens, this was not so much something the family wanted, as a reflection of Indian perceptions of what was fitting – and of local mores as to what a given servant might nor might not do. A bearer's caste allowed him to serve drinks, but not to wait at table because he could not touch food cooked by those of other castes. Only the sweeper could empty chamber-pots – but if a pet guinea-pig died, he could not dispose of the corpse ("a boy of a special sect had to be called in from the bazaar; he put on his best shirt of marigold-coloured silk to do this grisly work"). How much of this was necessary, it is hard to know – but the Goddens state that their father was responsible for meeting the cost of this household himself, although the Company paid for the house. So it is hard to see why he would have had such a large household had he not been constrained by custom to do so. It may however explain some British expatriates in the Empire, who, in time, grew to know no better: "Primrose ideas take root with frightening ease; …the big house and garden, the ponies, the muslin dresses we changed into every afternoon, the way [the staff] attended us everywhere we went …all added up to a princess quality." It did not prepare the girls for their eventual return to Britain, which would be a rude awakening.

Yet the children also faced dangers that would, in their words, "have horrified parents living in England or America." Malaria, dysentery and dengue fever featured, as did having one's tonsils taken out on the dining-room table by a Welsh doctor who seems to have taken it all in his stride, as did their parents. Neither were they always shielded from the harshest aspects of life in India. In one powerful chapter, titled simply *Cain*, the sisters describe how they became exposed to the harshness of the world: the beggar-boy in the bazaar who has been deliberately deformed, so that he can beg; the endless lawsuits that drain the servants of their wealth; the accidents in the jute mills and the fires in the bazaar; and their household sweeper, who fathers a child on his own daughter then beats her to death when she seeks solace with a better man.

One year when they are in a hill station to avoid the hot weather, trouble flares between Hindus and Muslims back in Narayanganj. Their father meets one of his steamers arriving there with Hindu pilgrims returning home; he warns them there is trouble and they should not disembark, but they disregard his advice. They do not reach their homes; passing through an apparently deserted street, they are ambushed and knifed to death.

This last incident is a reminder that Partition lay years in the future. In 1947 Narayanganj was to become part of East Pakistan, now Bangladesh. It is a Muslim country. But in 1914 millions of Hindus and Muslims alike lived in places where they are no longer to be seen. Moreover the vast Indian Empire stretched from the Khyber Pass to the borders of Thailand (Burma was part of it until 1937, when it became a separate territory). Within this huge area people could move freely, and did, the more so as the railway network grew. One night in the bazaar:

A couple of tall Kabulis, holding their long staffs, pushed contemptuously through the crowd, which parted uneasily in front of them; we knew that they were moneylenders, hated and feared, come from the mountains of Afghanistan to collect the exorbitant interest on their loans, but we could not help admiring their height and swagger.

I wonder how many people know that Afghan moneylenders ventured as far as Bangladesh a century ago. There is a sense in which our globalised world has become smaller even as it has, for some, been knitted together.

*

It was usual for British families to decamp to the hills in the hot weather, heading for hill stations such as Ootacamund, Darjeeling and Simla. Every few years, of course, a man would have home leave, but the First World War prevented this. One summer – it seems to have been 1917 or 1918 – the Godden's father took a long leave in Kashmir instead, hoping to hunt. The family took a houseboat at Srinagar and later, when the weather was hotter, embarked on a trek into the mountains, where their father fished for mahseer and hunted bears.

The children were left largely to their own devices. They were told not to go too far away, but of course they did. "We went deep into the sweet-smelling woods, following woodcutters' paths or paths made by animals, losing ourselves and knowing a few moments' panic... Once we saw what we thought was a huge grey dog slipping away from us between the trees..." Their father confirmed that it must have been a wolf. Today they have been hunted to extinction and when I lived in the Himalayas in the 1990s, I was told that an epidemic of destructive wild boars then troubling the

country was a consequence. The boars now had no natural preda-
tors. A century ago, however, wolves would have been quite usual
in the Himalayas. The bears are still there. That summer, the Goddens' father shot three. It is a cruel pursuit perhaps, but no-one
would have objected to it at the time. Indeed the Goddens recall
that a slain bear would be tied to a pole and carried back to camp
by villagers whose crops it had raided, and who were delighted
with its demise.

These summer retreats involved long journeys; it is many hundreds of miles from Narayanganj to Kashmir, and indeed to other
hill stations, and the family would spend days in a compartment
on a train, washing and cooking as best they could. The vastness of
the country affected them:

*...In the brief Indian twilight ...a curious sadness would fall on us, when
we all ...grew still. Then the compartment seemed suddenly small, the
train infinitesimal as it travelled over the vast Indian plain. ...A fire flick-
ered in a lonely village that, in a moment or two, was lost to sight...*

Reading this, I was reminded of a bus journey I took from Siliguri
to the Bhutanese border at Jaigaon many years ago. It was a cool
afternoon in November. As the countryside slipped by, the sun began
to sink, and the landscape was transformed. I enjoyed everything: the
long grass catching the light and the shadow, the quiet shacks by the
roadside, sleepy village shops, sparkling village ponds, lush bright
fields, palm fronds, boys playing cricket and laughing. A man wheel-
ing his bicycle slowly back from the fields. A path winding away
from the road and disappearing, between trees, to nowhere. Orange
lorries, white cars, a thin young man with glasses riding on top of a
truck's green tarpaulin, a train standing in the middle of the fields,
birds by the Brahmaputra. Then dusk, a round red sun above green-

yellow fields, and darkness, and Jaigaon with flickering lights in the main street, food stalls, rickshaws, chaos, slowly ambling crowds with white shirts that shone in the darkness. In India you can lose yourself in a journey.

*

Two Under the Indian Sun is an outstanding memoir of childhood. But as the First World War ended, the sisters were entering their teens; stresses and strains developed between them, not least because Jon was the glamorous one and got all the male attention. (This rivalry would be the theme of Rumer Godden's later novel *The River*, which would be filmed with great success by Jean Renoir.) In any case, the war had given them a reprieve; now, in 1920, they would be returned to England to be educated, as was the normal way. On a cold grey morning they berthed at Plymouth. "Everything was grey, wet, colourless ...We travelled third on the train to London. 'Then in England do we travel third-class?'"

Two Under the Indian Sun ends there. But Rumer Godden's strange and brilliant life was just beginning. For five years she attended schools and college in England, not always with happy results, but was lucky enough to meet a teacher who recognised her writing ability and urged her to develop it. She also developed an interest in dance and took classes, but her progress was slowed by a childhood injury. She recounts this period in *A Time to Dance, No Time to Weep*, the first volume of her autobiography (the title is adapted from a passage in Ecclesiastes). It includes an account of a sojourn in France that would give rise, years later, to one of Godden's most successful novels, *The Greengage Summer* – which also became a film; it was, it turns out, barely fiction at all.

In October 1925 Godden's older sister Jon returned to India and, overcome with nostalgia, she decided to go too. But she was no longer a child; Narayanganj seemed dull and ugly, and the garden and busy river that had fascinated her as a child no longer did. Unsettled, perhaps, she embarked on an abortive engagement that she quickly broke, leaving her guilty and restless. Now 19, she began for the first time to question the British presence on the subcontinent. She had read *A Passage to India* and it shocked her. "Were we, the English in India, really like ...those righteous, insensitive characters?" she asked herself. Godden blamed her father for telling them nothing of India, or Indian life, in their youth. In *A Time to Dance*, written decades later in old age, she acknowledged that this was unjust. Her father was well-liked by his large staff and his boat captains, and spoke Hindi and Bengali, and some Assamese.

He found her work in an agricultural research establishment in Dacca, but not long afterwards most of the family, including Godden herself, returned to England and remained there until the autumn of 1929. During this period she trained as a dance teacher, and on her return to India set up a small dance school in Calcutta. The British community did not approve ("In Calcutta's then almost closed society, 'nice girls' did not work or try to earn their living.") Worse, dance schools had a reputation because they were run by Eurasians – people of mixed race, who found themselves in a difficult position in India. A British man who married one would be asked to resign from the civil service or his company. Godden worked with and taught Eurasians and also employed a troupe of dancers from that background; she found herself ostracised as a result. "I quickly learned who my real friends were," she wrote nearly 60 years later. This anti-Eurasian prejudice was to figure in one of her earliest books, *The Lady and the Unicorn* (1937), and in a much later one, *The Dark Horse* (1981).

Godden had other problems besides ostracism. She became pregnant by a British stockbroker in Calcutta, Laurence Foster, and they married – there were few alternatives in 1934. The child, a boy, was born prematurely and died four days later. Meanwhile the marriage proved unfortunate. They were not always unhappy and had two other children, both daughters. But Foster proved feckless. Quite early on they had to leave a pleasant apartment in Calcutta because he had simply not bothered to pay the rent. A keen sportsman, he spent heavily on playing golf when on leave in England, although their finances were stretched. Then the second daughter proved delicate at birth and had to be nursed carefully for some months at a family home in Cornwall.

It did not help that Godden still felt uneasy about the British in India, about the worsening political situation and the poverty that she saw all around her in Calcutta. Moreover, unlike her father, who at least genuinely liked and understood India and its people and spoke two of their languages, Foster and his friends cared little for such matters.

Yet it was hard to ignore the growing demands for independence and the undercurrent of violence. A policeman friend was stabbed in the back by students as he played rugger with them; a student went up to collect a prize from the Governor, and tried to shoot him. "Yet I could not help sympathising with them. Who would not want, I thought, to be free? 'Idiots. They're far better off under the British,' said Laurence and his friends."

This alienation, for Godden, went deeper. She talks, in *A Time to Dance*, of the concept of *darshan*. This involves travelling to, and contemplation of, a holy or miraculous place or person – she cites Gandhi or Kanchenjunga – not to photograph or physically record, but simply to let it seep into one's soul. Foster lacked this side to his nature and so did his companions. "It slowly dawned on me that not only did they not know, they seemed unable to feel any sense of wonder, ecstasy or awe," she wrote. That Godden was different – that *dar-shan* did exist for her – would later become clear in one of the strangest and least-known books she ever wrote. But that lay several years in the future.

*

Meanwhile, the monkey-shit seesaw also went the other way. Godden's career as a writer was beginning.

Shortly after the marriage to Foster, Godden had had a novel accepted for the first time (it was *Chinese Puzzle*). In 1938, on her way home to deliver her second daughter, and not feeling social, she decided to turn in at the same time as her older daughter, Jane, at six o'clock; and, while Jane slept, her mother wrote. On arrival at Tilbury 18 days later she had the draft of a novel. Her father was sceptical.

"Fa, I'm writing a book about nuns."

"Don't," said Fa. "No-one will read it."

But *Black Narcissus* has never been out of print.

According to Godden's own account in *A Time to Dance*, the book's genesis went back to when she was 18 and visiting Shillong, a then fairly remote town at over 5,000ft, or about 1,500m, that was then in Assam (the borders of which have since changed; Shillong is now the capital of the state of Meghalaya). The story took root on a picnic to a deserted cantonment in the mountains. Wandering away from her companions, Godden chanced upon the grave of a nun, marked only with her name and her dates; she had died at 23. No-one seemed to know who she had been and there was no mission nearby, but the villagers seemed to have made a shrine of the grave. It seems the grave piqued Godden's curiosity; 10 years later, *Black Narcissus* was the result.

Although far from the only novel Godden would write set in India, it is still much her best-known. Published in January 1939, it passed largely unnoticed at first but as the weeks went by it attracted increasing critical attention. In 1946 it was to be filmed by Powell and Pressburger, no less, starring Deborah Kerr. Godden did not like the film version but viewers disagreed, and still do; it has become something of a classic period piece, with its seething sexual tensions in an isolated community of Anglican nuns, high in the Himalayas. But in 1939 the book's success took its author by surprise. Godden, who by some oversight had not even been told it was published, wandered into Foyle's in Charing Cross Road to find a table piled high with copies.

But the monkey was about to shit again.

Godden had planned to fly back to India in the autumn of 1939. The flight was cancelled. But as the war situation worsened, it became clear that the children would be safer in India, where her husband still was. "If you are to go at all, you must go now," Godden's father told her. In June 1940 she embarked on the *Strathallan* with her two infant daughters and a much-loved Swiss-Italian nanny. As with so much in *A Time to Dance*, the voyage is made wonderfully vivid, although Godden was writing nearly half a century later. There is a knack here for resurrecting those details that bring her memories alive, and discarding those that do not. This time, everyone was very conscious of the danger the ship was in, and Godden recalls that the passengers – mostly women, often with children – were frightened and frequently sought solace in the bar, or with one of the stewards. They were not wrong; like the *Persia*, the *Strathallan* would also be sunk some time later (again, Godden does not mention this). They spend "an uneasy week" in Mombasa; "There are two cruisers and other battleships in the harbour and the Italian planes come over every night, attacked fiercely by ack-ack fire." Yet as always Godden is conscious of beauty, sneaking on deck at night when she can to see the phosphorescence in the water as she stands in the bow.

The journey ended with an apparently happy reunion in Calcutta. Over the next few months Godden's husband seemed more settled than he had been, and harder-working. Then one night in June 1941 he came home and announced that he was in the army; asked whether by choice, he did not say. Somewhat surprised, Godden saw him off to training camp at Bangalore, only to return to the house and find lines of tradesmen waiting with bills and writs. Foster, left in charge of the family finances, had simply not paid the bills. Meanwhile he had gambled on the Stock Exchange, had lost, and had used the firm's money to recoup his losses and had lost that too. Godden resolved to pay off his debts. The earnings from *Black Narcissus* were gone, and so was her husband.

As luck would have it, Godden had already arranged to borrow an isolated bungalow in the Himalayas for the hot weather. A few weeks later she, her children and the few remaining staff headed for the hills, and instead of returning for the cool weather, she remained there. The result was a strange, little-known but magical book, *Rungli-Rungliot*.

*

One December day in 1993 a friend and I travelled by bus from Jaigaon on the Bengal plain to Kalimpong in the mountains and then across to Darjeeling. It is never cool on the plain, even in winter, and besides the bus had a quite enormous stereo. In that year the big Bollywood hit was *Khal Nayak* (The Villain), a melodrama that included a dance number, *Choli Ke Peeche Kya Hai*, noted for its suggestive lyrics. (The title, roughly translated, means "What's beneath my blouse." There was dancing to match.) I rather liked it but found it palled somewhat when heard for the tenth time in one day. As the driver fiddled with the volume control, my friend suggested we go on the roof. We scrambled up the ladder at the back of the bus and perched on the rack with the luggage; it is a good way to travel in hot climates.

The bus wound its way past Siliguri and into the mountains towards Kalimpong. We climbed; the air grew cooler, the country around us greener; and after some time we crossed the Coronation Bridge, a large prewar single-span bridge across the powerful River Teesta, which lay many hundreds of feet below us in a gorge. At this time of year, it was a startling bright cobalt blue. The river was visible for less than a minute, but the sight was not one to forget. Later the bus passed slowly along the narrow road that clings to the contours between Kalimpong and Darjeeling, passing close to Tiger Hill, the vantage point from which one admires sunrise on distant Kanchenjunga – again, not something one forgets if one has seen it, which to my delight I have.

Somewhere between Kalimpong and Tiger Hill, we will have passed a small village with a police post. This was Rangli-Rangliot.

Rungli-Rungliot, as Godden spells it, means "Thus far and no farther", and was the phrase spoken – she says – by a Buddhist monk at some point in the past to stop the flooded waters of the Teesta reaching the hilltops and drowning all and sundry. (Godden states that the words are in Paharia, but it is not clear which language she meant by that word; it can refer to several dialects and even to Nepali.) She arrived there in the summer of 1941, broke, without her husband but with two children, the Italian-Swiss nanny, her husband's Sikkimese bearer and his family, and one or two servants, for all of whom she was responsible.

Later in the war she would publish her short book, *Rungli-Rungliot*, based on the diaries she kept, and it was republished shortly after the war. But it was then mostly forgotten until, like *Two Under the Indian Sun,* it was put out in a new edition in India by Speaking Tiger. The book includes charming illustrations by Tontyn Hopman, a Dutch artist stranded in India by the war who became a friend of Godden's a year or two later (and who died as recently as 2016, at the age of 102).

Rungli-Rungliot is a curious book. Godden's other autobiographical work is marked by its clear, straightforward prose; it dazzles by the clarity and quality of her memories, not by tricks of presentation, and seems effortless although there is, in fact, not a word out of place. *Rungli-Rungliot,* written much earlier, has a less sure touch and can even seem overwritten. It is still memorable. Climbing slowly northward into the mountains on the narrow-gauge railway that runs to Darjeeling: "After the rains, in the winter, the river would be blue; first a chalky blue and then a blue with a grape-green tinge from the ice water. It is a dangerous cruel river, as cruel as it is beautiful.."

Godden's retreat is not at Rangli-Rangliot itself but in a so-called "out-bungalow" some miles away, where one of the tea-planters would be stationed and would live when, as she put it, not drinking or hunting. She refers to the place as Chinglam. Like Rangli-Rangliot, this is a real place, eccentrically spelled; in *A Time to Dance* she uses the correct spelling, Jinglam. It is isolated; it can be reached by car but via a vertiginous road on which one had to strain in first gear. An expedition to Darjeeling, for mail or shopping, is an undertaking.

Yet Jinglam is, it seems, its own reward – a place of staggering beauty, with the valley falling away steeply thousands of feet in front. The Swiss nanny, Giovanna, takes to yodelling; the sound "rings right across the valley" and before long the workers in the tea-plantation start to do it too. Behind the house there is a high saddle behind from which Godden and her children can see the eternal snows of Kanchenjunga. When tiring of this they can come back to a warm and welcoming bungalow, lit softly by Victorian oil lamps she has bought from Thieves Bazaar in Calcutta. The planters are mostly gone to war, but the head planter remains and is kind and popular. A keen naturalist, he "had a python in his chicken-run. It was a full-sized python but there was no need to be afraid ...because it was anchored in the middle by a deer that it had eaten, which was progressing, by degrees of slow digestion, towards its tail."

There are few other Europeans around, but there are of course her staff. ("The cook was very turbulent, and left partly because he was turbulent and partly because he had foot-rot.") And there are plenty of visitors; pedlars, wandering Lepchas from Sikkim and people from the plains and two Bhutias (Bhutan is quite close by). She presents the latter as wild and savage people. I wonder if they were; the Bhutanese are rather civilised. But in 1941 they would have had little contact with outsiders.

In fact *Rungli-Rungliot*, brief though it is, is a haunting snapshot of a quite recent past. But it is also the account of an idyll, in one of the most beautiful places on earth, suspended between the bright blue of the Teesta river and the eternal snows of Kanchenjunga, bathed in the soft light of a Victorian oil lamp or the sparkling air of a crystal winter's morning. *Rungli-Rungliot* drips with *darshan*. Yet it is leavened with wit and never cloys. It is mostly forgotten now, but Godden would write over 40 years later that this book had brought her more letters than anything else she had written.

*

Jinglam may have been an idyll, but early in 1942 Godden left. She doesn't say why in either book, but implies that she had to. According to her biographer, Anne Chisholm, this was not the case; in her excellent 1998 life of Godden (*Rumer Godden: A Storyteller's Life*)

Chisholm says it was her own decision, but the reasons for it are not quite clear.

At any rate, Godden now found she headed what was described, in wartime India, as an 'abandoned family'. This was less dramatic than it seemed, meaning simply the dependants of someone who was normally based in India and was serving for now in the Army, which had thus become responsible for her. She was told to choose somewhere in the Indian Empire to which she would be relocated, and would remain for the duration under the protection of the Provost Marshall (the head of the military police). She chose Kashmir, thinking it to have a good climate; clearly the long summer in the mountains described in *Two Under the Indian Sun* was not forgotten. She also felt that its location in the far west of the Empire would be safer. This was not fanciful. The Japanese would soon overrun Burma and would push west into India, and would eventually be only a few hundred miles from Jinglam. They would not be repulsed until 1944.

In March 1942 Godden arrived in Kashmir with her children – a move recorded in *A Time to Dance* as one she and the children made on their own; in fact, Chisholm says that Laurence Foster was with her and took leave to try and settle the family. (In general, the marriage does not seem to have broken up quite so finally and quickly as Godden would later suggest.) In any case, Godden was reminded that she had not been to Kashmir in winter: "Peasants shuffle in rags, thin shawls and straw sandals and the light tongas move as silently as sleighs ...The women's cotton robes are filthy but the colours are blended by the very filth, dull blue and muted green, a prune colour or purple; they wear white veils and not one silver earring but bunches of them hanging either side of the face."

These quotes are from letters that Godden wrote at the time and later included in the later parts of *A Time to Dance*; often they were to her sisters. However, it is not just these snapshots from the time that are vivid; the book lacks the strangeness of *Rungli-Rungliot* and the prose is straightforward and undramatic, and yet its author, in her 80s when it was published, seems to be sitting with you, not writing but speaking, a little steam rising from her tea, her eyes on you one minute and then focused elsewhere as some long-ago joy or misery comes to her.

One wonders why Godden took so long to write *A Time to Dance*, but perhaps she did not want to recall everything, including her troubles; yet felt unable to write it without doing so. Her wartime life was very harsh. In Srinagar she, her children and their adored Swiss-Italian nanny, Giovanna, were quartered in two rooms in a bad hotel, surrounded by other wives of officers who had formed a small world to which Godden could not adjust. Worse, the hotel was insanitary and the entire family got dysentery, one child got typhoid and the youngest and weakest had a contagious disease that forced them all to move out. At length Godden herself contracted jaundice. She had little money but knew that somehow she had to find somewhere for them all to live. Then she remembered a house she had seen from a great distance, across the lake, lost among the trees high on a mountainside.

Godden moved in with her daughters as soon as she could. She writes in *A Time to Dance* that she should have liked to stay there for ever. Like Jinglam, it seems to have been a place of astonishing beauty. "I have had several cherished houses; always, by circumstance not by desire, I have had to leave them but never have I loved a house as I loved Dove House." In a letter at the end of May 1943 she describes dusk in the mountains, the lights slowly appearing around the lake below, and from the garden comes "a gust of sweetness, the scent of flowers. Tonight I am grateful from my head to the soles of my feet ...for living here, for being allowed to live here."

*

But Godden was to stay there for less than two years. The monkey curse struck again in June 1944, when a servant poisoned her and the children in an apparent murder attempt.

Exactly what happened is not clear. In *A Time to Dance* Godden states that she met an accomplished British woman, a painter, by the name of Olwen, and eventually agreed that they would share Dove Cottage and the cost of running it; Godden was as short of money as ever. Bit by bit Olwen's servants displaced her own and Olwen's bearer recruited a new cook, Salim, a man who, Godden wrote, never seemed quite as he should be. Both Godden and Olwen became very unwell, and it was clear that Godden, at least, was being fed drugs of some sort; she was to remember walking around the grounds wearing a Norman Hartnell ballgown. At length the Provost Marshall appeared at the house, removed both women, forbad them to return and arrested Salim who, unbeknownst to either woman, had a past record of making himself indispensable to English ladies and relieving them of their belongings. Charges were brought against Salim but it became plain that the court would not convict, and that the women might face counter-charges for slander. Advised to leave Kashmir, Godden slipped away, leaving Olwen to face the music – something of which she later admitted she was not proud; Olwen, she said, did not forgive her.

That last part, it seems, was true; according to Chisholm's fine biography, Olwen – whose real name was Helen Arberry – did feel that she had been treated badly. They never met again. Other parts of the incident may not have been quite as Godden wrote them. In particular, Chisholm's account, which draws on Godden's own letters from the time, suggests that the cook Godden calls Salim (his real name was Siddika) had not been recruited by Arberry's bearer as

Godden wrote later, but had been employed by Godden herself before Arberry moved in.

In the early 1950s Godden wrote a fictionalised account, a novel called *Kingfishers Catch Fire,* in which some at least of the episode is very true to life. A headstrong young widow and mother, Sophie, becomes badly ill in Srinigar and is cared for with her children by the Mission next to the graveyard. Then, in spring, largely recovered, she insists against local advice on taking a hillside cottage away from the town. This is very much what Godden did. Once in the cottage, Sophie fails to understand the dynamics of the nearby village, and causes trouble between the local peasants. She also wilfully refuses to understand her young daughter's fear of the local children, which turns out to be all too well-founded. Her life in the cottage ends badly, as she is poisoned by her cook.

Is this how Godden herself saw this episode? Probably not. Neither her own books nor Chisholm's careful account suggest that Godden was prone to self-criticism of this sort. One could ask why, in that case, she wrote *Kingfishers Catch Fire* if not in expiation; but that one is easy to answer – writers never waste good material.

What *Kingfishers* is, though, is a good novel. Chisholm rates it very high, suggesting that, as a portrait of the British in India, it ranks alongside *A Passage to India* and *The Jewel in the Crown.* This is high praise, and is based in part on the way Chisholm feels the book respects the locals themselves. In fact, I am not sure it does; I thought Godden's depiction of the villagers had, by her standards, quite dated and imperial overtones. Where *Kingfishers Catch Fire* is a success, however, is in its vivid portrait of a woman who has misunderstood her Indian neighbours in a hundred different ways, while also offending against the conventions of her own community; the latter is fiercely critical of her decision to move to an isolated location amongst people she does not understand. In this sense, the book is true to life. Mollie Kaye – better known as M.M. Kaye, the author of *The Far Pavilions* – was in Kashmir herself at the time; they do not seem to have known each other well then, though they did become friends in later life. Kaye was to remember that the British community had thought the move was unwise and that no-one was very surprised that Godden had had trouble. It was even suggested that no-one had really tried to poison Godden and Arberry at all, though on that score at least Godden – and the Provost Marshal, and the Kashmiri police – seem to have had no doubts.

Whatever really happened at Dove Cottage, it cast a long shadow over Godden, and she was still nervous of entering Kashmir when she returned with the BBC Bookmark crew in the 1990s, not long before she died. According to Chisholm (who accompanied her to India), Godden demanded assurances from the Kashmiri authorities that she would not be subject to any proceedings if she returned, and she was not willing to revisit Dove Cottage. Yet her description of her life there in *A Time to Dance* suggests a beauty so profound that it seems to have transfixed her even as she wrote of it 40 years later.

*

That beauty must have sustained Godden as she left India via a stinking, diseased transit camp near Bombay in the summer of 1945 – a difficult time that she describes in her second volume of autobiography, *A House With Four Rooms*. She was not finished with India; her sisters were still there, and she would return soon after independence, in November 1949, with the distinguished French film director Jean Renoir, to make his much-loved film of her novel *The River*, for which she wrote the screenplay. Her last visit to India was with the *Bookmark* team in 1994 at the age of 86. But she was not to live there again. She spent the rest of her life in Britain, in Sussex and later in

Dumfriesshire, producing more than 60 books, including some well-received children's titles. A number of her novels, notably *Coromandel Sea Change* and *In This House of Brede*, were highly successful, and several – including *The River*, *Black Narcissus* and *The Greengage Summer* – were filmed. She continued to write until the end of her life and her last novel, *Cromartie* vs. *the God Shiva*, was published as late as 1997.

Rumer Godden died in November 1998 at the age of 90. One of Britain's most successful ever novelists in her lifetime, she is probably less read now, but still has a following and in time, like J.B. Priestley, she will be rediscovered as a quintessential English writer. In fact the rediscovery is under way; a number of her novels have now been republished by Virago.

For me, however, it always will be her vision of India that astonishes and delights; the clear-eyed but loving childhood memoir in *Two Under the Indian Sun*, and the thoughtful beauty of *A Time to Dance, No Time to Weep*. The latter is written with the clarity of old age and filled with people who were already long dead but, to her, very much alive. It is a book that sometimes comes quite close to perfection.

And there is the mystical, forgotten *Rungli-Rungliot*. I read it in December 2017. I took it with me when I reported to a hospital in New York for a heart procedure that I knew might not work (it did.) As I left the house in the early hours, I remembered that I should take a book; there is a lot of waiting to do in hospitals. *Rungli-Rungliot* had just arrived, and I slipped it into my bag and felt it bumping against my hip as I walked through the pre-dawn streets. Later that morning, checked in, monitored and waiting in my cubicle, I reached for the book. I came to Godden's description of her climb to Darjeeling on the narrow-gauge railway from Siliguri on the Bengal plain. Sitting in a cubicle in a New York hospital, frightened of what lay ahead, I

71

let my mind wander back to the journeys I had made to Darjeeling myself, over 20 years earlier. There was the one via Kalimpong and past Rungli-Rungliot itself, across the Coronation Bridge, the Teesta river a glacial blue many hundreds of feet below. There was another when we climbed by road, slowly, in the wake of round, stately Hindustan Ambassador saloons in green and grey, packed with Indian families.

Once, we rode the train. The engine, painted bright blue, had a plate that proclaimed its date of birth in Britain: 1877. It may have hauled Godden and her family upwards, through Ghoom and Tung, past hamlets of clapboard and corrugated-iron roofs, just as it took me on a sunlit afternoon in 1992, the deep green of the Himalayan foothills all round us. An Indian guard clapped me on the shoulder. "Your great-grandfather built this," he said. There was another passenger, an elderly Englishman in a sports-jacket. The late sunlight bounced around the carriage and lit his face, and he was smiling with what looked like wonder, and I knew that he had been here before, a long time ago.

The Butler Did It. Or Did He?

Some months ago, tired and worried after months of lockdown (and in the middle of a health scare of my own), I decided that a detective novel seemed a good way to relax. So I downloaded a collection of early Agatha Christie books. I had read one or two of hers before, of course; most of us have – but I had forgotten just how good they could be. It was the start of a journey into a peculiarly English phenomenon – the Golden Age of Detective Fiction.

That golden age is widely accepted as having been between the two world wars. That is not to say that no good crime novels have been written since. That would be absurd, as anyone who has read P.D. James, Ian Rankin, Colin Dexter, Ruth Rendell or a host of others will happily attest. Neither was it solely British; the "hardboiled" style of American crime fiction had its golden age too, led by Dashiell Hammett and Raymond Chandler – both still widely read. But there is something essentially English in the world of Agatha Christie, Dorothy L. Sayers, Ngaio Marsh and Margery Allingham that is of its time and place. It's a world of bodies in libraries, ingenious poisons and genteel murderers. And of quaint Cotswold villages full of unseemly death.

It reflected the English newspaper reader's preoccupation with a certain type of real-life crime, defined by George Orwell in his 1946 *Tribune* piece *Decline of the English Murder* as committed by: "A little man of the professional class – a dentist or a solicitor, say – living an intensely respectable life somewhere in the suburbs ... He should go astray through cherishing a guilty passion ...Having decided on murder, he should plan it all with the utmost cunning, and only slip up over some tiny unforeseeable detail." In Orwell's view, interest in real-life crimes of this kind had declined partly because in line with the times, crime had become more violent and nihilistic. He also commented that "the violence of external events has made murder seem unimportant" – which, in 1946, it had. If he was right, then a waning interest in genteel, cerebral crime fiction was also a result.

Much later, P.D. James wrote a piece in *The Spectator* titled *Who Killed the Golden Age of Crime?* (December 14 2013). She did not answer her own question directly, but it seems clear that she, too, saw Golden Age stories as the product of a vanished world in which we can no longer believe. "The world these writers portrayed was one [in] which ...any sense of the world outside the comfortable confines of conventional English village life was absent," she writes. "Readers expected the detective to be a gentleman in all senses of the word." Those detectives were, she points out, often wealthy aristocrats. She quotes an Alan Bennett character's description of English literature as "snobbery with violence", which seems to fit the inter-war detective novel. Besides, she says, policing is different now and the copper's relations with the community rather more complex. "The best of the Golden Age stories have survived and will continue to survive," she wrote, "but they they are not being written today."

I am sure that both Orwell and James are right. The TV news and the Internet confront us constantly with sordid realities of life – so they must be reflected in fiction, or we can't suspend disbelief. We are also less squeamish; I don't believe 1930s readers would have easily accepted a book like P.D. James's own *Innocent Blood* (1980), which features the sexually motivated murder of a child. I wonder, too, if the audience has changed in other ways. Before 1939, fairly ordinary middle-class families would have been able to afford domestic help – so women, in particular, may have had more time to read (a point made in Colin Watson's book about the

Golden Age, actually called *Snobbery With Violence*; more on that book later). After the war, detective fiction may have had to seek a broader, less genteel class of reader. Suddenly, the Golden Age detectives were dated.

On the other hand the best writing will always be worth reading, or why would we read Shakespeare – or Orwell, or Graham Greene? James herself says in the *Spectator* piece that the best Golden Age detective stories "have survived and will continue to do so". Besides, the success of the "cosy mystery" in our own time – not just in print, but with TV series like *Midsomer Murders* and *Rosemary and Thyme* – suggests that the Golden Age of murder still has a place in our hearts. Why? I decided to take a break from heavier reading and find out for myself. Should one still be reading Golden Age detective fiction today? Or does it belong in the museum?

I started with Agatha Christie. One would, after all.

*

Christie was born in 1890 and brought up in a comfortable home in Torquay. Although she is a quintessentially English figure, her father was American. Born and brought up in New York, he had inherited money from the family business. But her early life was quite troubled; her father died when she was 11, and with no formal skill or career – a well-to-do girl wouldn't have them, then – she married at 24. In the 1920s, her marriage failing, she famously disappeared for 11 days, turning up in Harrogate, where she had booked into a hotel under the name of her husband's mistress; she claimed to remember nothing. Her brother Monty, too, would cause her endless worry – a spendthrift who couldn't cope with life; at about the same time she parked him in a small house on

Dartmoor to keep him out of trouble. But in 1929 he decamped with his housekeeper to Marseilles, where he died not long afterwards after suffering a stroke in a bar.

But a much happier second marriage followed. Moreover, by the time of the Harrogate incident, Christie was already a successful writer. During the First World War, with her first husband away on active service, she had had time to occupy; liking mystery stories, she decided to write her own. *The Mysterious Affair at Styles* was written in 1916 and benefited from her wartime work in a dispensary (she would do that again in the second war, updating her knowledge of poisons). The book was not accepted by a publisher until 1920. But it was then quite a hit. Agatha Christie was on her way.

I decided to begin with *The Mysterious Affair at Styles*, since she did. A young officer, Hastings, has been wounded on the Western Front and is invited to spend part of his convalescent leave with an old friend at the latter's country home, Styles. Very soon the mistress of the house dies horribly in the night, as one does. However, Hastings has found that a distinguished Belgian refugee detective of his acquaintance is staying nearby. Hercule Poirot has arrived, and the "little grey cells" are deployed for the first time.

The lady has been poisoned. Forensic science is not where it is now, but no matter – M. Poirot has other tools of deduction, from a random footprint to a fragment of burned paper in the grate. Clues are scattered where the attentive reader will find them and others will not, which is part of the fun with a book like this. The characters come alive. There are complex motives and red herrings aplenty.

In fact, *The Mysterious Affair at Styles* is rather good. I needed no encouragement to read Christie's second book, *The Secret Adversary* (1922).

It disappointed me. It is as much an adventure story as a detective novel – but that is fine if one can combine the two; John Buchan could. But M Poirot is, regrettably, absent. Instead we have Tommy and Tuppence. The former is a somewhat stolid middle-class English chap, a little dim but a good egg; Tuppence is the impoverished daughter of a country deacon, but an awfully good sport. They are so relentlessly jolly that I wanted to throttle them both. The narrative concerns a desperate attempt to foil a wicked Bolshevist coup in which, through either wickedness or stupidity, Labour leaders have become complicit. Perhaps, in 1922, this was popular with middle-class readers, but it has not aged well. Moreover one or two plot devices do not really work. For example, much turns on the text of a secret treaty, now abandoned, that must on no account be made public lest it bring down the Empire; Christie never troubles to tell us how it could have done so. The book was quite well received in 1922, and was even made into a silent film in Germany. But it was clearly not Christie's best.

Still, she only used Tommy and Tuppence in five books; M. Poirot featured in over 30, and Christie's evergreen heroine Miss Marple, the nice old lady with a mind like a razor, in 12. I decided to go in search of something better. I knew where to look.

In 1928, the year in which her divorce became final, Christie travelled to Iraq – presumably to get away from personal troubles and to catch some sun. When there, she met a young archaeologist, Max Mallowan; they married in 1930. This second marriage was far happier and lasted nearly fifty years, ending only with Christie's death. Mallowan's work would take them back to the Middle East more than once. On at least one of these trips, Christie spent an extended stay at the Baron Hotel in Aleppo.

The Baron, like the city, is a storied place, and I often drank in its bar when I lived in Aleppo in the 1990s. Opened in 1911, it soon became the hotel of choice for Europeans passing through the ancient city; they included T.E. Lawrence, who, as a young student, was studying the fortifications of the Crusader castles in the region. After 1919, Syria ceased to be part of the Ottoman empire and was instead occupied by France; as with the British occupation of Palestine, this was either done under a League of Nations mandate or was a colonial land grab, depending on your point of view. In any case, the Baron weathered the changes and continued to welcome the great and the good, who sometimes arrived via the Orient Express from Paris to Istanbul and thence to Aleppo on the Taurus Express. They included Christie and Mallowan. In *Murder on the Orient Express*, M. Poirot makes this journey in reverse.

Agatha Christie wrote the book at the Baron in 1930 – officially in room 203, which retains the writing-desk on which it is said to have been written. In fact, I believe some of it at least was written on the terrace. I knew it well; in the winter I sat at the cluttered bar, which had changed little since Christie's day, and imagined Kim Philby drowning his sorrows there in the last months before his defection (which, apparently, he did). But in summer one could sit outside and hope to catch some cool breeze in the stifling Syrian summer. I suppose Christie did the same.

Murder on the Orient Express opens in Aleppo station on a freezing night; M. Poirot has been in the city to render some unspecified service to the French military and is being wished on his way by a French officer. They do not know each other well, and would clearly happily be rid of each other, but are too polite to make this clear.

Eventually the Taurus Express pulls out bound for Konya and Istanbul via the Cilician Gates, the mountain pass that admits it from the Middle East to Anatolia. It is a spectacular journey. It would be made some years later by Richard Dimbleby, who took

the same train on a tense journey through Vichy territory and neutral Turkey in 1941, and described it in *The Frontiers are Green*
(1943).

M. Poirot's eye, however, is caught not by the scenery but by
an English governess and a straight-backed British officer who
have travelled, together and yet apart, from Iraq. Poirot will go on
with them on the Orient Express from Istanbul and, in a snowdrift
in the Balkans, there will be murder most foul in the sleeping-car.

It is a wonderful setting; a cast of exotic characters who cannot
leave the train, and one of them must be the murderer. Is it the
Hungarian diplomat, Count Andrenyi? The Russian Princess Dra-
gomiroff? The English governess? I knew the solution; I had seen
the film. I was drawn in nonetheless. This is so much better than
The Secret Adversary and shows just how Christie has captivated
generations, although the world in which her books were set has
long gone. Pick the plot apart and one can find the holes; but why
would one wish to? It really is such splendid fun. It is not surprising that, at about the same time, Graham Greene used the Orient
Express for his own adventure story, *Stamboul Train*.

So Agatha Christie is still worth reading – if you get the right
book. To be sure, her books are dated now; but while *The Secret
Adversary* grates for that reason, in *Murder on the Orient Express* this
glimpse back into a vanished world is part of the appeal. In any
case, readers are still in no doubt. In 2019 they bought 20 million
copies of Christie's books in the English-speaking world alone –
adding to the two billion already sold. We still cannot get enough
of either Poirot or Miss Marple. Neither are they just in print; they
have made both the big and the small screen. Poirot has been portrayed most notably by David Suchet, but also by Albert Finney,
Peter Ustinov, John Malkovich and Kenneth Branagh, amongst
others. Marple has been played by Margaret Rutherford, Angela

Lansbury, Geraldine McEwan, June Whitfield and, amazingly, Gracie Fields – the latter for American TV.

But what about Christie's rivals? Do they stand the test of time?

*

After Christie, I suppose one would turn to Dorothy L. Sayers. Just three years younger, she too began to publish in the 1920s. She would never be anything like as prolific, and her detective fiction is sometimes seen as far more cerebral. To some extent, that reflects the women themselves; although clearly extremely intelligent, Christie was not an intellectual. Sayers was; she won a scholarship to Somerville College, Oxford, and in later life translated Dante's *Divine Comedy* and wrote extensively on Christian theology. But she also spent some years as an advertising copywriter, and there is no doubt that her detective fiction was intended to entertain. Much of it features her aristocratic amateur detective, Lord Peter Wimsey, who is introduced in Sayers's first book, *Whose Body?*, published in 1923. So once again I decided to start there.

The book starts with a body in Battersea. To be precise, it has appeared in the bath in someone's flat, in one of the big 1890s mansion-blocks face the south edge of Battersea Park, along Prince of Wales Drive. (One of the blocks was the scene of a notorious real-life murder that remains unsolved – that of Thomas Weldon Atherstone, a music-hall performer, in 1910.) In *Whose Body?*, the flat's resident appears to have no connection with the crime, or with the body; and, flustered, he accepts the help of the aristocratic amateur detective Lord Peter Wimsey, with whose mother he is distantly acquainted. In the meantime Lord Peter is also trying to solve the disappearance of a well-known London financier, Sir Reuben

Levy. The body in the bath is, it appears, not Levy's; but are the two matters connected?

I confess that the first 50 pages or so of this book did not impress. Lord Peter is too much the lordly fool; his logorrheic banter is so dated that now and then it flummoxed even me (and I am only 30 years younger than the book). To be sure, Sayers wishes us to see the fatuous ass before we glimpse the ruthless brain beneath, but it seemed to me overdone. In contrast, his loyal valet and confederate, Bunter, has an intellect and skills that would surely have fitted him for a career with more prospects. Meanwhile the doltish detective assigned the case, Sugg, appears a cypher, a straw man from the lower classes set up as a foil for our posh hero.

One is reminded of Raymond Chandler's skewering of Sayers in a 1944 essay in *The Atlantic*, titled *The Simple Art of Murder*. As I noted briefly at the beginning, the American detective story had its own golden age at roughly the same time – the 'hard-boiled' style of which Chandler was a prime exponent, along with Dashiell Hammett, James M. Cain and others. Chandler wrote that Sayers had "an arid formula which could not even satisfy its own implications. ...if it started out to be about real people..., they must very soon do unreal things in order to form the artificial pattern required by the plot. When they did unreal things... They became puppets." For Chandler, the hard-boiled American style is clearly more realistic so works better; Sayers is trite.

Is that fair? Reading *Whose Body?*, I would at first have said yes. It seemed as if it may have pleased readers in the 1920s, but was a dated confection that was best left there. But something made me think I should read on. And I was right. In fact one wonders if Orwell had read this book; he might have been less sure that the English murder was quite so cosy, because – without revealing too much – this book has an undercurrent of Gothic horror that admits one to the darkness at the heart of the human condition. I think Chandler missed something.

Moreover there is a chilling insight into the psychology of crime that tells us how Sayers herself saw the world. Speaking through one of her characters, she tells us that a mechanistic view of the human character – a belief that one's motivations are purely biophysical – leaves no space for morality, or for a conception of good and evil. It seems to Sayers that we need a dimension we do not understand if we are to refrain from evil. A humanist would not agree with this view, but Sayers was religious and it was probably deeply held.

A more serious criticism of Sayers than Chandler's is that Sayers was antisemitic. *Whose Body?* is sometimes cited as the book in which this is most evident. There is a *prima facie* case there, and there are antisemitic remarks in some of her private letters. However, some writers on her disagree with this; and as a young woman she had a long affair with a Russian-Jewish poet, John Cournos. Sayers's relationship with antisemitism is actually complicated – and there seems to have been a link with her private life. It's a topic discussed with sympathy and insight in an essay by American critic Amy E. Schwartz, *The Curious Case of Dorothy Sayers & the Jew Who Wasn't There* (2016). Sayers's private life was itself complicated; in 1924 she gave birth to an illegitimate child, who was fostered by relatives, but who she adopted some years later without telling him she was his birth mother. (He did eventually find out.)

Sayers might not be so easy a read as Agatha Christie, but *Whose Body* suggested to me that she more interesting. To see if that was true, I decided to read two more books – *The Unpleasantness at the Bellona Club* (1928) and what devotees consider her finest work, *The Nine Tailors* (1934).

The first of these opens in a London club, one of those old-fashioned institutions where men used to gather to read the papers, have a drink, dine and, if from out of town, stay overnight. A few still exist. One day an elderly member, sitting in his normal place in front of the fire, turns out to have died. No-one is very surprised. Then it turns out that the precise time of death might be of some importance to his legatees. Wimsey is asked to establish it. He finds he has opened a rather nasty can of worms.

Once again, there is more to this story than one might suppose. As in *Whose Body?*, Wimsey comes across as a fatuous ass, but in that first book Sayers hinted that he might be more complicated than he seemed. In *The Unpleasantness at the Bellona Club* this is confirmed. "I find you refreshing, Wimsey," says an acquaintance. "You're not in the least witty, but you have a kind of obvious facetiousness which reminds me of the less exacting class of music-hall." The reader sees that it is a front.

Meanwhile the Bellona Club is the haunt of old soldiers and there is a certain tension between the older members, with their Victorian and Edwardian imperial values, and those who have served in the recent war; some of the latter, including Wimsey himself, have been seriously injured and are suffering, sometimes very badly, from what we would now call PTSD. Sayers writes to entertain. But she is not trivial.

The Nine Tailors, meanwhile, is something else again. Wimsey and his man Bunter skid off the road in heavy snow one New Year's Eve in some Godforsaken part of the Fens. Seeking refuge in the parsonage in a nearby village, they find that their host, the vicar, is an ardent campanologist. *The Nine Tailors* has nothing to do with tailors. It is (in part) about bells. To the traditional bell-ringer, 'Tailor' is a corruption of 'Teller", or toller – the largest, lowest-register bell in a church, which is used to toll the news of a passing; so many for a man or for a woman, then the tally of their years. The plot of *The Nine Tailors* concerns a long-ago theft and a murder, but is set around the almost uniquely English discipline of change-ringing – the art of making church bells peal in different sequences.

The Nine Tailors is gripping, and infuriating. It is gripping for its claustrophobic tension; almost all the story takes place in the cramped confines of a Fenland village, set on a low rise that is an island in the sinister drained flatlands around it. We thus know that the murderer is near at hand. But this book is also infuriating, as Sayers plays mind-games around the mathematical sequences in which bells are to be rung to produce various traditional peals. And the huge, ancient bells themselves – the medieval Batty Thomas, the 17th-century Tailor Paul – are among the characters. It isn't hard to see why Sayers fans think this very original book is her crowning achievement.

The Sayers devotee would have you believe that the intellect behind the books is the attraction, but I think it is subtler than that. In the three books by Agatha Christie, I foresaw the culprit in only one; in another, I was taken by surprise, and in the third I already knew but would not otherwise have guessed. Sayers is different. In all three books I did guess at least part of the solution, and at first I was pleased with myself for doing so, then realized that this was exactly what Sayers intended – that the attentive reader would uncover the truth at the same pace as Wimsey himself and would share his thought-processes without being told what they were. It works beautifully, making the reader identify with Wimsey and holding their attention. Forget the mind-games; Sayers's real strength is to put you in her hero's head, and keep you there.

I asked whether Agatha Christie's rivals had also stood the test of time. Sayers has, although she appeals to a narrower readership.

What of Margery Allingham and Ngaio Marsh?

*

Margery Allingham's parents were both journalists; her father Herbert Allingham was also a prolific writer of pulp fiction. Writing was in her blood and she pursued it from an early age.

She was born in 1904 in London, but the family soon moved to Essex, where she would spend most of her life. Its coastline, with its damp foggy estuaries and sinister marshes, would exercise a pull on her imagination that is evident in her books, beginning with her first effort, *Blackkerchief Dick* (1923), a tale of smugglers set on the county's Mersea Island, which Allingham knew well in her youth.

That book was not a success, but she broke through with *The Crime at Black Dudley* (1929). In it, we are introduced to amateur detective Albert Campion, who would feature to a greater or lesser extent in pretty much all her books. Like Sayers's Lord Peter Wimsey, he is an aristocrat (of, it is hinted, most noble origins). And, like Wimsey, he is – on the surface – a fatuous ass. He so strongly resembles Wimsey in concept that when Agatha Christie read *The Crime at Black Dudley*, she wondered if Allingham was Sayers writing under a pseudonym. In fact Campion is thought to have been meant, at first, as a caricature of Wimsey, but he soon acquired a life and character of his own.

Allingham is a much-admired writer, but *The Crime at Black Dudley* was nothing special. Like so many crime stories of its time, it is set at a country-house weekend. This is a posh function that middle-class readers of the day would probably not have attended themselves, but would have understood. The hero is not Campion but another young man, Abbershaw; Campion, however, rather steals the show as the assembled bright young things find themselves imprisoned in a decaying medieval Suffolk mansion, embroiled against their will in an international criminal conspiracy. There is snobbery and violence aplenty. But the plot is not believable, driven as it is by evil masterminds, creepy mysterious foreigners, hidden doors and secret passages. And the characters are hackneyed stereotypes of their day; frightfully decent overgrown schoolboys partnered by girls who are, of course, complete bricks. This is Enid Blyton for adults and it has not aged well.

You can't condemn a well-loved writer on the basis of one book. So I went on to her next one, *Mystery Mile* (1930) – one of eight Albert Campion stories adapted long afterwards for TV (by the BBC in 1990; I never saw them). This is set partly on a remote near-island off the Essex coast, thought to again be Mersea, on which Campion has decided to sequester an American judge that someone is trying to kill. Meanwhile Campion sets about finding who that someone is.

Mystery Mile, too, was a disappointment for me; too many jolly japes, an implausible adventure or two, and characters too much stereotyped according to the conventions of their time. Yet in this book, there were things that did grab me. The setting – the salt flats, the treacherous mud, the sea mists – did have a ring of truth and as we have seen, Allingham loved that landscape for most of her life. Moreover the final scenes in which Campion must confront the villain are very well done, and there is a sub-plot concerning the death of a parson that is neatly tied up at the end. Could I be wrong about Campion – and his creator? After all, she is still widely read, and Agatha Christie herself was generous in her praise of Allingham when the latter passed away.

At this point I came across an article by literary historian Jane Stevenson in *The Guardian* (*Queen of Crime*, August 19 2006) that compares her favourably with both Christie and Sayers. "All Allingham novels (except perhaps the first two) will, like those of Dorothy Sayers, stand a good deal of rereading," she writes. But Sayers, she says, "is made hard to read by her snobbery and racism ...and she was profoundly anti-semitic [as we have seen, this is disputed]. This is not a problem with Allingham, who was a person of genuinely wide human sympathy." A charwoman in one of her books, says Stevenson, is a "precisely observed character with a history and something of an inner life, presented without condescension." Moreover, as Stevenson says, Allingham's first two books – the ones I had read – are not her best. Ask Allingham's fans which one was, and they all seem to have the same answer: *The Tiger in the Smoke*.

Published much later, in 1952, it is set in the midst of a London November smog, five or six years after the war. A beautiful young war-widow, Meg, is about to remarry. But mysterious messages arrive suggesting that her late husband is far from dead. There are even photographs and newspaper-clippings that purport to show him. Is she being blackmailed? If so, what does the blackmailer want? Is her husband really still alive? As the book opens, she is in a taxi, on her way to Paddington Station to meet a train on which he may, it has been hinted, be travelling. Meanwhile a violent and extremely dangerous convict has escaped and is somewhere nearby, killing people. He, too, is interested in Meg; why, and is she in danger?

The Tiger in the Smoke has been highly praised, not least by fellow crime writers such as H.R.F. Keating and Susan Hill. In her foreword for the 2015 Vintage edition, Hill comments that "There are not many crime novels more genuinely frightening." And Hill should know, having written *The Woman in Black* (1983), the creepy 1989 TV adaptation of which still has the power to shock. Hill also praises the power of Allingham's villain. "In real life," she writes, "criminals are rarely very interesting ...but detective fiction usually benefits from having a murderer who exerts a terrible fascination." *The Tiger in the Smoke* has the escaped convict, Havoc. "He is her most repellent, dangerous, evil, and unusual killer," says Hill, "a man with a wounding childhood, and a strange past history, without emotion or empathy or conscience, and yet not entirely without humanity, cold-blooded, shocking, brutal, and yet perhaps, just perhaps, redeemable."

Moreover, as Jane Stevenson points out, you know early on who the criminal is, and "the interest is transferred to questions of the villain's psychology and how, or if, the detectives catch up with him." Or as Hill puts it: "This is not a whodunit, it is a why-dunnit, a complex novel of character. It is also, at its core, about the essential Biblical, and specifically, the Miltonian, conflict between good and evil: the devil in the shape of Jack Havoc, and an angel, the saintly Canon Avril." (The latter is a clergyman who confronts Havoc towards the end of the book.) Hill praises, too, Allingham's sense of place and the way in which she uses the London smog to create a sinister backdrop that seeps through the narrative. The book is, she says, a masterpiece.

At least some of this is true. The way Allingham co-opts the notorious London smog as a character in her book is indeed masterful, and reminded me of Iris Murdoch's sinister *The Time of the Angels* (1966); this too is wreathed in a wintry London fog through which the nature of evil slowly becomes apparent. Hill and Stevenson are also surely right that this book isn't simply a whodunnit; it is a complex novel of motive and morality, with a big dollop of religion thrown in. I myself felt that the book was not so much Agatha Christie, more Graham Greene – it reminded me a little of *Brighton Rock*. Yet there is also plenty of complex plotsmithing, with twists and turns of which Dorothy Sayers would have been proud.

Greene himself did not like the book. Travelling in Africa in February 1959, he noted in his diary that friends had "lent me *Tiger in the Smoke* – a most absurd unreal story by Margery Allingham. It didn't even pass the time; it was an irritation" (*In Search of a Character; Two African Journals*, 1961). This is rather ungracious; perhaps Greene felt Allingham was muscling in on his territory. That said, some of the praise for *Tiger in the Smoke* does seem overdone. Albert Campion and his extended family take up too much bandwidth; in fact Campion himself isn't even essential for the plot (the 1956 film adaptation omitted him altogether). A group of street musicians plays a large part in the story, but for me they did not come to life. There were two or three other characters who did not seem right. Even so, *The Tiger in the Smoke* is rather good. It's not hard to see that for some, it might be Allingham, not Christie or Sayers, who was the true Queen of Crime.

It seems to have done her little good in life. Julia Jones's 2009 biography (*The Adventures of Margery Allingham*) records that she worked and worked. This was driven in part by a strong work ethic – she was from a journalistic family that had always lived from one commission to the next. But it also reflected her material support of others, including her husband, who was not faithful and may have had a son with the journalist Nancy Spain. Allingham herself struggled with thyroid and weight problems and eventually died of breast cancer aged 62.

*

So to the last of these four, Ngaio Marsh.

Her first novel, *A Man Lay Dead*, appeared in 1934 but Marsh had written it three years later, while running an interior decoration business in Knightsbridge. As I had started with the first novels by the other three, I started with this one. In some ways it is a disappointment. It is set, like far too many other such books, at a country-house weekend, and (like Christie's *The Secret Adversary*) it involves a conspiracy by various sinister Russians. There's also an aristocratic detective. It all seems rather hackneyed.

But there may be a reason for that. Marsh had just read a detective novel, and as it was a rainy Saturday, she decided to see if she could write one too. It was, it seems, just a jape to pass a wet weekend. Marsh later said that the book that inspired this prank was by either Christie or Sayers, but in fact *A Man Lay Dead* bears a striking resemblance to Allingham's first, *The Crime at Black Dudley*, and perhaps that was the book that Marsh had just read. She may even have set out to write a parody.

Yet the characterization is stronger – Marsh's detective, Roderick Alleyn, who would continue to feature in her books, comes to life better than Albert Campion. The victim is also believable. He is a man who has long played with fire, and is finally burnt – and at the end we see clearly why. We also see a tendency to kill the victim in ingenious ways. In future Ngaio Marsh books they would be murdered while life modelling or drowned in the mud of hot springs; in one case, the owner of a sheep farm turns up at auction in one of her own bales of wool. (The latter book bore the splendid title *Died in the Wool*.)

In later years, Marsh herself would dismiss *A Man Lay Dead* as implausible and the characters shallow. She may even have been surprised it was published. But Ngaio Marsh's mischievous wet weekend had launched her on a new career.

Marsh had tried writing earlier, but had been dissatisfied with her own efforts. It hadn't occurred to her before to try crime fiction.

In 1934 she was already 39, and her life so far had been as a painter and then in the theatre. Also, unlike the other three, she was not from a privileged background; her father had been a bank clerk. There is another important difference; her books seem as quintessentially English as theirs, but although she spent long periods in England, she was born and eventually died in Christchurch (Ngaio is a Maori word for a type of flowering tree). In fact her relationship to England was ambivalent; she was quite at home there but also felt drawn back to New Zealand, and it was there that she would eventually spend most of her life. Yet, of her 33 books, only four would be set there.

One of these four was the book I read next – *Colour Scheme* (1943), set at a run-down hot springs on North Island. The resort is owned by a genteel, somewhat incompetent English couple who have spent most of their lives in India. The Englishman is in hock to an unpleasant local businessman who dies a very Marshian death; he is pushed, one night, into a pool of simmering mud – an event that elicits a blood-chilling scream from the victim and a visit, eventually, from Inspector Alleyn. The plot, like the mud, thickens as the motive is uncovered. Was it debt? Or the victim's habit of thieving sacred Maori artifacts? Or even espionage – has someone been signalling to Japanese submarines in the bay? (This last was not fanciful; two or three Japanese submarines, and one German U-boat, did conduct operations in New Zealand waters.)

Colour Scheme seems different to other Golden Age fiction. It has been said that it shows Marsh as a progressive figure who did not much like the Empire and Commonwealth, and cared more than most New Zealanders of the time about Maori tradition and culture. The latter may be true. I'm not sure about the former. Marsh split her time between New Zealand and the UK and wrote about New Zealand for the Collins series on the Commonwealth.

As for *Colour Scheme*, I thought it inventive and well-constructed but a bit sinister, and found it hard to love some of the characters. Still, I wanted to read a third book, as I had for Christie, Allingham and Sayers. And I hit on the right one.

Artists in Crime was published in 1938 and was Marsh's sixth detective novel (a lot of work in just four years). It opens as Alleyn nears the end of a long leave, which he has used to travel to New Zealand. He is now returning to England via the United States. The liner has called at Fiji. As it leaves Suva astern, Alleyn stumbled across an artist, Agatha Troy, who is painting the docks on an upper deck. Troy will become the love of his life. But she is not especially friendly. Then, back in the Home Counties, Alleyn is summoned on official business to Troy's country house, where she gives private courses for moneyed aspiring artists. A beautiful but unlikeable life model has been murdered in a most ingenious fashion (best not to give this away but as we have seen, Marsh often had great fun with this). Any of the artists could have been the murderer; so could Troy herself. What follows is a terrific yarn, with well-drawn characters, red herrings, random clues and finally a grisly, haunting climax in a dark, grimy prewar Brixton.

Ngaio Marsh would eventually write over 30 detective novels, along with a number of shorter pieces and some non-fiction; late in life she would even write for TV. It's quite an achievement for a woman whose first field was not fiction, or even writing, at all. She had been an art student when young, but was a competent painter rather than a really good one, and did not pursue it as a career.

Her real love was the theatre. Unable to travel during the war years, she spent them in New Zealand and became a noted producer and director, especially of Shakespeare. The theatre plays a key role in several of her novels. She was enormous fun to work with, according to Ray Neumann, who designed the set for one of her productions in Christchurch in 1962, when she was in her late 60s. She also had style. Years later, Neumann would tell journalist Linda Herrick that Marsh "drove a black XK120 Jag with white sheepskin upholstery and she'd bring her lunch each day – chicken sandwiches, a bottle of lager and a cigar" (Linda Herrick, *The Mystery of the Crime Writer*, *New Zealand Herald*, August 23 2008).

But she was also very private. She had published an autobiography, *Black Beech and Honeydew,* in 1966 but it contained few personal revelations, and she destroyed all her papers before she died. One of her biographers, Joanne Drayton (*Ngaio Marsh: Her Life in Crime*, 2008), told Herrick that Marsh remained an enigma in some ways, and that she may have been hurt by the fact that her own country never quite accepted her the way Britain did. (She was a huge success in the UK, where she remains well-known). She may also have found theatre people more accepting of the fact that she was (probably) a lesbian – something she always denied; for most of her lifetime it was not acceptable, and besides she may understandably have thought it was her own business.

Marsh was also the only one of the four women from an ordinary background. Agatha Christie had been born wealthy, Allingham had connections in journalism and publishing, and Sayers's father was the chaplain of Christ Church Cathedral, Oxford; she herself attended Somerville College. But Marsh was the daughter of a bank clerk from the other side of the world. All of these four women are interesting as individuals, but Marsh perhaps most of all – yet we'll never know quite who she really was.

*

How did these four women find such a huge audience? They were, of course, good at what they did. But that cannot wholly explain their extraordinary success.

The answer lies in the publishing industry between the wars. It is explained by Colin Watson in his book on the phenomenon, *Snobbery With Violence* (as stated earlier, the phrase is Alan Bennett's; it's from *Forty Years On*). Watson, a journalist in Lincolnshire, published 12 detective novels of his own – with some success; the BBC adapted eight, four for TV and the rest for Radio 4. *Snobbery With Violence* was published in 1971 and has since been reissued as part of the excellent *Faber Finds* series. Watson felt the popular fiction of the day gave an insight into the mentality of the inter-war years, during which he grew up; he was born in 1920. He quotes the 18th-century writer Lady Mary Wortley Montagu (herself a fascinating figure) as follows:

Perhaps you will say I should not take my ideas of the manners of the times from such trifling authors; but it is more truly to be found among them than from any historian; as they write merely to get money, they always fall into the notions that are most acceptable to the present taste.

This is exactly what Watson does in his book; define the interwar years by their reading interests and prejudices. It is most revealing.

Popular fiction was of course not new; neither was adventure or detection – Wilkie Collins had set the ball rolling in the mid-19th century with books such as the splendid *The Moonstone* (1868), which still feels fresh and original today. Conan Doyle, who was still active in the 1920s, had published his first Sherlock Holmes in 1887. But between the wars a number of factors sent the number of books read to stratospheric new heights. Watson argues persuasively that the growth in commuting, by bus and train, gave middle-class men time to fill; in the meantime, middle-class women were at a stage where labour-saving devices were appearing in the home, yet domestic help was still widely available – giving them, too, far more time to read. Books had competition, of course; Watson says little about the alternatives, but there was the cinema and from 1922 BBC radio. But the cinema meant going out. Radios remained expensive (they did not become really cheap until the transistor radio arrived in the 1950s), and there was little choice of stations until after the war. BBC TV started in 1936 but only in London, and again, sets were very costly; by 1939 there were still just 10,000.

So people read. The number of books published a year was 12,500 in the early 1920s (Watson says just a quarter of these were reprints); by 1939 they had reached about 17,000. A reader would therefore have 180-210 new titles to choose from *every week*. And they were accessible; besides municipal libraries, one could pop into WH Smith or Boots, both of which ran lending libraries from many of their branches, to which one could subscribe for a modest fee. (Boots only closed its last such library in 1966.) Importantly, the vast majority of books were read for entertainment. As Watson puts it, this vast and mainly middle-class interwar audience "read for pleasure rather than for education, and to kill time, not ignorance (with which, in any case, they were not conscious of being burdened)."

Perhaps inevitably, this tsunami of adventure and detection was sometimes of doubtful quality. Watson gives the example of Sydney Horler, whose character Tiger Standish was a vehicle for many of Horler's own opinions; these included a loathing of foreigners and a big dash of antisemitism. Reviewers such as Dorothy Sayers herself and Compton Mackenzie were unimpressed, but the public lapped it all up and Horler published nearly 160 novels. He did not, in any case, hold other authors in high esteem, saying that too many books were being written by "half-witted Oxford under-graduates, man-obsessed old maids, homosexuals with polished periods, and pin-heads of all descriptions."

Meanwhile rival H.C. McNeile, who wrote under the pseudonym "Sapper", created his gentleman adventurer Bulldog Drummond, whose xenophobia and antisemitism matched his own. It did not bother his readers; McNeile sold 400,000 books between the wars. Neither were they troubled by the rabid racism in Sax Rohmer's books, which featured his hero Nayland Smith and his adversary, the Oriental master criminal, Fu-Manchu. Watson quotes one passage: "At last they were truly face to face – the head of the great Yellow movement, and the man who fought on behalf of the entire White race..." It was nonsense but the public lapped it up; Rohmer published 13 Fu-Manchu books. They were also filmed; one – *The Brides of Fu-Manchu* – was released well into my lifetime and as a child I saw it in the cinema. Even more prolific was Edgar Wallace, author of the *Sanders of the River* series, which would have appealed to the imperialistic sentiments of the time. Wallace, who had been born in poverty, was at least a nice man; Daphne du Maurier, a family friend, records his kindness in her memoir, *Myself When Young* (1977). He also wrote the script for *King Kong*, though he died before it was made. Unlike most of the others, he is still read to some extent. But his work has not aged well.

There were better writers, of course. Conan Doyle managed some late Sherlock Holmes stories in the 1920s. Many of G. K. Chesterton's *Father Brown* stories also date from the inter-war period, although some were written before 1914. Chesterton wrote short stories, not novels, but they were substantial enough to be filmed in our own time, and have remained popular on TV. One should also note Scottish writer Elizabeth McKintosh, who published mostly as Josephine Tey, and is very highly regarded by some Golden Age enthusiasts. I have not discussed her here as her output was relatively small; as with Ngaio Marsh, her first love was the theatre, and she wrote at least as many plays. There were only eight detective novels. But their quality was high, and she should not be ignored.

Others included the distinguished left-wing economist G.D.H. Cole, whose chair at Oxford would later be filled by Isaiah Berlin. Cole produced a huge number of non-fiction books, articles and pamphlets with titles such as *Guild Socialism – A Plan for Economic Democracy* (1921) and *Some Essentials of Socialist Propaganda* (1932). For light relief, he found time to co-author 29 detective novels with his wife Margaret (in fact, each one had been written by either one or the other). But it is not clear whether anyone still reads them, and they seem mostly to be out of print. Others included "Nicholas Blake", actually C. Day Lewis.

In the main, though, it's the Big Four – Agatha Christie, Dorothy Sayers, Margery Allingham and Ngaio Marsh – whose work has survived, and is still enjoyed today, both in print and on TV. Why?

*

The main reason is that they were good. As we've seen, all four of them had the odd misfire, especially with their earliest books. But in general, if you have a dull wet weekend ahead or a long flight, you can just download an Agatha Christie or Nagaio Marsh and you'll get almost Toyota-like quality control. Moreover, while modern readers would find the bigotry of the Fu-Manchu or Sapper books distasteful, these four are *mostly* free of it, at least in their books. As we have seen, Dorothy Sayers has been charged with antisemitism, though this has been debated; and there can be a certain whiff of prejudice in the way some characters are depicted in her books and Christie's. In the main, however, these four do not reflect the racism and jingoism of the time. And although the books are entertainment, the best of them have plenty of character development and are good on motivation. In this respect Marsh's *Colour Scheme* and Allingham's *Tiger in the Smoke* stood out for me; and as I said earlier, Sayers's *Whose Body?* includes glimpses into the human condition that are terrifying.

By 1939 Dorothy Sayers had stopped writing detective fiction altogether (although she lived until 1957). But the others continued for much longer. Margery Allingham wrote until her death in 1966. Agatha Christie also went on nearly to the end and wrote her last book in 1973, when she was 83; but she had gone on too long – *Postern of Fate*, which featured the wretched Tommy and Tuppence, was apparently not very good and showed signs of cognitive decline. However, it wasn't the last to be published; several works written much earlier, including the last Poirot, were published after her death in 1976, as was a well-received autobiography. The last detective novel by any of the four was Ngaio Marsh's *Light Thickens*; she completed it in 1982 when she was 87, and died that same year. It was published posthumously. With Marsh's death, the Golden Age of detective fiction was truly over.

But it had really ended in 1939, and certainly by 1945. As Orwell wrote, the horrors of the real world in that year were too much for it. P.D. James was right; although the Big Four's best work will always be read, it would not be written now. The world (and policing, and forensics) has changed and the best writers reflect it. Neither should we regret that old world's passing; as Colin Watson showed, vast numbers of books were sold but many were dire, and

were steeped in the prejudices of their age. These four writers –
and a few others, such as Josephine Tey and G. K. Chesterton – did
deserve to survive. But they were outliers.

Who will be today's?

On Whether He Warned Us

Stefan Zweig was an Austrian middlebrow writer known for his novellas and for his historical biographies. His work was widely translated between the wars and was immensely popular. From quite a young age he travelled widely, especially in Europe, and had friends in the arts in much of the continent. But he was Jewish and in 1934, sensing what would happen in Austria, he went into exile in England – ironically, one of the few Western countries where he was not well known. In 1940 he moved to the US and eventually to Brazil, where, despairing of Europe's future, he committed suicide with his wife in Petrópolis in February 1942 at the age of 60.

Until recently Zweig, once a best-seller, was largely forgotten in Britain (though not in Austria or Germany). In recent years, however, there has been a revival – and this time it has extended to Britain, where he has been championed by the Pushkin Press. The latter has brought out new editions of much of his oeuvre, both his biographies of historical figures, and his fiction.

Some years ago Pushkin published a new edition of Zweig's autobiography, *The World of Yesterday*, begun in 1934 and finished just before his death in 1942. It is less a conventional autobiography, more a sentimental journey through Zweig's world as a cosmopolitan young writer before the First World War, when he knew figures such as Rodin and Rilke. The book describes, too, the war itself, its aftermath and the gathering storm of fascism. Pushkin has now brought out *Messages From A Lost World*, a collection of lectures and articles Zweig produced between 1916 and 1941, translated by Will Stone. Much of this material has hitherto been unavailable or never existed in English.

Why this sudden interest in Zweig? He is long dead and, although very popular in his lifetime, was not a literary heavyweight. He had languished for years in obscurity; I only discovered him myself when searching for someone else (Arnold Zweig, the pro-Soviet author of *The Axe of Wandsbeck*).

But now it seems we cannot get enough of him. There is a clue as to why in a brief piece by George Prochnik, one of Zweig's biographers, in *The New Yorker* (February 6 2017). "The American people are confused and benumbed by a flood of fake news and misinformation," he remarks. "Reading in [*The World of Yesterday*] how, during the years of Hitler's rise to power, many well-meaning people 'could not or did not wish to perceive that a new technique of conscious cynical amorality was at work,' it's difficult not to think of our own present predicament."

In other words he resonates with those who hold certain views about our own times. This seems to be the case also from Nicholas Lezard's adulatory review of Pushkin's reissue of *The World of Yesterday* (*The Guardian*, December 4 2009). He called it "a long lament for a lost world, … [it] is essential to our understanding of history. For it was as an enthusiast for the pan-European cultural project that Zweig found his greatest motivation and, eventually, his greatest pain..."

Here we have Zweig used as a stick with which to beat Trump in the US and also, though only by implication, to support European integration in the UK. If I wished to be cynical, I would say that the Zweig revival was nothing more than the anglophone liberal establishment co-opting a long-ago Austrian writer in order to make points of their own, exploiting the pathos of his death to do so. But is that fair? And even if it is, does that make Prochnik, or Lezard, wrong to see Zweig in a way that resonates today?

It doesn't help that Zweig divided the critics during his own lifetime. His sales were enormous. In Brazil, he received a state funeral in the presence of President Getúlio Vargas (himself to commit suicide a few years later). Yet in a highly critical piece in the *London Review of Books* (*Vermicular Dither*, January 28 2010), German poet and translator Michael Hofmann excoriated Zweig and pointed out that other writers of the era had had no time for him. "There is an unusual consensus here," wrote Hofmann. "Mann, Musil, Brecht, Hesse, Canetti, Hofmannsthal, Kraus – [all considered that], save in in commercial terms, [he was] an utterly negligible figure." Hofmann seems to imply that Zweig cannot justify his new fame. And one does feel that to do so, Zweig would have to bring us some message of his own from the time in which he lived.

There are two ways one can do this from the grave: as a witness; or as a prophet. *The World of Yesterday* would be his claim to the first role. *Messages from a Lost World*, his lectures and articles, would establish his claim to the second. Do either of these books succeed on those levels?

The answer to that is, in fact, quite messy.

*

Zweig's memoir *The World of Yesterday* was published not long after his death. It has never really disappeared, but has come back into vogue of late. It is alternately infuriating, charming and gripping. It is, at its best, profoundly vivid.

One reason for its impact today is simply that Zweig was well-connected, and the book includes pen-portraits of many figures who are still historically important. Many are literary or artistic. We meet Romain Rolland (who Zweig knew well) and Auguste Rodin; in one of the book's best passages, Zweig sees the master at

102

work in his studio, so absorbed in his work that he forgets the young writer's presence, and is startled when he realises that Zweig is still there. Hugo von Hofmannsthal, Richard Strauss's librettist, appears, and gets more generous treatment than he ever gave Zweig, who he despised (one of the good things about Zweig's own memoir is that it is largely spiteless). Richard Strauss is also in the book; Zweig briefly succeeded Hofmannsthal as Strauss's librettist, to the mortification of the Nazis. Neither are all Zweig's acquaintances from the arts. He knew, and warmly describes, German Foreign Minister Walter Rathenau, who he saw not long before his tragic assassination in Berlin – an event supposed, by some, to have helped set Germany on the road to Nazism. There is also a memorable description of Theodore Herzl, the father of Zionism, who was Zweig's first editor.

But *The World of Yesterday* can often grate. Zweig is an incorrigible name-dropper. As Leo Carey remarked in a 2012 review in *The New Yorker* (*The Escape Artist*, August 20 2012), it is sometimes "tempting to see his sedulous gathering of eminent friendships as a counterpart of his manuscript collecting" (Zweig was a noted collector of scores, manuscripts and memorabilia). Late in the book there is a long list of those who, he says, stayed with him in Salzburg (including not only Hoffmanstahl but also Thomas Mann, who does not appear to have liked him much either).

There is also a whiff of cant. Early on he claims that he wondered if he should ever have dared submit his early work. Later there's more evidence of this false modesty when he recounts how gobsmacked he is when Maxim Gorky is to write an intro to his work, or he affects to have been humbled to have been approached by an American publisher (it was the influential Benjamin Huebsch of Viking). "Such apparent success was apt to confuse one whose faith, hitherto, had been in his good intentions rather than in his ability and the efficacy of his work." Oh, do shut up. After all, there is an undercurrent of ego simply in making one's work available.

One is also irritated when he 'modestly' praises his own writing, citing his "distaste for everything redundant and long-winded... I had always felt it incumbent on me to study the causes of the influence of books or personages within their own time, and I could not but ask myself in hours of reflection to what particular characteristics my books owed their, to me, unexpected success." He then says that it was his concision, which is scarcely evident in that passage. In fact, Michael Hofmann goes so far as to refer to his "abundant, facile and unhindered lifelong logorrhoea." That is not fair, but it is true that Zweig could be wordy.

Neither is Zweig always a reliable witness. He spent the latter part of the First World War in Switzerland (for reasons that will be discussed below). In *The World of Yesterday* he recounts how he returned across the Austrian frontier to a most poignant moment. A train rolls slowly into the station:

...not the customary, shabby, weather-beaten kind, but with spacious black cars, a train de luxe ...Then I recognized behind the plate glass window of the car Emperor Karl, the last emperor of Austria standing with his black-clad wife, Empress Zita. I was startled; the last emperor of Austria, heir of the Hapsburg dynasty which had ruled for seven hundred years, was forsaking his realm!

It is a wonderful moment – but a few pages later he describes how the cold autumn air came through the broken windows of his own carriage as he rode on into Austria. But the Emperor did not leave Austria in the autumn but on March 24 1919; moreover he entered Switzerland with a British escort, something Zweig would surely have noticed. In short, Zweig was probably not there.

Oliver Matuschek, author of an absorbing recent biography of Zweig, *Three Lives*, does not mention these disparities, but notes it is strange that Zweig had never mentioned this incident before. He is reluctant to accuse Zweig of lying, but concludes: "The most likely explanation is that Zweig's account is not to be taken literally, as a description of events that he actually witnessed, but rather as a narrative allegory." Which is a polite way of saying that Zweig made it up.

Matuschek is a little harsher regarding an episode from 1911 that is not in *The World of Yesterday*, but which Zweig had recounted elsewhere. In April 1911, the dying Gustav Mahler was brought home by his wife and family aboard the German liner *Amerika*; the young Zweig, who had been visiting New York, happened to be aboard. Zweig's account of the voyage in the presence of the dying composer was emotional. But in fact he only saw him once, from a distance, on disembarkation. He had sent an offer of help to the family, but Alma Mahler was suspicious of his motives and later said that far from helping, Zweig had disappeared rapidly at Cherbourg.

Once again, however, Matuschek seems to suggest that Zweig is not being overtly dishonest; rather, that he felt he had a duty to chronicle what he saw as his presence at history. He may be right. The fact remains that, as the work of a witness, *The World of Yesterday* must be found wanting, and it is therefore hard not to call much else in the book – the distinguished friendships, for example – into question.

But if Zweig did wish to capture history in *The World of Yesterday*, he succeeded – not in his relentless name-dropping, or in his portraits of the great and the good, or in moments such as the departure of the Emperor, but when he was not trying so hard. It is in these passages that he tells us most.

Thus he goes to the quiet Austrian resort of Baden to enjoy the summer: "Throughout the days and nights the heavens were a silky blue, the air soft yet not sultry, the meadows fragrant and warm, the forests dark and profuse in their tender green..." One day, reading in the park, he senses a flurry of disturbance; the band stops playing; people press towards a news placard. What has happened is the assassination of the Archduke in Sarajevo. But nobody seems terribly upset. Franz Ferdinand, adds Zweig, had never been popular in Austria.

He was never seen to smile, and no photographs showed him relaxed. ...My almost mystic premonition that some misfortune would come from this man with his bulldog neck and his cold, staring eyes, was ...shared by the entire nation ...Two hours later signs of genuine mourning were no longer to be seen.

Zweig sees no reason to change his plans and trots off to visit friends in Belgium, where the Belgian army has started to prepare for war; even this seems slightly farcical (in a charming detail, we learn that their machine-guns are mounted on carts pulled by dogs). It comes as a shock when he realises that war really is imminent, and he takes the last train to cross into Germany. The atmosphere of that summer – the insouciance regarding the assassination, the doubt there will be war – is well expressed.

And yet Zweig had sensed an undercurrent. For the last year he has been uneasy. First there is the arrest of Alfred Redl, a spy at the heart of the Austro-Hungarian intelligence machine (this is a fascinating episode, well described by Fitzroy Maclean in his book *Take Nine Spies*). Then he finds himself watching newsreels in a cinema in Tours and is taken aback when the Kaiser and Franz Joseph appear on the screen:

A spontaneous wild whistling and stamping of feet began in the dark hall. Everybody yelled and whistled, men, women, and children, as if they had been personally insulted. ...I was frightened to the depths of my heart. For I sensed how deeply the poison of the propaganda of hate must have advanced through the years...

It may be these incidents did not alarm Zweig so much at the time as he would have us believe. Even so, resonance can be retrospective, and he is telling us a lot here. This does echo in our own time; the media politics of hate, a rottenness at the heart of the establishment, and a failure to know when they are coming home to roost. One wonders if we will recognize the beginnings of the third world war. Could it be taking shape in some current crisis as yet understated, just as in July 1914?

It goes on. Zweig's description of the aftermath of the First World War is an excellent read. As the Austrian currency collapses, Germans stream over the border to Salzburg to quaff multiple steins of virtually free beer. Then along comes the German inflation of 1923 and the Austrians, in their turn, stream into Bavaria to get tanked up. On a visit to Berlin, Zweig finds that the great inflation has destroyed all values, not just monetary ones:

In the dimly lit bars one might see government officials and men of the world of finance tenderly courting drunken sailors ...Whoever lived through these apocalyptic months ...sensed the coming of a counterblow ...For the German people, a disciplined folk, did not know what to do with their freedom and already looked impatiently toward those who were to take it from them.

Is that us, bored with our cheap booze, porn and wide-screen TVs?

Is the election of Trump, and Brexit, a result of sheer boredom and frustration with ourselves? If so, *The World of Yesterday* did warn us.

I began by saying that, to justify the new attention being showered on him, Zweig would have to justify his stature as either a witness or a prophet. His claim to be a witness rests mainly on *The World of Yesterday*. It is flawed. Sometimes it is long-winded and discursive. At other times Zweig tries too hard to insert himself into history, in claiming (for example) that he saw the last Emperor leave when he almost certainly didn't.

Yet maybe Matuschek is right to forgive him, for in a broader sense, *The World of Yesterday* really is an extraordinary work of witness. For the moment, with reservations, I'm with the defence.

*

But what of those who see Zweig as a prophet, trying to warn us from the past? For this we turn to the second book, *Messages from a Lost World*.

The title does implicitly claim, for Zweig, the mantle of a prophet. However, it isn't his title, and he did not publish the book; it is a modern anthology of Zweig's articles and speeches put together in 2016 by the Pushkin Press. The pieces in *Messages from a Lost World* vary in subject, but mostly reflect on Zweig's sense of loss for the cosmopolitan, unified Europe of his youth, and his wish to see the borders come down again. Given this subject matter, and the circumstances of Zweig's death, it's easy to see why Pushkin would think this book relevant for 2016, with its rising nationalisms and threat of European disunity.

On first reading I was rather impatient with the book. Translator Will Stone suggests in his detailed introduction that Zweig's internationalism was really just a series of personal connections, and there is some evidence for that in this collection, as well as in *The World of Yesterday*. The phrase that kept occurring to me was "liberal elite". There also seemed to be a hefty dollop of nostalgia. Zweig seemed to hark back to a pre-WW1 Europe that was indeed united for the educated and multilingual, but a place of division for the rest. This contrast has a nasty modern resonance.

This is evident in one of the earlier pieces in the book, *European Thought In Its Historical Development*, a lecture given in 1932 in Florence. Zweig traces several divisions and reunifications of Europe. The fall of Rome splits Europeans asunder, but they are reunited, to some extent, by the founding of the universal Church, which replaces temporal power with a spiritual one. Then Latin revives and "spiritual men across Europe ...can now correspond with each other again ...It matters not in the epoch of Humanism whether you study in Prague, Oxford or Paris." Well, it does if you happen to be an illiterate goatherd, or even a modestly prosperous merchant, but this dimension seems not to have engaged Zweig. Instead he recounts the continuing atomization and reunification, as he sees it, of the continent for people like himself. The Reformation splits civilization apart again; music reunites it, but the introduction of nationalism into music shatters the surface once more, according to Zweig. In fact, national music was the expression of a struggle for freedom from empires, and cannot be regarded as simply a divisive or retrogressive force. And in general, these arguments present Zweig as an elitist whose concept of European unity was meaningful for his class alone. Worse, they present him as a reactionary. Not long after reading *Messages From A Lost World* I happened also to read Mark Lilla's *The Shipwrecked Mind*, in which he analyses a certain type of intellectual conservative – one who believes that all was well before The Fall, whatever, for them, that

Fall happened to be (and he quotes the Reformation as one example). Is that all that Zweig was? If so, translating these pieces was a waste of time. Worse, there is the feeling that Zweig is serving a class interest – a project of an international elite.

But Zweig may have understood this himself, at least at some level. In *European Thought In Its Historical Development*, he comments that "only a slender allegiance by all states to a superior governing body could relieve current economic difficulties, reduce the propensity for war – [but] ...For until now it has been the domain ...of a selective higher class and its roots have not yet penetrated the roots of the people." Yet this sentence also reminds me of Slavoj Žižek's 2016 book *Against the Double Blackmail*. When Western liberals point the finger at working people in their own countries for being bigoted peasants, says Žižek, this is part of the "culture wars" fuelling movements such as Trump's (he could have added Brexit in Britain, had he written the book a few months later). At times it seems that all Zweig is doing is unconsciously confirming Žižek's present-day analysis from the depths of the last century.

It does not help that for a man being praised for his foresight on fascism, Zweig actually did little, in the public space, to fight it. Leo Carey, in his interesting piece in the *The New Yorker* referred to earlier, comments that Zweig was often asked to support anti-Nazi and Jewish causes, but was "anything but outspoken ...his silence frustrated other writers of the time and has been much criticized since." Hannah Arendt was contemptuous. In 1943, not long after Zweig's death, she condemned him in the strongest terms for not fighting for the Jewish people. "Without the protective armor of fame, naked and disrobed, Stefan Zweig was confronted with the reality of the Jewish people. From the "disgrace" of being a Jew there is but one escape – to fight for the honor of the Jewish people as a whole."

This passage, from Arendt's 1943 review *Stefan Zweig: Jews in the World of Yesterday* (Zweig's book had just been published), is probably far too harsh. It seems to suggest that Zweig's suicide was driven by shame at being Jewish. True, Zweig never seems to have bought into Zionism, despite knowing and admiring Herzl when he was younger. But there is no evidence I know of that Zweig felt ashamed of his Jewishness. His suicide was driven by his despair at the death of the civilised world he had known.

Where Arendt may have a point, however, is the suggestion that Zweig's fame and prosperity had put him into a protective bubble in which he did not feel the brutal reality of Nazism until quite late; although he went into a sort of precautionary exile in London in 1934, he continued to visit Austria right up until *Anschluss*. As Arendt also wrote in the same review: "The world that Zweig depicts was anything but *the* world of yesterday; naturally, the author of this book did not actually live in *the* world, only on its rim. The gilded trellises of this peculiar sanctuary were very thick..."

But Zweig *had* paid his dues, in the First World War if not against fascism. He had written a pacifist play during the First World War; it was by all accounts not very good, but could have got him into serious trouble, especially since it was produced during the war in neutral Switzerland (this was why Zweig was there when the war ended). As to the narrow nature of Zweig's internationalism, even Arendt acknowledged that Zweig did, in the end, understand that he lived in a changed reality. Reading *Messages from a Lost World*, one does see when Zweig's thinking evolved before he died. The *European Thought* essay is not the best thing in this book. There is also a remarkable lecture called *The Historiography of Tomorrow*, given during a lecture tour in the US in early 1939. This is seven years after *European Thought*; much had happened in between, not least that Zweig had been forced into exile. In the intervening period, Zweig appears to have moved from a theoretical support for closer international cooperation to the idea of a totally different world in which the nation-state simply does not play the same role.

In *Historiography* he explains how, while moving house, he has found an old history book from his schooldays and is taken aback that its chief objective is to impress upon the pupil the greatness of the Austrian empire in which s/he has been raised. "But twelve hours by rail from Vienna ...in France or Italy, the school textbooks were prepared with the directly opposing scenario: God or the spirit of history laboured solely for the Italian or French motherland." The key dates, he says, are all wars. "It is deeply pessimistic and depressing."

As this lecture progressed, Zweig argues for a new set of values on which to base the study of history. In a telling passage, he points out that in 1797 Napoleon defeated Austria on Italian soil at Rivoli – but that victory, the type of event lauded in history schoolbooks, has long collapsed into insignificance, whereas in the same year and region Alessandro Volta produced the first feeble spark from his first battery, an event of far greater weight. More important still, Zweig states that: "I still remember the revelation I experienced many years ago, from a book which completely overturned [my] conception of history." It was, he says, Kropotkin's *Mutual Aid*, in which the theory of a struggle for existence is challenged by the notion that evolution is actually the product of cooperation. So Zweig is not driven solely by solidarity with an international elite of which he is a member; there is something deeper here. And he is certainly not a mere nostalgic – at least not by the end of his life.

Even in the pieces in which Zweig *is* driven mainly by nostalgia, he has a message for us. Almost the last piece in *Messages from a Lost World* is titled *The Vienna of Yesterday*. It is a lecture given in Paris in April 1940, just a few weeks before the fall of France. In it, Zweig talks of the artistic identity forged by a Vienna whose best and brightest came from elsewhere. The fact that they did, did not negate the city's genius; it *was* its genius. "Gluck," he says, "came from Bohemia, Haydn from Hungary, Caldara and Salieri from Italy, Beethoven from the Rhineland, Mozart from Salzburg, Brahms from Hamburg, Bruckner from High Austria, Hugo Wolf from Styria." The important point is not that they didn't come from Vienna; it is that they went there. Eighty years later, in a time of Brexit and rising borders, this is something London would do well to remember.

Zweig is a fragile figure in some ways. He was successful in his lifetime, but it does sometimes feel that his suicide, its reasons and its circumstances has since lent him a weight that his career alone would not have done. Yet his contemporaries were – being jealous of his huge readership, perhaps – unfair. Reading his fiction today, one finds a tendency to exposition rather than inference. But there are interesting psychological insights (Zweig was an associate of Freud); I found his novella *Burning Secret* very satisfying for that reason. He is not perhaps a great writer. But he is a good one. And he is indeed a witness; *The World of Yesterday* is fascinating, even if its perspective is narrow and its facts open to dispute.

As for *Messages from a Lost World*, these essays and lectures have been revived because they appear to make a link between our own times and Zweig's, rather than for any intrinsic merit of their own. They aren't really great literature; the early selections, in particular, are quite verbose, and nothing in them is a true revelation.

On first reading I rather dismissed them. But I should not have done, for there is a fascinating evolution in these pieces, from nostalgia for a lost world to, in his last months, an understanding that the way led not back to that world but to a different concept of global organization.

Besides, although these pieces are mostly not great writing, there are times when they make you sit up. *Messages from a Lost World* includes a 1936 essay called *1914 and Today*. In it, Zweig writes that he had visited slaughterhouses in Argentina and seen the beasts in their enclosures, grazing quietly, while "on the floor above you saw the flashes, heard the hammering of machines that ten minutes later would kill them, chop, carve, slice, disembowel and dismember them. But then the animal ..has no idea to where it is led. Our human herds in Europe, who are today much closer to the butcher than they realize, have no excuse."

At the beginning of this chapter, I asked whether the Zweig revival was nothing more than the anglophone liberal establishment exploiting a long-dead middlebrow writer for their own purposes. To an extent I think that is true. He cannot really bear the weight that is now being placed on his shoulders. It is our own job to find our own arguments for our own time. Indeed I wonder if Arendt would make just that point, were she still with us.

But that does not mean Zweig has nothing to tell us. The last piece in *Messages from a Lost World* is *In This Dark Hour*, an address given to the American PEN Club in My 1941. You don't know what you've got till it's gone, Zweig told his audience. It was, he said, necessary for "this dark hour" to make everyone realize that "freedom is as vital to our soul as breathing to our body."

Or, as he also said on that occasion: "Darkness must fall before we are aware of the majesty of the stars above our heads."

Flying, Fighting, Writing

As *Washington Post* publisher Philip Graham said back in 1963, journalism is "the first rough draft of history". That hasn't changed; new books about Donald Trump and Brexit pour off the press or onto our Kindles almost weekly, and they are often by journalists – Bob Woodward and CBS correspondent Major Garrett are the latest. In a year or two their books will be out of date and out of print. But in time, historians will go back to them as primary sources.

The Second World War was no different. Publishers fell over themselves to commission the topical. Sometimes, these commissions went to the well-known – people such as war correspondent Ernie Pyle and journalist and socialite Ève Curie, who slugged it out for a Pulitzer in 1943; Pyle won, but Curie's book is a *tour de force* (we will come to it in a later chapter). In Britain, Richard Dimbleby published two books during the war – *The Waiting Year* (about the run-up to D-Day) and the splendid *The Frontiers Are Green*. Novelists also got stuck in; John Steinbeck, for example, got books out on the war while it was on (for example *Bombs Away*, about an American bomber crew, and a rather good short novel, *The Moon is Down*).

But publishers know an expanding racket when they see one, and they didn't just publish the great and the good. A number of serving RAF pilots wrote about their experiences during the war. The best-known were *Enemy Coast Ahead* by Guy Gibson, published just after the war; *The Last Enemy*, by Richard Hillary; and Leonard Cheshire's *Bomber Pilot*. (Cheshire survived the war; the other two did not.) There was much they could not talk about while hostilities were still on. Airfield names are omitted, for instance, and sometimes the names of other pilots. And of course they could not talk about the extraordinary electronic war that the RAF was fighting in the skies over Germany; some of that remained secret for some time after 1945. But they could give civilians a taste of the war being fought above their heads.

Books like Hillary's and Gibson's are still in print, but most have vanished. The two writers reviewed here are less well-known. Their books are not remembered as literature, but they do offer flashes of fine writing. And they give an acute flavour of the war and what it was like to fight it in the air.

First, R.C. Rivaz's *Tail Gunner*.

*

Richard C. Rivaz was born in 1908 in India, where his father had been a civil servant. In the 1930s he tried to earn his living as an artist, but made little money, and turned to teaching. When the war began he volunteered for the RAF and was disappointed to be told that he was too old for pilot training. But he was accepted as an air-gunner. In the summer of 1940 he was posted to an operational unit; as it was wartime he did not name the squadron or the airfield in the book, but it was 102 Squadron at Driffield, north of Hull.

Arriving late, he is put in a room with an officer who is already asleep but has left his possessions scattered all over the room. "I was awakened next morning by the buzzing sound of an electric razor ...After a few moments I said 'Good morning'... and was fa-voured with some sort of grunt in reply...." Not long afterwards he is assigned to fly with this unfriendly character, who then makes himself quite charming. Rivaz gives his first name, Leonard, but not his second, which was Cheshire. At the time he wrote his book,

Rivaz would have known that Cheshire was to be a successful pilot, but not just how famous he would become.

Before he can get off the ground, however, Rivaz experiences a fierce air attack on the airfield.

I saw a party of men digging furiously around a shelter that had received a direct hit: the ambulance was there... and the orderlies were lifting a man — with his tunic, face, and hair covered with earth — on to a stretcher. ...I noticed that his legs were in an unnatural twisted position. ...I saw two more men crushed — with faces nearly the same colour as their tunics — between sheets of corrugated iron: they were both dead.

It was August 15 1940 and Driffield had been attacked by a large force of German bombers; 14 RAF personnel were dead, including the first female RAF fatality, and 12 British aircraft were destroyed.

These were details that Rivaz couldn't give, but it doesn't matter – his description of the raid is very vivid. So is much else in the book; Rivaz was to see a lot of action, and there are few dull moments. Flying over Cologne, his aircraft is hit and a flare explodes in the rear of the plane, temporarily blinding the crew, injuring one terribly and blowing an enormous hole in the fuselage; Rivaz, in the tail turret, must struggle past the damage and try to put out the flames. Cheshire eventually regains control of the aircraft and brings it home, a feat that will win him the DSO. Later, Rivaz would twice fly on missions against the *Scharnhorst* at Brest, daylight attacks on a heavily defended target. He was not to know that in the first of these raids, in July 1941, armour-piercing bombs of the type he was carrying did damage the ship quite badly. They may have come from his aircraft. He also "ditched" twice and was rescued from the sea, both times in winter; on one of these occasions, he only barely survived.

Rivaz flew as rear-gunner in two types of aircraft. Again, he was writing in wartime so says little about them, but he does identify them. At Driffield it was the Armstrong Whitworth Whitley, a twin-engined type that had been introduced in early 1937. In a time of rapid change, this meant it was already outdated. But it was not unsuccessful as a bomber, and later variants were also used for sub-hunting and for clandestine long-distance transport. What it wasn't, was fast. Rivaz records that on one raid, to Leuna in Saxony, they were in the air for 11 hours. Life in the rear turret must have been extremely uncomfortable (and he does mention the extremes of heat and cold). Later he transferred, like Cheshire, to 35 Squadron at Linton-on-Ouse; this was the first squadron to fly the new four-engined Handley Page Halifax Mk I.

Rivaz's writing is inconsistent. But at its best it is excellent. He was a thoughtful and observant man; at one point he describes, in detail, taking off on a different mission to Cologne on a March night. The Whitley's engines are being run up. "The ground crew were standing by, watching: one stood too near the slipstream and had his hat blown off... it was rolling over and over behind the aeroplane, and he was chasing it. ...A large pool of water by my turret was being thrown up into a fine spray, and some bits of oily rag were flying about in the air." They move off; the tail lifts in the air; the plane sways from side to side as the pilot keeps it straight with the rudder; then they are crossing the airfield perimeter, the lights glowing yellow and red below. Rivaz, as a gunner, is alert, knowing that enemy intruders have sometimes attacked bombers as they take off. Yet he sees his surroundings. He was, after all, an artist: "The sky above us was a green-blue... and the western sky was lit by a glorious red sunset. ...They would have lost the sunset from the ground by now... but up here it was as vivid as the ground was obscure." He gets on the intercom to the captain, to remark upon the evening's beauty.

But this night would not end well. By early morning the captain would be dead. Rivaz does not identify him; in fact, his name was Clive Florigny and he was from Streatham, South London. Rivaz also does not say, and probably did not know, that Florigny's brother, also a Whitley pilot, was to be killed later the same day. Their names are on the Air Forces Memorial at Runnymede, along with other aircrew with no known grave.

*

At about the time Rivaz was reporting at Driffield, Arthur (Art) Donahue was arriving at his own first operational station; like Rivaz, he does not name it, but it was Kenley in Surrey, on the southern approach to London. It was a rapid transition. As he recalls in *Tally-Ho! Yankee in a Spitfire*, also published in the middle of the war, just six weeks earlier he had been at work on his father's farm in St Charles, Minnesota. He had applied to join the US volunteer reserve very soon after the war began in Europe, but had heard nothing. Now, hearing that France had collapsed, he decided that, as an American, he could wait until his people were forced to fight, as they surely would be; or he could join the battle now. He travelled to Canada to join up and just 10 days later he was on a liner to Britain. "I didn't have any of the qualifications of a soldier. I was neither big nor very strong; I was quite mild-tempered and absolutely afraid to fight, and I was more cautious in my flying than the average pilot then."

This may be modest. Donahue, then 27, had been a Depression-era barnstormer but was also a serious pilot; when the war broke out, he was instructing. Even so, the speed with which the RAF got him off the boat and into combat is astonishing, given the very long training that most RAF pilots had to undergo. On arrival, he was sent straight to an Operational Training Unit (OTU) – again, he does not say which, but it was No. 7 OTU at Hawarden. OTUs were what their name suggests – advanced training units from which newly trained pilots would undertake their first missions. After a brief period flying trainers, he was unleashed on a Spitfire, a plane that cruised at twice the speed of anything he had ever flown before.

As in *Tail Gunner*, there is hardly a dull moment. Donahue began his combat career by chasing a Messerschmitt 109 across the Channel and engaging it, he says, at Cap Griz Nez – a hot pursuit that I'd always thought Battle of Britain pilots avoided, not wishing to be lured into combat over enemy territory. Which is what happened to Donahue, who caught the fighter but was then bounced by its friends. He escaped, and landed at Hawkinge on the Kent coast with serious damage to his aircraft. Then just a week later his aircraft caught fire after being hit in combat, forcing him to bail out with serious burns to one leg. By the time he returned to flying, the Battle of Britain was essentially over. Yet he had taken part in it – one of only about 10 American pilots to do so.

Of the two, Rivaz is the better of the two writers. But now and then Donahue, too, captures the imagination. A dawn flight from Kenley to their advanced base at Hawkinge: "Wicked blue flames flared back from the exhausts of all the engines as I looked at the planes in formation about me. ...The sun ...made weird lights over the tops of our camouflaged wings. We were like a herd of giant beasts in some strange new kind of world."

There is also striking detail on the life of a fighter pilot. They were clearly very organised. Donahue describes how, preparing for a period on readiness, he puts his parachute on the aircraft's tailplane, as that is where he can grab it quickest if he's scrambled.

He even arranges the straps so that they will fall easily to hand. In the cockpit he hangs his helmet over the control stick and plugs in the radio and oxygen leads, making sure that they are hanging in the right way so they won't slow down the business of putting the helmet on. The seat and shoulder straps are similarly arranged. Then Donahue methodically sets various valves to the open position so that he will not have to waste time doing so when the call comes. There are many more checks, all of them – by his account – meticulously carried out.

Donahue was apparently a strict Catholic and teetotaller (he mentions neither in the book), and one wonders how he fared with the hard-drinking RAF pilots; well enough, it seems. Also, he recounts in the book that he went to Canada to join the RAF but does not mention that he claimed to be Canadian, almost certainly because he faced losing his American citizenship for serving under a foreign flag. In fact, the US rescinded this threat only a few weeks later. But it may explain why there are different stories as to how many US nationals flew in the Battle of Britain (between seven and 11, depending on where you look; more joined the RCAF/RAF soon afterwards).

*

Rivaz's *Tail Gunner* ends with the second daylight raid on the *Scharnhorst* at Brest (he gives no date, but it was in January 1942). At the end of the book, Rivaz staggers ashore after a ditching – his second; this attack, it seems, proved as hairy as the first one.

Rivaz still wanted to be a pilot, and finally persuaded the RAF to post him for training. The result was a second book, *Tail Gunner Takes Over*. It describes his training in Manitoba, and ends with his posting back to Britain. *Tail Gunner Takes Over* is not as good as *Tail*

Gunner; there's some padding, and the details of his training are now really only of interest to historians of wartime flying. Rivaz was a good rather than great writer. But the first book is gripping – not least because he was in the thick of the air war at the start of Bomber Command's offensive against Germany. The casualty rate was high, and relatively few of the early pilots can have survived to write of those early raids in Hampdens and Whitleys. Later aircrew were more likely to, by virtue simply of having less time to get killed.

Moreover Rivaz could be quite thoughtful, and was fully aware of the destruction he was causing below. On Cologne:

There would be people dead or dying... there would be people burned there. ... There would be people with arms and legs blown off... and people with their stomachs blown open... and people with half their faces blown away. They might have to wait hours or even days until they were found...

Did Rivaz have doubts about what he was doing? He might have done; he was clearly aware of its consequences. Nearly 700,000 Germans would die in the air bombardment before the end of the war, and Rivaz was right – they would not always die mercifully. In practice, though, he probably felt, as others did, that the Germans had started the war, and besides had bombed us, and others; they could hardly complain that bombs were being thrown back. Most members of his generation still had no sympathy when I was growing up.

*

Donahue's book ends a year or so before Rivaz's, early in 1941; the

Battle of Britain had really ended by the time he recovered from his injuries, and he was reposted to another squadron in the south of England. Here there is much that Donahue does not say, hinting only that he was transferred more than once. In fact, it seems that he was posted to an embryonic squadron for American RAF volunteers. It is said that he disliked it; no planes had arrived, and the other Americans were somewhat louche and not to the taste of the strict Catholic from the farm. But he does not say this in the book, and it is hard to confirm.

At any rate, he gets himself posted again and as the book finishes he is flying offensive fighter sweeps over Northern France. These became more common in 1941 as the RAF, stronger now, looked for ways to strike back. They were not without losses; Douglas Bader, flying a Spitfire V, was captured on a sweep of this sort after his plane collided with a German in combat. Still, the fierce fighting of the previous summer was over. *Tally Ho* ends there.

Donahue's flying career, however, didn't. Like Rivaz, he was to write a second book. Unlike Rivaz, he would have plenty of action to speak of therein.

In the autumn of 1941 he was transferred, apparently at his own wish, to a squadron that was going overseas; he wanted to fight. The squadron set off on a troopship, to be united with their new aircraft at their destination. They weren't to be Spitfires but Hurricanes, which Donahue had not flown before.

The Hurricane had entered service a little earlier than the Spitfire. It too was a fast modern monoplane with retractable undercarriage and eight guns, but instead of being all-metal, it was – like older aircraft – partially fabric, with a linen skin stretched and shrunk over a skeletal framework. This had its advantages, as it could be repaired more quickly, but it was also more prone to fire, and most RAF fighter pilots who suffered terrible burns did so in the Hurricane rather than the Spitfire. It did not help that the fuel tank was sited right in front of the pilot. (Though Messerschmitt 109 pilots actually sat on theirs, which may have felt worse.)

Donahue never learns where the squadron was supposed to have gone. In fact, it seems to have been the Middle East. But in South Africa they learn of Pearl Harbour; also, that they have a new destination. Arriving in the Dutch East Indies, they collect their new planes, and at the end of January they arrive in Singapore.

In his second book, *Last Flight from Singapore*, Donahue recalls his first sight of the island, under "heavy, blue black storm clouds" that forced his squadron to fly lower and lower. They see at once that the airfield is spotted with filled-in bomb craters. The next two weeks are intense. There are only a few Hurricanes, and less capable Brewster Buffalo fighters, on the island. Although they fly daily, the Hurricanes are rarely able to get high enough in time to get above the Japanese bombers, as there are now no observers in Malaya to warn of their approach; the peninsula has been occupied by the Japanese, and on his first night Donahue is woken by the sound of British engineers blowing up the Johore causeway onto the island. Singapore is now under siege.

It is a bizarre time for the pilots, fighting for their lives in the day and then returning to the luxurious Seaview Hotel, where they are served wonderfully cooked multi-course meals and live in sumptuous suites. Meanwhile the pilots encounter snobbery from the colonials, with one elderly man who was waiting to be evacuated protesting that they should not use the swimming pool because they had not been 'introduced'. "His dislike for us was made obvious quite often," records Donahue, adding that besides "fighting to keep the Japs off his head now, we would quite likely have to patrol and perhaps fight over his ship later, to keep him from being sunk." Donahue becomes aware that terrible mistakes are being made in the defence of Singapore and that the decadence of the British in the East is not helping. "There's no need denying that I was terribly disillusioned by much of what I had seen and experienced out here — things that I have avoided or passed over in this story because it isn't in my province as a member of the forces to speak of them, and because I could only do harm by telling about them now," he writes.

Yet there is also a poignant unreality. One day, with the Japanese already fighting on the island, he and another pilot watch an "exotic, dark-haired English girl" exercising two greyhounds on the hotel lawn, as if nothing has happened. "Her movements and theirs were so graceful that I thought she must be a dancer, but someone said she was a nurse. It seemed that either she or the approaching enemy and the terrible fighting must be unreal. It just didn't make sense — but neither did a lot of things, in the last days of Singapore." Later Donahue would wonder what became of her, as well he might; the Japanese would kill a large number of staff and patients at the British military hospital a week later, on February 14. (Although it was the Chinese community in Singapore that would suffer most; tens of thousands would be killed during the occupation.)

The battle for Singapore was brief. A week after Donahue's arrival, the Japanese landed on Singapore. Two days later, on February 9, orders came to evacuate the last fighters to Sumatra, and he took off with two other Hurricanes and a Buffalo from an airfield that was already under ground attack, the crack of rifle fire only a few hundred yards away. It appears that this was indeed the last flight from Singapore, and there were no further Allied air operations over the island. It fell five days later.

Donahue continued to operate for a few days from Sumatra,

but before long this too was invaded. On February 16, with other pilots, Donahue attacked the invading troops as their boats came up the Musi River towards Palembang. Hit by ground fire and seriously wounded, he managed to land his aircraft, and was evacuated to hospital in Bandung and finally embarked on a hospital ship. *Last Flight from Singapore* ends there; he wrote it shortly afterwards in India and in Ceylon (Sri Lanka), where he had rejoined his squadron.

*

What were these men like?

Rivaz, the artist, seems to have been the more worldly; Donahue was from rural Minnesota and proud to be, and his letters home talk of the pigs on the farm there, and of the eggs and potatoes that the airmen produce on the base. But both were men of substance. Neither had had to fight; Rivaz was too old, and Donahue was a national of a neutral state. They were also, in the manner of the time, quite modest. Rivaz says nothing about his prewar career; though he'd made no money as an artist, he must have been a good one, as he had studied at the Royal College of Art and is known to have exhibited at the Royal Academy. But he mentions neither in the book. Donahue nowhere says that he had qualified as a commercial pilot at just 19, at a time when flying in the States was extremely dangerous. Moreover both write warmly of other men's courage but speak little of their own. They do not reveal in their books that they had both had the Distinguished Flying Cross – Rivaz for his conduct on the first daylight raid on the *Scharnhorst*, when he destroyed an enemy fighter and saved his own plane, and Donahue for that last desperate low-level attack on the Japanese in Sumatra.

One wants of course to know their eventual fates.

On completion of his pilot's training, Rivaz was posted back to Britain – not, to his disgust, as a combat pilot, but to the forerunner of Transport Command. He survived the war. In October 1945 he was a passenger on a Liberator that crashed on takeoff from Melsbroek, now part of Brussels Airport. All 31 passengers and crew died, including Rivaz; he is buried in Brussels Town Cemetery.

Art Donahue stayed for some months in Ceylon, but in August 1942 he returned to Britain and was posted to 91 Squadron at his old airfield of Hawkinge in Kent. On September 5 he wrote to his family in Minnesota: "Well, I think …I'll be with you for Christmas this year! I hope to have a month in the States, possibly more, so don't go planning any celebration but keep it in your hope chest anyway."

Five days later, on September 11 1942, Art Donahue took off in his Spitfire to chase a Ju 88, which he caught; it later crash-landed in Belgium. But his own aircraft must have been damaged in the encounter, and a brief radio message was received saying that he was ditching off Gravelines. His body was never found.

The Polish Anne Frank

The Second World War ended 75 years ago, and there are now few people alive who lived through it as adults. They won't write more books. What does come to light, now and then, is a manuscript in a trunk – or a diary.

Renia Spiegel kept one until she was murdered by the Gestapo in Poland in 1942, aged just 18. Her diary was brought to the US by a survivor sometime in the 1950s, and eventually reached Renia's surviving sister, Elizabeth Bellak. She could not bear to read it, and it lay in a safe-deposit box in New York for 40-odd years. Then Bellak's daughter, Alexandra Renata Bellak, persuaded her to let it be translated into English. The project also had the encouragement of filmmaker Tomasz Magierski, who has since made a documentary, *Broken Dreams*, about Renia and her sister. *Renia's Diary: A Holocaust Journal* (the American title) has now been published in English.

Like Anne Frank's diary, it's full of the musings of a girl growing up; boys, friends, crushes, introspection, the trials of adolescence. But, like Anne's, it's also an historical document – in some ways a remarkable one. It keeps alive a young woman who was highly intelligent and well-read, and was also a vivid and thoughtful poet.

*

In 1918 Poland emerged as an independent state for the first time since the 18th century, formed from the wreckage of the empires around it. The new state was promptly attacked by the USSR, which nearly succeeded in snuffing it out. In the end, however, the Poles inflicted a heavy defeat on the Red Army. In March 1921 the war ended with the Treaty of Riga, by which Poland acquired some of what is now Belarus, and a large part of modern Ukraine, running south to the Romanian border. It was in the latter region that Renia Spiegel was born in 1924.

Although not originally assigned to Poland at the Paris Peace Conference, the region did contain Poles as well as Ukrainians. The two populations were intermingled. They would come into conflict after 1945, but between the wars they seem to have lived together happily enough. Renia was Polish. She was also Jewish.

When Renia was very young her parents acquired a manor house and farm at Stavki, on the Dniester River, not far from the border with Romania – again, in the region that Poland had acquired from the USSR in 1921. It seems to have been an idyllic childhood.

It is not clear what went wrong to end this, but at some point her parents split up, apparently as a result of Renia's father's affair with another woman. Her mother left to tour Poland with Renia's younger sister, Ariana (now Elizabeth Bellak), who was making a career in film as "the Polish Shirley Temple". Renia found herself parked with her grandparents in Przemyśl, a former Austro-Hungarian garrison town on the San River some way to the west. (Przemyśl, unlike Stavki, is still in Poland.)

The city had had a difficult recent history, having undergone a long siege by Russian forces during the First World War; it eventually fell. Many of its people were Jewish. They had been there a long time. The YIVO Institute for Jewish Research, founded in Vilnius between the wars and now based in New York City, records that a Jewish community began to establish itself in Przemyśl as early as the 13th century. By the late 18th century they were a quarter of the city's population.

But there were anti-Jewish riots in the city in the 16th to 18th centuries. Despite this, the YIVO Institute estimates that nearly 30% of the city's population was Jewish by 1910 – and that they were later as much as 38.8% of the population. It also states that the Jewish community won 18 of the 48 seats on the city's council in 1926. According to the Holocaust Research Project, they accounted for as many as 24,000 out of the 60,000-odd prewar population. But there was continuing antisemitism; this was expressed at times through boycotts of Jewish businesses.

We don't know to what extent Renia would have known all this, or cared. We do know that she was not ecstatic at being dumped on her grandparents in Przemyśl. In her first diary entry, dated January 31 1939, when she was 15, Renia laments in a poem the loss of the peaceful manor at Stavki. But in this first entry, just like Anne Frank, she also describes the girls in her class, rather frankly and with a certain relish. There's Irka ("I don't like Irka and it's in my blood") and Luna ("she thinks of herself as a very talented and unearthly creature"), and Ninka, who's quite nice but "arranges meetings in dark streets, visits lonely men and is proud of it". Meanwhile Renia and her best friend Norka have a crush on the Latin teacher.

Comparisons with Anne Frank's diary are inevitable. Yet this is a very different diary from Anne Frank's in one key respect: Anne was in hiding, whereas Renia was not. Anne did hear the radio and was aware of the progress of the war; in fact, she records surprising details – for example that Churchill had had pneumonia and that Gandhi was again on hunger strike (the BBC must have been franker than one expects). Anne also kept up with the news of the occupation outside. But she was not part of it. Renia, by contrast, was out in the world. So we see the situation around her unfolding much as a Pole would have, in the first half of the war.

At the same time, these two diaries are both just that – diaries;

there is no hindsight. *Renia's Diary* has a concise and thoughtful foreword by the Holocaust historian Deborah Lipstadt, in which she points out the difference between a memoir and a diary; the author of the first knows how the story ends, whereas the diarist does not. "A survivor may recount the details of an event in order to stress a particular point, a point whose importance only became evident to her well after the fact," says Lipstadt. Thus Renia is desperately miserable at being with her grandparents and losing Stavki; if she had known what was to come, these would have been the least of her problems.

Anne did know all too well what her fate might be; as early as October 9 1942 she wrote that "English radio" was saying that Jews were being transported to be gassed. "Perhaps that's the quickest way to die," she mused. But Anne didn't know for certain what lay ahead. Renia had even less idea, strengthening Lipstadt's comment that diaries give a different perspective sometimes; the diarist sees the tragedy unfolding in real time, without knowing how it will end. Thus in April 1939 Renia writes a witty poem for her little sister. A few days later she describes the slightly farcical air-raid precautions being organised as Przemyśl prepares for a gas attack. But she is more worried about her chemistry class.

All that changed on September 1 1939, when Germany attacked Poland. As Przemyśl was overrun, Renia, her younger sister Ariana and their grandfather fled eastwards on foot to Lwów, the major city of south-east Poland (today Lviv in Ukraine). They walked for three days. On September 18 1939:

We've been in Lwów for almost a week... The city is surrounded. Food is in short supply. Sometimes I get up at dawn and stand in a long line to get bread. Apart from that, we've been spending all day in a bunker, a cellar, listening to the terrible whistling of bullets and explosions of bombs. God, please save us.

On the 22nd, Lwów surrendered – not to the Germans, but to the Red Army. As part of the Nazi-Soviet Pact a few weeks earlier, Hitler and Stalin had cynically agreed to carve up Poland between them; Germany would take the western half and the USSR would occupy the east, including the territories it had lost to Poland after its ill-advised war against the country in 1920-21.

Renia records that Warsaw, and some Poles in Lwów, were still fighting. The September war is sometimes a footnote in the history-books, and it was indeed short. But the Polish resistance was, in fact, very stiff. A country with indefensible borders, attacked on two fronts by two enormous neighbours, it fought for only a month. But during that month, it extracted a heavy price from its invaders. The Germans lost 285 aircraft, not many less than the Poles themselves. About 20,000 German soldiers were killed or missing, and quite a lot of their armour was destroyed. Poland never actually surrendered.

*

Renia, Ariana and her grandparents returned to Przemyśl. But their home was not in German-occupied Poland. It was in the Russian sector, and the border with the German-run General Government ran along the River San – right through the centre of Przemyśl. Their city had been cut in half. As they could not cross the bridge to the German zone, they were cut off from Renia's mother, who was in Warsaw.

For a Jewish family, the Russian zone was a much better place to be. They appear not to have been discriminated against. They may even have been better off than before in some ways; Renia went so far as to write in her diary that people couldn't call her "you lousy yid" any more (the implication being that they had before). Before long, things seem to have been oddly normal; she returned to school, and went on going to parties, worrying about her lessons and having crushes. She was even able to travel to see her father, who was also in the Russian zone – although his estate had been confiscated, he was safe. But communication with her mother in the German zone was difficult and potentially dangerous. On October 27 1939 she writes: "We haven't heard from her. I had a terrible dream that she's dead. I know it's not possible. I cry all the time…"

But in fact Renia's mother was alive. She seems to have had both charm and wit, because with the help of friends, she managed to secure fake papers as a Catholic woman, and found a job as assistant manager of the Europejski – which was, and is, one of Warsaw's poshest hotels.

Meanwhile the Russian occupation, benign for Renia, was much less so for others. Many Poles, both soldiers and civilians, had been taken prisoner, and the following spring the NKVD murdered more than 20,000 of them in a notorious massacre, disposing of the bodies in the Smolensk region's Katyn forest, after which the killings are now named. The dead included many of Poland's officers, intellectuals, businessmen and landowners. Many Polish prisoners who were not killed were shipped elsewhere in the USSR, where the authorities kept some in prison camps and seem simply to have abandoned others. (Many would eventually leave the USSR under General Anders and fight alongside the British in Italy.)

Renia seems to have been aware of at least some of what the Russians were doing. On April 24 1940 – actually during the Katyn murders, though she did not know of them – she wrote that: "Terrible things have been happening. People were rounded up and sent somewhere deep inside Russia. ...There was terrible screaming at school. Girls were crying."

The Jews who had fled across the San from the German zone seem to have fared little better; the Russians deported them. On July 6 1940 Renia records that they had come in the night to arrest people in the house opposite. "The arrests were led by some fat hag who kept yelling in Russian... They were told the journey would take four weeks. ...Poor refugees from the other side of the San. They are being taken to Birobidzhan." It is not clear how Renia knew this, but she was probably right. Birobidzhan was, and remains, an autonomous Jewish oblast in Russia's far east, on the border with Manchuria. The Soviets had attempted to start a Jewish homeland there, with mixed results. The YIVO Institute states that about 7,000 Jews from Przemyśl were deported to Russia during this period.

Renia knew, of course, that the war was still being fought, in the West and North Africa, but does not seem to have followed it as closely as Anne Frank and her family, who clustered round the radio just outside their secret annexe. But Renia did make her feelings about the war known. On October 12 1940 she writes, apparently of war in general:

Who is stifled, killed, destroyed by you
forever remains free
...those who're alive have broken hearts
...you howl, you infuriated beast,
"more, I want blood to fill my snout."

*

134

Anne Frank and Renia Spiegel were very different, and their situations were different too. Anne had a more supportive family. When they went into hiding in the Secret Annexe, she found that her father had brought her postcard and movie-star collection there beforehand, a thoughtful and loving gesture; and her mother tried to care for her though Anne was indifferent to her. In this sense it was harder for Renia, whose father had gone off with someone else and whose mother was in Warsaw and had been absent for years anyway, touring with Renia's younger sister Ariana.

There was also a difference in their sense of identity. According to Ariana (later Elizabeth Bellak), the family went to synagogue and observed the major holidays, but was not especially religious. Renia was certainly aware of being Jewish, and later passages in the diary show that she was very aware of anti-semitism. But she does not seem to have seen being Jewish as something that defined her.

Anne Frank didn't either, but seems to have thought more about being Jewish, as a result of her family's experience in Germany. "Fine specimens of humanity, those Germans, and to think I'm actually one of them!" she wrote. "No, that's not true. Hitler took away our nationality long ago. And besides, there are no greater enemies on earth than the Germans and the Jews."

They had different personalities. Anne described herself as a chatterbox. In the very last entry of her diary, on August 1 1944, she writes: "I'm guided by the pure Anne within, but on the outside I'm nothing but a frolicsome little goat tugging at its tether." One gets the feeling that her father saw the Anne inside but that others around her did not. Renia seems to have been more intense. But her pictures usually show her smiling, and maybe they were more similar than their diaries suggest.

Certainly they both had a deep need to express themselves in writing – and both were very good at it. Anne was the more imaginative prose writer (and wrote a number of stories while in hiding). She also eventually realised her diary might be published, after hearing a Dutch minister in exile, Gerrit Bolkestein, say in a radio broadcast that evidence such as diaries would be wanted after the war. Renia had no notion that her diary would be published, and it is entirely confessional; she complains of her family and her girlfriends and her social failures, and at times, to be honest, there can be too much of it – this was a teenager's diary and was not intended to be read. But Renia had a talent Anne does not show so much, at least in her diaries: as we've seen, she was a poet, and rather a good one.

It helps that the many poems in *Renia's Diary* seem to have been beautifully translated (the translators were Anna Blasiak and Marta Dziurosz). They do make one wonder what might have followed had she had a lifetime to write. On June 18 1939:

If a man had wings
If souls could be in all things
The world would lose its temper
The sun would shower us with embers
The people would dance beyond the beyond
Shouting, more! We want to abscond!
What we need is wind and speed
The world is dark, stifling, squeezed

In one key respect, besides their desire to write, these two girls were similar – both were sexual beings, and expressed this in their diaries. Some of this would be excised in the early editions of Anne Frank's diary, but is now restored. Thus on January 6 1944 she writes of a friend: "I could no longer restrain my curiosity about her body, which she'd always hidden from me ...I also had a terrible desire to kiss her, which I did. Every time I see a female nude, such as the Venus in my art history book, I go into ecstasy. ...If only I had a girlfriend!" This has been used to suggest that Anne may have been a lesbian – but she was only 13 when she went into hiding, and 15 when she wrote that passage. Moreover she was just about to become strongly attracted to Peter van Daan, who lived in the annexe with her. We don't know if she would have been lesbian or bisexual. Still, she had erotic feelings and now and then expressed them.

Renia did so much more strongly. This is evident in several of her poems. One, for instance, seems to be a reference to masturbation. Then on June 15 1942, the 18-year-old Renia writes an explicit verse ("A bloody spring fruit you resemble ...I will absorb you, I will writhe and adore, I will kiss you like a lithe whore"). It would be prurient to dwell on this when it is only one part of Renia's personality. But it is a part of her story, because there was no doubt about whom she was writing: Renia Spiegel was in love.

Sometime in September or October 1940 she had formed an attachment to Zygmunt Schwarzer. Zygu, as Renia calls him in the diary, was a doctor's son from Jarosław, a city not far away and also on the San river, but under German occupation; the family had thus fled to Przemyśl. Aged 17 in 1940, Zygu was a year older than Renia and according to Elizabeth Bellak, he was very handsome.

A huge strength of *Renia's Diary* is the commentary that Bellak has provided in the back of the book. Matched to the diary by date, it explains events that would otherwise be puzzling, date by date, giving essential background. It is warm, gentle and humane, and seems full of love for the sister she last saw when she was 11 and Renia herself just 18.

Bellak has no doubt that her sister was in love. According to

137

Bellak, Zygu had "black, curly hair, bright green eyes, and dimples on the sides of his cheeks that got deeper every time he smiled – which was a lot. ...I always felt warm and comfortable around him." There is no doubt how Renia herself felt.

The course of true love didn't run smooth. Perhaps at that age it never does. The diary is peppered with doubts; he was dragged away by someone else; he was not here this evening; he loves me, he loves me not. Now and then friends got in the way. Schwarzer's good friend Maciek Tuchman seemed to be in love with her too. ("He walks me home ...constantly has something to whisper in my ear, or a speck to brush off me"). But slowly Renia and Zygu drew together. On June 21 1941 Renia wrote that they had kissed amongst the pine trees. In the early hours of June 22, she later recorded, he blew her a kiss as she stood on the balcony, watching him walk away; a Montague slipping away from his Capulet love.

Then four hours later a shot rang out. The war between Germany and Russia had begun. War needed more blood to fill its snout.

*

Things changed quickly.

On July 1 1941: "Tomorrow, along with other Jews, I'll have to start wearing a white armband. ...to others I will become someone inferior, I will become someone wearing a white armband with a blue star. I will be a Jude." Ariana (Elizabeth Bellak) also felt this deeply, although she was only 10 and did not need to wear an armband herself. "When I first saw one, something in me died," she wrote nearly 80 years later. "My family and friends and neighbors who wore them weren't people anymore. They were objects."

Renia herself records on July 28 1941 that: "Yesterday I saw

Jews being beaten. Some monstrous Ukrainian in a German uniform hit every one he met. He hit and kicked them, and we were helpless, so weak, so incapable." But on the same day she had written of the troops of wounded Germans that passed every day, and jhow sorry she was for the young boys far from their homes and families. In a poem on that day she talked of seeing a young wounded German soldier, and wrote: "Who can explain to me why ...I curse the thousands and millions ...And for the one wounded, I cry?"

Reading that, one is filled with rage that this young woman did not survive.

But she didn't. In July 1942 the Germans designated a part of Przemyśl as a ghetto and forced all the city's Jewish people into it. Shortly afterwards they allocated work permits to those they thought might be useful, and took the rest away. Some were sent to an extermination camp at Bełżec near Lwów. Others, probably including Renia and Ariana's grandparents, were taken into the countryside and shot. Zygmunt Schwarzer's parents did not have work permits and neither did Renia. In actions that must have taken insane courage, Schwarzer first smuggled 10-year-old Ariana across the San to the family of a Christian friend, then hid Renia and his parents in an uncle's house. Then the father of Ariana's Christian playmate, also with great courage, got her to Warsaw, where her mother arranged false papers for her; they made their way westwards near the end of the war, and eventually emigrated to New York.

Renia was not so lucky. The Gestapo found her, and Schwarzer's parents. Bellak does not say how, but in a memoir published nearly 70 years later, Schwarzer's friend Maciek Tuchman said they were betrayed by the building janitor; he did not know why. They were shot there and then. It was July 30 1942.

139

*

The Holocaust Research Project states that, of the 24,000 Jews living in Przemyśl before the war, just 300 survived. Other sources put it a little higher, but not much. The YIVO Institute records that there were some 22,000 Jews in the Przemyśl ghetto when it was closed off in July 1942; about 10,000 were deported to Bełżec at about the time Renia was murdered, and had she not gone into hiding she would have gone with them anyway. The remainder of the ghetto was liquidated between September 1943 and February 1944. Some limited Jewish life did restart in Przemyśl after the war but by the beginning of the 21st century, only a handful of Jewish people lived in the city.

The best revenge is to survive and thrive. Both Schwarzer and Tuchman survived the war, though not easily; Schwarzer went to Auschwitz, while Tuchman went to Birkenau and worked as a slave-labourer for Siemens. In 1945, as refugees, they were offered the chance to study by UNRRA, and studied medicine in – of all places – Germany, in the ancient university town of Heidelberg. In his memoir (*Remember: My Stories of Survival and Beyond*, Yad Vashem, 2010), Tuchman explains that they didn't really have anywhere else to go; even the US was taking a restricted number of displaced persons, and Israel did not yet exist. So they formed a lively community of Jewish students in Heidelberg, many of whom went on to successful careers.

They included Tuchman and Schwarzer, who eventually reached the United States. Both married and had children. Tuchman practiced medicine in New York for many years and died there in 2018, aged 96. Zygmunt Schwarzer became a paediatrician. Tuchman records that after service in the US Air Force,

140

Schwarzer practised in New York, where he developed an interest in, and published on, the infectious diseases of children.

Ariana – Elizabeth Bellak – also remained in the US and still lives there. In her commentary on the Diary, she writes: "It's been almost 80 years since I last saw my sister. That's a lifetime since I saw her looking up from one of her leather notebooks, her bright blue eyes shining... Yet her presence is one of the largest in my life."

As for Schwarzer, at times in the *Diary* Renia seems to doubt his love, or to worry about his feelings for her; but she was wrong. Bellak records that he kept photocopies of the *Diary* in the basement of his Long Island home, and that every few days he would go down to look at them. In 1989 – 47 years after Renia's death – he wrote the following words in the back of the original *Diary*: "Thanks to Renia I fell in love for the first time in my life, deeply and sincerely. ...It was an amazing, delicate emotion ...I can't express how much I love her. And it will never change until the end."

He died three years later, aged 69.

In 2015 Elizabeth Bellak started the Renia Spiegel Foundation, the objective of which is to promote tolerance and Polish culture, and keep Renia's story alive for future generations. It can be found at http://www.reniaspiegelfoundation.org/.

War Tour: The Incredible Journey of Ève Curie

Early one morning in November 1941, a Pan-American Airlines Clipper flying-boat lay moored off New York's Long Island, preparing for an historic flight. Outside, reporters gathered and photographers' flashbulbs split the predawn darkness. The *Cape Town Clipper* was to pioneer a new route for PAA, to British-controlled West Africa.

The flight was not secret, but its real purpose was not made explicit. In fact, many of the 58 passengers were young men who were more often in uniform, while others were logistics experts. The British had set up an air route to ferry planes across Africa to the desert war. Now PAA was quietly helping the British and the still-neutral US government to strengthen it from the west.

In the darkness inside the plane was a passenger PAA preferred to keep hidden, as she was not supposed to be there. "We will carry you to Nigeria," she had been told, "but just try to forget how you got there." It had not been hard to arrange. This petite, charming woman had a famous name and powerful friends. A few weeks earlier she had met the Roosevelts at the White House, and the year before she had dined with Churchill at Chequers. A little after five on the morning of November 10, she was escorted on board. Between now and February, she intended to go round the world, visiting the fighting fronts and reporting on the war. She carried all the luggage she was permitted: 29lb (about 13kg), including a brown silk dress, a typewriter and a book called *Brush Up Your Russian*.

She would not get round the world. But she would visit almost every major front, and would write a book, *Journey Among Warri-*

ors, that would narrowly miss a Pulitzer. Today it is mostly forgotten, yet it is a wonderful piece of writing that bears extraordinary witness to the war and to those who fought it.

*

Ève Curie was French, but was half-Polish; she spoke both languages. In November 1941 she was just short of her 37th birthday. Pictures and newsreels from the war years show her to have been slim and elegant, with striking dark eyes. Unlike her sister, Irène Joliot-Curie, she had not shown her famous mother Marie Curie's aptitude for science. But as a child she had been a gifted pianist, to the extent that Paderewski was impressed when she played for him aged six. As a young woman she gave concerts in Paris and elsewhere, but she does not appear to have felt herself good enough for a concert career. Instead she turned to journalism. After Marie Curie died in 1934, Ève Curie wrote a biography of her that was extremely well-received and remains in print. By 1939 she was well-known in France and on the outbreak of war was co-opted into a senior post in the Ministry of Information.

In the spring of 1940 Curie visited the US, where she addressed audiences on France and the war. She then returned to France via Lisbon on another PAA flying boat. (That time her luggage didn't make it, being left on the quay by mistake; the moment she was told this was somehow captured by a *Life* photographer). She arrived back in Paris in June 1940 – and left again, this time in a hurry. Leaving Paris on June 11, Curie escaped from France a week later on board the P&O liner *Madura*, which had been diverted to pick up refugees from Bordeaux. She never wrote of this voyage so far as one knows, but others did so; badly overloaded, the ship survived air attack and reached Falmouth two days later with about 1,400 refugees. They included not only Curie but Baron Rothschild;

also Hugh Carleton Greene and assorted other British journalists. According to Daphne Wall, who was a child at the time and was on board, some of the media corps had a bibulous voyage (*The World I Lost: A Memoir of Peace and War*, 2014).

Curie spent some months in Britain, working with the Free French and also visiting the Free Poles, then returned to the United States. There was another lecture tour, and Eleanor Roosevelt gave a dinner at the White House in her honour. The woman who sat in the dark interior of the flying boat *Cape Town Clipper* in November 1941 was now an exile and a nomad, but she was a jolly well-connected one. She had now been commissioned to write for the *Herald Tribune* and for a British group that included *The Sunday Times* and *The Daily Sketch*. "This intrusion of mine in the Anglo-Saxon press, the best in the world, impressed me frightfully," she wrote. "For the first time, also, I was to attempt to write a book in English.... The water whistled under us and we took off. New York, the United States, vanished in the chilly mist."

Ève Curie's *Journey Among Warriors* had begun.

*

The length and complexity of that journey are lost on us now. The regular JetBlue service from JFK to Bermuda takes two hours and nine minutes; from New York to Banjul is about nine and a half hours. Curie's Clipper took five hours to Bermuda and would take three days to reach Bathurst, as Banjul was then known, via Bermuda, Puerto Rico, Belém and Natal. Nonetheless Curie expressed a sense of wonder at arriving in Bathurst just three days after leaving New York, and at the time she was right. The huge British Short flying boats had shrunk the Eastern hemisphere, the even bigger American Clippers the Western.

In West Africa Curie found the British busy shrinking Africa. There was a desperate need for planes to reinforce the Middle Eastern front. Quite early in the war they had started to ferry planes across from West Africa, and by 1941 the Americans were also heavily involved in the logistics. In fact, reading this book, one realises that in the months before Pearl Harbor the United States was just barely neutral. Had it still been neutral when *Journey Among Warriors* was published, Curie would have been much less frank about what she saw.

Curie is also frank about the differing views of her American travelling companions. On the flying boat a young Californian pilot tells her that the administration was "muddling into this war against the will of the people, when America is not menaced. ...A war with Japan?" he sneers. "It is not in the interest of our good friends the English, so the English will see to it that it does not happen." Other pilots and Pan American staff express a very different view. One comments that America must organize a full-scale war industry without being at war, and wonders if that is possible. In less than a month this debate would end with Pearl Harbor, which none of Curie's companions could have foreseen. But history is written by events, and only a book like this can show you how the world was seen just before they occurred.

Curie moves east across the continent, on a succession of planes. It is as she crosses Nigeria that she starts to use her descriptive skills. In Kano:

The deep red mud houses of the native town, which dated back to the fifteenth century ... were so much like an African legend that it was difficult to believe they were true. ... Complicated carvings ornamented some of the doors. It was all very rough, savage and virile – indeed beautiful.

A European's Africa. Later, the British Resident introduces Curie to a man she describes as "the local Emir". It is explained to him that her parents had discovered "a thing called radium", which was "very important in science and medicine". She continues: "The black ruler worded his courteous answer so that we should not gather whether he had, or had not, heard of radium before." Although Curie does not name him, he was almost certainly Abdullahi Bayero, who had reigned since 1926 and had considerable autonomy, which he used to encourage industry in Kano. He had also, early in his reign, provided water and electricity across the city although the colonial administration regarded it as too expensive; in fact he made it pay for itself.

Curie wonders how much the people of Kano know and understand about the war. She comments that educated Africans "were keenly aware – much more so than the Arabs – of what Hitler's racial theories had in store for coloured people." This is quite possible, but one wonders how she knew. But the fact is that in 1941 many Europeans would not have asked themselves these questions, or cared greatly about the answers. It is also clear that Curie has no time for the colour bar. It is a matter of pride for her that the Governor of the French colony of Chad, Félix Éboué, is black, born in Martinique, she says (wrongly; he was born in French Guiana). It was because Éboué has declared for de Gaulle that the crucial air route is possible; had he sided with Vichy, it could not have crossed Chad. Curie does not meet Éboué, and sadly he would die of a heart attack in Cairo not long after *Journey Among Warriors* was published.

Curie pushes on across the desert with BOAC, the forerunner to British Airways, arriving in Cairo soon after the beginning of Operation Crusader. This was Auchinleck's offensive against Rommel, which had begun on November 18 and appeared to be going well. Curie wanted to go to the front and see the fighting. However, "the military men to whom I spoke did not seem to think that to send me to the front was the most urgent war measure that ought to be taken." They might have been right.

However, as always, Curie is well-connected. She is staying with diplomat Michael Wright, who had been a friend when he was posted in Paris, and who she describes as "now secretary at the British Embassy in Cairo" (actually First Secretary; he would later, as Sir Michael Wright, serve as ambassador to Iraq). She also had "off the record" talks with a number of "the great and the good", including Air Marshal Tedder, who commanded the RAF in the Middle East; Sir Walter Monckton, a future Minister of Defence who was head of propaganda in Cairo; and Oliver Lyttleton, Minister of State in the Middle East. "In the preceding twelve hours," she writes, "quite a few obstacles to my trip had been levelled." She is told Randolph Churchill, the Prime Minister's son, will pick her up at seven. "Now remember," says Lyttleton at dinner, "I have *not heard* that you are going to the desert tomorrow." One wonders how the old-fashioned war correspondents felt about this. Moreover, while Curie was never afraid to be near the fighting, it is also clear that she did not think too hard whether she might cause complications there. This was especially so in the desert, where the situation could change rapidly in a few hours – as she and Churchill soon find; Operation Crusader has stumbled somewhat, and communiqués describe the situation as "confused" as both sides used armoured columns to probe each other's defences.

On a sandy airstrip in the middle of nowhere Curie interviews young pilots as they leap out of their Hurricanes and Tomahawks. "One could see that their guns had been used. The men were gay and excited, also tired, somewhat out of breath." She cannot get them to take themselves seriously, and seems to like them for it. There is some surprise at seeing a woman in the desert. A Polish pilot standing beside his Hurricane is even more surprised to be addressed in Polish, then announces he has read her book. A German pilot who has been taken prisoner is puzzled that she is French. "He turned toward me and said severely: "May I know what Marshal Pétain would think of a Frenchwoman being here with the British? He would not be too pleased, I suppose!"

The Free French are a recurring theme in this book. Curie clearly prefers them to the British; but they were, after all, her people, and she was in exile. They were also a reminder that the humiliation of the surrender had not been total, because some Frenchmen had decided to fight on. When she talks of the Allied invasion of Syria, the fact that British forces were also involved is hardly mentioned, but perhaps she can be excused for that; the Free French had to shoot at other Frenchmen. But some British soldiers who fought in that campaign will also have found that hard. John Verney, who took part in the invasion as part of a Yeomanry regiment, later wrote that he only cried once in the war, after a bad day's fighting in Syria.

Curie and her party emerge unscathed from the desert; the only casualty is Randolph Churchill's silver whisky flask, crushed by someone's typewriter. It would perhaps have helped had this happened more often in his life. (Curie mentions that only the unexpected presence of Auchinleck could shut him up.)

By this stage of the book one is getting a better picture of Curie. It is a mixed one. She is a French chauvinist, but one of great charm and poise that she clearly uses, along with a massive social network, to get help from the English who (at least collectively) she does not really like. But she is also shrewd, and, although writing in wartime, honest; she is quite frank about the Allies' problems with the Arabs, for example. In fact her political antennae seem un-usually sharp. Moreover she clearly has some quite serious balls. To be sure, she pulled strings to get into the desert, but her drive to see the war, and to share its discomforts, was real. As for the bulging contact book, it would have been useless without enter-prise. She shows this in her next port of call – Tehran, where she meets the new ruler of Iran.

*

In December 1941 Tehran was a very strange place. It was neutral, but alleged pro-German rumblings, and the need to open a supply route to Russia, had led the British to invade it in August. In this they had the help of their new Soviet allies, who took over the north-west of the country. In the process the British deposed and deported the ruler of Iran, who had come to power in 1921 and had himself made monarch, or Shah, in 1925. His 21-year-old son was placed on the throne in his stead. Iran found itself under much the same position as Egypt; nominally independent and neutral, but under the thumb of the British, and humiliated. A few weeks later the Ambassador in Egypt, Sir Miles Lampson, with whom Curie had lately lunched in Cairo, would force King Farouk (who was the Shah's brother-in-law) virtually at gunpoint to dismiss his gov-ernment. These are incidents that the British have forgotten; the Egyptians and Iranians have not. But they paved the way for much that has followed since.

Curie was not the first Allied journalist to interview the new Shah; in fact not the first woman journalist. That had been the gutsy English reporter Clare Hollingworth, who in 1939 had been the first to report that the Germans were about to invade Poland. Hollingworth had interviewed the young Shah very soon after the invasion the previous August – an encounter should would describe 50 years later in her own book, *Front Line*. She seems to have got little from him, not least because he then spoke no English; he had been educated in French. Curie, however, does seem to have warmed to him, perhaps for that reason. "In his handsome face, the eyes were very dark, sensitive and proud, the features sharp, the nose high-bridged. ... [He was] as graceful as the oriental princes about whom I had read when I was a child."

Curie finds the young Shah unsure of himself: "He often left a sentence in suspense, as though he found it unwise to express his whole thought about a subject about which he felt strongly." He had, says Curie, just gone through a disturbing chain of events, being dragged onto the throne by the British on the same day that they sent his father, who he admired, into exile in Mauritius. Curie senses strongly how upset the new Shah still is about this. One wonders if anyone else did. The quiet young man who has been educated in Switzerland has found himself nominally in charge of a country that was in reality occupied by two ruthless empires. At one point he asks Curie what the world thinks of Iran's "non-resistance" to the invading powers (in fact there has been a little limited resistance). "I was almost sure to make a blunder, whatever I answered," writes Curie. She answers sincerely that her own country is overrun by Germans and that she would be delighted to have the Allies there temporarily instead, just as they now occupied Iran. The Shah accepts this eagerly, saying that it has been to avoid "the fate of countries doomed by Hitler" that Iran has accepted "the present arrangement". It is a revealing interview; as with so much in this book, Curie seems to perceive the future implications of what she hears and sees in ways that others perhaps did not.

In one respect, the Shah does disappoint Curie. "It was amazing," she writes, "to come all the way to Iran, a country of glamour, of legends, and to be received by the Shah in a dull office that could just as well have been located in the Rockefeller Center." In this, Clare Hollingworth had fared better. She was to write in *The Front Line* that the Shah had "welcomed me in a small study ...where he had a range of bound books on military history and strategy." Invited to stay to lunch, she "rather cheekily compared the 'flash' entrance hall of the palace to a Lyon's Corner House." The Shah takes this as a compliment and later asks her if she really thinks it is that good. Hollingworth would see the Shah change, for she would interview him again several times, in Tehran and finally in Marrakesh in 1979 after he, too had been sent into exile. Yet there is something especially poignant about Ève Curie's description of a young man adrift in a new world that foreshadows the struggle he would have to make sense of it.

*

But Curie does not intend to stay in Tehran. She has an appointment in Samara.

The central Russian city of Samara has since 1935 been known as Kuybyshev, in memory of an old revolutionary who had died that year, although probably not accidentally. Since October it has been the administrative capital of the Soviet Union; the embassies, government departments and much of Moscow's industry have been evacuated there as the Germans surround Moscow (where Stalin has remained). A Russian-crewed DC3 is said to travel between Kuybyshev and Tehran, but Curie's foreign friends assure her it is semi-mythical. After several weeks' wait she is summoned to the airport, to the jeers of fellow-guests at her hotel, who assure her she will be back for lunch. She is not.

It is about 1,750 miles (over 2,800km) from Tehran, and it is the depths of winter. After an overnight stop in Baku (where Curie joins the locals for a well-attended opera), the plane pushes north via Astrakhan, and the temperature starts to drop. It can fall to below -40 deg F (-40 deg C) in Kuybyshev in January; Curie is going to experience that in a hotel room with no heating. But she will also see what it means to fight a war in this climate. Just to keep machinery going is hard, and the crew must drain the oil from the engines at night, heat it and pour it back warm in the morning; charcoal stoves burn under the engines to stop them freezing. Coal stoves are also used in the ambulances that bring wounded soldiers from the front.

It is in Russia that Curie's writing starts to reach heights that mark *Journey Among Warriors* as one of the great war books, and from then on the standard never drops. It is clear to her that that the USSR is engaged in total war. In Samara she meets the USSR's preeminent ballerina, Olga Lepeshinskaya, who is also mobilized; she is secretary of the Anti-fascist Youth Committee. Beautiful, committed, urgent, she tells Curie, "I am twenty-five – about the age of the Soviet regime. I am a daughter of the October Revolution I have never known anything else than the fight of the Russian people against capitalism and fascism."

One wonders if Curie gulps a little at this, but she accepts an invitation to a children's party, where Lepeshinskaya will dance for the young evacuees. The accompaniment is poor, the floor imperfect, but it does not bother Lepeshinskaya: "She danced the most difficult steps with a delighted smile ...as if she felt like leaping higher and whirling much faster still. ...She was Youth herself."

The next morning Curie leaves for Moscow.

*

As always, Curie wants to reach the front. No-one from the Press Corps has, and in Russia her society links are of little use to her. But the name Marie Curie is.

On January 15 1942 her daughter Ève and her Russian companions drive out of Moscow in search of the fighting. This had come very close to Moscow in December, but the Germans, ill-equipped for winter, have been driven back by a determined counter-offensive. The Red Army is now hoping to retake Mozhaisk, about 70 miles west of the city. Its strategic position on the east-west highway means that this would end the battle for Moscow.

Curie records a mass of evocative detail. There are the destroyed houses of which only the stove and chimney remain. There are soldiers on skis, stranded tanks, the skeleton of a crashed plane, men fishing for mines. Destroyed bridges are being replaced with wooden ones that the engineers throw together with manic speed, using tree-trunks hauled by peasants. German corpses lie scattered in the snow (Curie takes a close look at a few, but is warned not to touch them; they are sometimes mined).

The destruction left by the retreating Germans appalls Curie. In one town of nine thousand people, Istra, just three houses are left standing. People from the town tell Curie that the Germans had forced them into the centre of the town as targets for the Russian shelling, and then lobbed grenades into the houses on their way out. In Volokolokamsk, 80 miles from Moscow, the Germans have burned the monastery, the School of Agriculture and the children's hospital. Late in January Mozhaisk does fall, and Curie enters it soon afterwards. The first person she meets is a wailing young girl who tells her that the Germans had driven two hundred people into the cathedral and blown it up. The general in charge, one Leonid A. Govorov, confirms to Curie that this has occurred.

I can't find any reference to this incident. But that does not mean it did not happen. Certainly Govorov was real enough (he would eventually take charge of the Leningrad Front, and finished the war as a Marshal of the Soviet Union). Maybe the dead of Mozhaisk were, in the end, part of a catalogue of destruction so long that some items have been lost in the intervening years. In general, Curie seems reliable. To be sure, she had no love of the Germans. But crude propaganda was not for her, and she wasn't afraid to argue with her Soviet hosts about politics. The Russian passages, like the rest of the book, have a ring of truth.

But there is a curious coda to her trip to the front. Near Volokolamsk she interviews one Major General A.A. Vlasov, "one of the young army leaders whose fame was rapidly growing ...in the USSR." Vlasov hasn't slept for five days but is hospitable and enthusiastic, showing Curie some of the regimental emblems and Iron Crosses that his men have captured, and gifts sent to him by the admiring people of the USSR – including an inscribed wristwatch. Then he takes a large map and a pencil and shows Curie how the campaign has been fought. Curie is impressed: "He kept muttering: 'Everybody, *everybody*, must fight the fascists.' Here was a man who waged war with something more than determination, something more than courage: he waged it with passion."

But Vlasov was to go over to the Fascists. Captured in July 1942, he changed sides in captivity and by the time *Journey Among Warriors* was published in 1943, he had already written a pamphlet describing his reasons for joining the fight against Bolshevism. Later he would try to recruit an army from Soviet prisoners – with limited success, for the German high command never really trusted him. At war's end he was arrested by the Red Army near

Dresden. Tried the following year, he was hung on August 1 1946. Vlasov's treachery was to become notorious, but it is possible that Curie did not yet know of it in 1943. She was later to say that he was not the same Vlasov she had met near Volokolokamsk. But he was. So it is hard to know if she was being disingenuous, or whether she sincerely believed that the two men could not possibly be the same. My guess is the latter.

For the most part, though, Curie is not credulous. She admires the Soviet war effort but has not forgotten the Nazi-Soviet pact, and reminds her hosts of it now and then. And she has not forgotten the Poles. In Kuybyshev she spends time with the Polish ambassador, who is trying to find out what has happened to a staggering one million Poles who are believed to be in the USSR. They are no longer its enemies, and are now supposed to be set free or allowed to join one of the new Polish units training in Russia.

The Poles Curie meets are reticent about their new allies. "Nobody said much," she writes. "Men who had suffered extreme hardships ...[and] had chosen to join their former jailers in the struggle against Germany ...felt they were the best judges of what the ...attitude towards Russia should be." Curie does not mention the Katyn massacre, but it was not widely known of in 1942 (a neutral mission would go to Katyn at the instigation of the Germans the following year). She does know, however, that there are Poles scattered in towns and camps all over Siberia. Now that the USSR is fighting Germany, the Poles are forming the former Polish prisoners into an army under General Anders, himself freed suddenly from captivity. But the Soviets say they cannot help locate all the Poles because they have simply lost track of them. Unbelievably, this seems to have been true; Curie meets a young man attached to the Embassy who wanders round isolated towns with a Polish eagle on his coat, finding Poles in rags everywhere, and making them help him find more.

*

From victory Curie goes to defeat. The British and their allies will win the war in Burma in the end, but in February 1942 they are retreating, and will soon lose the entire country.

Curie flies on a Chinese airliner to Lashio in the Northern Shan States, and then battles her way south by train and car towards the advancing Japanese against the tide of humanity fleeing in the opposite direction. In Rangoon (now Yangon) she finds quiet panic. Nothing works; shops are closed and the hotel staff have fled. She pushes on to the front with an Indian liaison officer, and interviews exhausted soldiers five miles from the fighting. A young British officer politely offers her tea, insisting that she have another biscuit. They are surrounded by teak trees, and an overwhelming silence. She returns to Rangoon, where the British governor of Burma, Sir Reginald Dorman-Smith, insists they plan to hold the city. But Curie has been in France in 1940 and can smell defeat. Rangoon falls three weeks later.

She is not polite about the British in Burma. "They did not, like the Russians, face the most appalling battles with an insane determination to win. They fought, and gave their lives, with something like resignation," she says. One wonders if she misunderstood something here. If he knows he must die, a Russian blesses the Fatherland; an Englishman returns his library books. But she may have been right about the civilians in the East, who she thought did not understand how the world, and their own country, had changed. In particular, she again notes the colour bar. Her Indian liaison officer, a volunteer who is committed to Allied victory, does not understand why he can't go into a restaurant with a white man.

As Norman Mailer was to write years later, British snobbery was forever building empires, then buggering them. Yet there are complexities here. Curie seems bemused to find that Mr Porter, the Commissioner for the Shan States, who is her host in Lashio, is half-Burmese. (This will have been Arthur William Porter. He had been made an OBE some years earlier, though Curie won't have known that. Sadly history records little else of him.)

The collapse in Burma has been very bad luck for a major ally, China. In April Lashio will fall, cutting the 700-mile Burma Road that linked it with Kunming in Yunnan. It also opens another front where Chinese troops will have to fight. They have in fact been fighting since 1937.

As Beijing (then known in the West as Peking) fell early on, the provisional capital is in Chongqing (again, then known as Chungking). Curie flies there from Lashio, again on China National Airways. As usual, she meets everybody. Now China at last has friends in the war, but they have disappointed her, and Curie hears rude things said of Pearl Harbour, Burma and Singapore. She also meets Chiang Kai-Shek and Chou En-Lai – and Madam Chiang (Soong Mei-ling), who seems very American and has been educated at Wellesley, graduating from it 52 years before Hillary Clinton, who she seems to have rather resembled.

Yet it is not her interviews with them that are memorable. What is striking about Curie's chapters on China is, first of all, her descriptive powers, evident in her picture of Chongqing, a very different city from the modern metropolis of 18.4 million. The second is Curie's acute sense of the future. A prominent Chinese businessman takes her to see China's one and only Bessemer converter in action. "The men who handled the containers full of liquid metal were barefoot ...Yet the work was being done. Steel was actually being produced."

157

As I write this, the last British blast furnace is about to be shut down and Chinese steel is glutting the world markets. But Curie would not have been surprised. "This was a solemn moment in the history of Free China," says Curie, and goes on to wonder whether the Chinese would "make the jump from the Middle Ages to the twentieth century without breaking their necks, ...or whether they definitely needed a transition period."

For the moment, an older China holds sway. On a visit to a military academy in Chengtu, she is told that it does have some tanks, "behind the dispensary". On the way back the car breaks down in the countryside. In search of food, she walks to a mud house where she finds "a half-crippled woman with a frightening face; one of her eyes was enormous, entirely red and blind. She looked like a Cyclops in a fairy tale." The party stop overnight in a village where she sleeps "in a wretched hovel" in which, for some reason, a dead squirrel is hanging on the door handle. "When I first grabbed it in the dark," she says, "I did not find this a very exciting welcome."

*

But the next chapter opens with Curie staying in the colonial splendour of Government House, Calcutta. It was once the residence of the Viceroy; the capital has moved some years before to Delhi, but it is still the home of the Governor of Bengal, Sir John Herbert, of whom she is a guest. There are no dead squirrels here.

The last 100 pages of this long book are amongst the most extraordinary, and of the most interest to an historian.

Up to now, Curie has given us vivid descriptions of the fighting fronts, their hinterlands and the swarm of soldiers, technicians and engineers united in the war on fascism. But although she has met many people of importance, they have not always told her much; or if they have, it has been in confidence (one suspects the latter, especially in Cairo). India is different. In Delhi, a week or two hence, she will alternate between the residences of the modern Viceroy, the Marquess of Linlithgow, and the Commander in Chief of the Asian theatre, General Wavell.

Linlithgow she describes as: "A tall man, with long arms, long legs, and a remarkably long head." She finds him modest and shy. History has not been kind to Linlithgow; he is remembered for bringing India into the Second World War without consulting Indian politicians (he was not obliged to join the war; the Raj was a separate entity under the Crown). He is also blamed for failure to respond adequately to the appalling Bengal famine of 1943. It is said that he had been exhausted by his long tenure as Viceroy and had already asked to be released. But Curie will have known nothing of this. In any case, she devotes more space to Wavell, who will eventually succeed Linlithgow and will be the last real Viceroy. As such, he will start by taking more vigorous action to address the famine (which nonetheless is to cost at least 1.5 million lives). But he will also struggle to make the Indian leaders find common ground between themselves. Still, that lies in the future. For now, Wavell's problems are solely military.

Wavell has a reputation for taciturnity, but Curie finds that when he does speak, he is frank and sometimes very charming. She does not mention that he also writes poetry (he will later edit an anthology of other people's, called *Other Men's Flowers*). Neither does she mention that he has recently suffered a serious back injury; an odd omission – it had occurred while he was boarding a flying boat at Singapore a few days before it fell, and at the time she met him he would have been in some pain. But she clearly likes Wavell, and history suggests that she is right.

However, Curie is in the unique position of being able to talk not only to the British high command but to the leaders of the Indian independence movement. In view of this, Curie's portrait of them is of enduring interest. It is "easy to get to see Jawaharlal Nehru, because he was utterly natural and simple and because he liked people." One could, writes Curie, "almost read his thoughts and guess what his mood was: gay or gloomy. His was a romantic face; also a witty one. It changed quickly, like the sky on a windy day."

Curie stays with Nehru in Allahabad. The family is immersed in preparations for Nehru's daughter Indira's wedding to Feroze Gandhi. Curie does talk to her, but might have done so more had she known what she would become. However, her extensive conversations with Nehru are riveting. In particular, Nehru is, in many ways, an upper-class Englishman; but he is fighting an emotional battle for India's separation. Yet it is clear that Nehru is himself very aware of this paradox and even amused by it. Also, he does not reduce imperialism to the idea of Empire; the concept of economic imperialism, as practised by the United States, is quite clear to him. Neither has he any illusions about the nature of Japanese expansionism. It is clear that Curie likes Nehru, and again, one feels that she is right.

Curie comes to Delhi at a crucial juncture in India's history: Sir Stafford Cripps is bringing a set of proposals for the country's leaders. Although she doesn't find out until later, they are an explicit statement of intent that India will become independent at the end of hostilities, and that although she will initially have Dominion status (like Canada or Australia), she will be able to modify that if she chooses. Curie has the curious task of interviewing Jinnah and Gandhi when they know the contents of the proposals, and she does not (the Indian leaders will eventually reject them).

With Jinnah, the conversation is one-way. That with Gandhi is far more interesting. He is welcoming and thoughtful. Curie presses him hard on his doctrine of non-violence. His response is courteous and shows great internal logic, yet seems, to her, ultimately sterile. She raises the question of the Poles, whose heroism is keeping their occupied country alive. "He dismissed the Poles, not without disdain, by saying: 'They are a race of fighters who have not the slightest notion of what a philosophy such as non-violence consists of. To fight is their only way of expressing themselves.'"

To Curie, who was half-Polish, this must have struck a rotten note. She urges him to accept that non-violence will not protect India from invasion. Gandhi replies – one suspects, with a certain hauteur – that the Japanese would be no worse than the British. It is an attitude that Curie finds infuriating amongst Indian independence activists. They have, she reflects, a relatively free press. They are also able to take part in politics; the British had by then introduced elections and limited self-government in much of India. Curie is not uncritical of the Raj, pointing to the medieval poverty that existed within its borders. It also seems clear that, in the long run, her sympathies lie with independence. But when she hears Indians say that British, Japanese and German oppression are the same, she is appalled. She notes that she is able to buy "two or three vitriolic volumes denouncing the sins of the British imperialists" in a bookshop, from an English clerk.

*

This long, final part of *Journey Among Warriors* that deals with India is fascinating, even compulsive, reading. It is especially so when

Curie writes of Wavell, Gandhi and Nehru, air-raid drills in Calcutta, and old-school expats mouldering in their clubs while other, younger men from Britain have come to forge weapons of war. Why has this book been neglected by historians?

Journey Among Warriors was published in 1943, in British and American editions. It attracted some interest, and Curie was in contention for a Pulitzer, but was beaten by the American war correspondent Ernie Pyle. The book was not reprinted after the war, apart from a French edition in 1947. It has since vanished.

Perhaps readers would find it a strange book now; the modern style of travel writing is as much about the writer as their environment, a sort of confessional. Curie belonged to a less self-indulgent age. And yet she is there in the book if you look for her. Now and then one is reminded how she must have felt. In Kaduna, Nigeria, she feels suddenly alone among so many Englishmen, who all over the world could meet people with the same language and habits "and who, most probably, knew one of [their] cousins or his brother-in-law." Meanwhile Curie has been stripped or her citizenship (and her flat) by the Vichy government and has no idea when, or even if, she will return to France. She can take little pleasure in the splendour that sometimes surrounded her. Travelling from Lashio to Mandalay, she is dazzled by the beauty of Burma: "The most beautiful country in the world, which the war affected in no way ...We passed silvery rice fields, then a swift river with jade-green waters." In Lashio, soon to fall to the enemy, she has breakfast on the porch of Porter's residence, the bright sun lighting the green hills around and the garden full of "red, exotic flowers ...It was one of those radiant mornings which seem to be the negation of everything cruel and gloomy." Yet her job is to leave every pleasant spot and go somewhere where there is trouble. In Allahabad she rests on the veranda of Nehru's house, hearing the wedding preparations around her, and realises that, for the first time in months, she is in a real home. But this too she must leave.

Hermione Ranfurly, who met Curie in Algiers later in the war, describes her in *To War with Whitaker* as extremely intelligent, multilingual with perfect English, and also very pretty, but "rather serious". The pictures and newsreels confirm that Curie was very attractive, and her English was indeed near-perfect. Mlle Curie is *soigné*, elegant, self-possessed, charming, and extremely well-connected, but also, one suspects, self-contained. She has many friends but is also alone, France and family lost, travelling the world like a restless spirit. One imagines her at dinner with the Minister of State or the Viceroy or the Commander-in-Chief or Randolph Churchill, the latter braying at someone to pass the salt; and suddenly one knows that sometimes, when no-one was looking, her gaze would fix itself on a wall or a painting, and she would not be there.

Early in *Journey Among Warriors* Curie is in the desert with Randolph Churchill, and a good-looking British officer approaches her: "He said: 'Don't you remember? We dined together in Paris, at Vera M---'s, and she gave us heaps of caviar.' ...Somehow, I felt that the ...caviar, and everything pleasantly artificial ...had very logically led us all here."

Curie was finished with caviar. By the time *Journey Among Warriors* was published, she had joined the Free French army. When Ranfurly met her in Algiers, she was a lieutenant in the medical corps, and had served in Italy. In 1944 she was awarded the Croix de Guerre. After the war she worked in journalism in France and later as special assistant to the first Secretary-General of NATO, Lord Ismay. In 1954 she married American diplomat Henry Labouisse, who became head of UNWRA and later

UNICEF, a post he held until 1979. During his tenure Curie devoted herself to travelling and working for UNICEF.

Labouisse died in 1987. Curie, however, lived to be a very old woman indeed. In December 2004 she celebrated her 100th birthday, an occasion marked by a visit to her New York flat by UN Secretary-General Kofi Annan. The following year she was made an Officer of the Légion d'Honneur in a ceremony at UNICEF House.

Among her many achievements, Curie left behind two books. One, her biography of her mother, is in print to this day. But *Journey Among Warriors* has vanished, forgotten, never reprinted. Why? It is one of the most extraordinary pieces of reportage to come out of the Second World War.

Ève Denise Curie Labouisse died at her New York home on October 22 2007. She was six weeks short of her 103rd birthday. She had lived an immensely full life; concert pianist, journalist, socialite, war correspondent, public servant and diplomat. She had much to remember. But one wonders if, towards the end, she thought sometimes of the long, strange journey by flying boat; the cold night in the Western Desert, the grandeur of the Viceregal residence, or the booby-trapped dead Germans in the snow; of late nights talking with Wavell or Nehru; arguing with Gandhi; the silence of the teak forests; or the red, exotic flowers in a garden where she sat wishing she could enjoy them, if only the war would end.

Since this was written a biography of Ève Curie has been published in French (Claudine Monteil: Ève Curie: L'autre fille de Pierre et Marie Curie).

Even Their Tears Froze

What was the worst-ever maritime disaster, in terms of lives lost? Some would say the *Titanic*, but they'd be quite wrong. Not even close. In fact, with just over 1,500 dead, it lies in fifth or sixth place even in the list of peacetime disasters (the worst was the ferry *Doña Paz*, which collided with a tanker when on passage from Leyte to Manila in 1987; the death toll was not far off 5,000).

If you count wartime disasters, the *Titanic* is a footnote; it is not even the worst loss of life on a British ship (that was the *Lancastria* off St Nazaire in 1940). But the worst of all was the *Wilhelm Gustloff* in January 1945. The death toll was twice that of the *Doña Paz*, and six times that of the *Titanic*; and many, possibly half, of the dead were children.

There is plenty of material available on the disaster in German. In English there is much less. However, a brief book by a British journalist, A.V. Sellwood, appeared in 1973. The "standard" work, *The Cruellest Night* (*Cruelest* in the US), by Christopher Dobson, John Miller and Ronald Payne, was published in 1979. Now there is a third account, Cathryn J. Prince's *Death in the Baltic* (2013). Finally, there is *Crabwalk*, the last novel by Nobel Prize winner Günter Grass.

All, in their different ways, shed light on a story that is barely known in the English-speaking world. And they invest it with an epic horror that makes the *Titanic* banal.

*

The *Wilhelm Gustloff* was large – over 25,000 tons (just over half as big as the *Titanic*). She had been built in the 1930s as a cruise liner for the Nazi Strength through Joy movement, and was launched in 1937. She was named after a Nazi official in Switzerland who had been assassinated by a Jewish student in 1936.

On January 30 1945 she lay in what is now the Polish port of Gdynia, where she was being used as a submarine depot ship. The city was on land that had historically belonged to Germany, but had been ceded to Poland as part of the Treaty of Versailles; between the wars, it was in the Polish Corridor that reached the sea between Pomerania and East Prussia. During this time, the Poles had built the port of Gdynia. The Germans had occupied it in 1939, but by the end of January the Soviet armies had effectively cut East Prussia off from the rest of Germany.

The commander-in-chief of the German navy, *Großadmiral* Dönitz, had foreseen this; unlike most of the German leadership, he had had the courage to plan for defeat. On January 23 he had signalled Gdynia with the single word: HANNIBAL. According to *The Cruellest Night*, this was the command for the submarine arm to evacuate Gdynia. In fact, it set in train the far larger Operation Hannibal, by which not only large numbers of troops but also hundreds of thousands of civilians would be lifted from what was then eastern Germany and out of the path of the Russian advance.

A number of large liners besides the *Wilhelm Gustloff* were pressed into service, including the pride of the Hamburg South America line, the *Cap Arcona*, said to be one of the most beautiful ships afloat; and a trio of large liners built in the 1920s for the North Atlantic run. These were the *Deutschland* and two slightly smaller liners: the *General Steuben*, and the *Berlin III*, remembered for its role in rescuing some of the passengers of the British liner *Vestris* in 1928. All of these ships would have a bad end, but in one case it would be long deferred.

The *Wilhelm Gustloff* was hurriedly readied for sea, despite

166

having lain at Gdynia for the best part of four years. The city was thronged with fleeing Germans, who fought for permits to board. Submariners took priority, but over 4,000 civilian refugees were allowed on board, along with several hundred women naval auxiliaries. There were also 162 wounded. According to Dobson, Miller and Payne, the final official list recorded 6,050 passengers and crew. However, as the ship drew away from the quayside, it was forced to stop:

...a number of small boats drew alongside, each one filled with refugees, mostly women and children. They blocked the ship and from their crowded decks came pathetic shouts and appeals. "Take us with you. Save the children!"

The ship put out nets and more people struggled on board; no-one counted them.

Their desperation is understandable. Some will have known how abominably their own forces had behaved in the East and will have understood what would happen when the enemy arrived. If they had had any illusions, they would have been dispelled the previous October. On the 21st of that month the Red Army had taken the village of Nemmersdorf in East Prussia. It was an early incursion into German territory, and did not last long; German troops soon retook the village and held the area for some time. In the meantime, however, the Soviets had carried out the notorious Nemmersdorf Massacre; 74 civilians, almost all women, had apparently been killed and it was alleged that some had been crucified, naked, on some barn doors. Exactly what happened at Nemmersdorf is disputed (including the crucifixions), but there seems to be general agreement that the Red Army did commit atrocities there. In any case, the German propaganda made the most of the incident in order to stiffen resistance. Understandably, many civilians wished to get away at all costs. Those who swarmed up the nets onto the *Wilhelm Gustloff* must have felt huge relief when they were pulled on board.

The ship did now leave Gdynia, in the company of another liner, the *Hansa*. It was early afternoon on January 30, and bitterly cold; there was hail, and one passenger noticed ice floating in the harbour. Shortly after leaving Gdynia, the *Hansa* and one of the torpedo boats developed engine trouble. The *Gustloff* initially hove to but was ordered to proceed alone, escorted only by the torpedo recovery vessel and a second torpedo boat. The authors describe the latter as "an ancient torpedo boat called the *Löwe* (Lion), which had been captured by the Germans during the Norwegian campaign in 1940." In fact, the *Löwe* was technically not a torpedo boat but a destroyer, and was not ancient; built by the Norwegians for their own navy in 1938, she was moderately well-armed and, when new, would have made over 30 knots. It was still not a powerful escort for a large target.

The Soviet submarine force had failed so far. According to Dobson, Miller and Payne, its 218 submarines in 1941 had made it the largest undersea fleet of the day, but it had sunk just 108 merchant ships and 28 small warships by war's end. Until 1945 it had been bottled up in the eastern Baltic. But by January 30 the Soviet submarines had re-emerged into the Baltic, using their new access to Finnish ports. From one of these came the *S13*, commanded by an able but unstable maverick called Sasha Marinesco. Just after 9 pm, he found the *Gustloff* off the coast of what was then Pomerania. Marinesko fired a fan of four torpedoes. One misfired. The remaining three struck home. The *Gustloff* sank in about 40 minutes. Most of the passengers did not know how to get out; the embarkation had been chaotic and although there had been an attempt at a safety drill, not everyone had heard it. The lifeboats were insufficient and in any case there were problems launching them, for the release and lowering mechanisms were iced over. There are several reports of passengers shooting their families before shooting themselves.

The *Löwe*, another torpedo boat, the T36, and the torpedo recovery vessel recovered some survivors; several other ships also participated, including the cruiser *Admiral Hipper*, which was in poor condition and being withdrawn to Kiel. How many people actually died in the sinking is not known. As *The Cruellest Night* points out, to know that, one would have to know exactly how many people were on board when she left Gdynia, and no-one really does. However, rough figures are possible. Writing in 1979, the authors gave an estimate of 8,000. "It is known that 964 people were picked out of the sea, some of whom died later," they say. "It is likely, therefore, that at least 7,000 people perished." In fact, it is likely to have been more. After the war, Heinz Schön, an 18-year-old assistant purser who survived the sinking, went on to research and write extensively about the disaster, and became the foremost authority on it. Schön, who was interviewed by the authors in the 1970s, later concluded that there were not 8,000 but nearly 10,600 on board, of which he thought about 1,230 had survived. He put the eventual death toll at 9,343. An unknown but very large number (Schön thought nearly half) were children.

*

The Cruellest Night was not, in fact, the first book about the *Gustloff* in English. British journalist A. V. Sellwood heard of the sinking from survivors when he was covering the Berlin Airlift in 1948. In later years, as he researched several books about the war at sea, he heard more stories, and began to get an inkling of what an enormous disaster it had been. His book *The Damned Don't Drown* was published in 1974.

Sellwood was a journalist, not an historian. He wrote a number of popular non-fiction books, sometimes co-written with his wife, Mary, or other writers. Most were on the war at sea but they included one on Victorian railway murderers, and a 1964 "startling exposé" called *Devil Worship in Britain*. This journalistic approach is very evident in *The Damned Don't Drown*. It sometimes grates. Sometimes he adopts the viewpoint of an eyewitness, which of course he was not, or writes as if he knew someone's thoughts: "In one of the few intervals he could spare... [Captain] Petersen found time to wonder briefly how the passengers were finding it. ...he felt a twinge of sympathy for their plight." Petersen did survive, but died a year or so later and won't have spoken to the author. There is also very little explanation of how the ship was caught by the submarine; Sellwood simply says that it was "waiting in their path" and saw them by accident. In fact Petersen was so worried about collision with other German vessels that he was not taking evasive action, and had the navigation lights on.

But it doesn't really matter, because that's not what you read this book for. The strength of *The Damned Don't Drown* is its survivors' stories. As the ship started to sink, literally thousands of people were trapped below deck, and the stories of those who did get out are gripping. So are the accounts of the fights to get into the lifeboats, the struggles to launch them from frozen davits, the attempts by the crew to keep order at gunpoint, and the bitter cold as the temperature dropped to (Sellwood says) -20 deg C.

There is cowardice. A Party official shoots his wife as part of a suicide pact, then lacks the courage to kill himself (a passing soldier, disgusted, does the job for him). There is brutish behaviour;

people on an already overloaded raft "used feet and fists to batter swimmers struggling to join them ...until finally the float itself was overturned. Dozens drowned in the ensuing panic."

But there is also great courage and selflessness. A teenager who Sellwood names as Ilse Bauer is being evacuated after being raped by Soviet troops in East Prussia. She is slipping down the icy, sloping deck into the sea when a sailor rescues her and wedges her behind a deck fitting, where an older woman hugs her to keep her warm; later, the woman gives Bauer her fur coat, then jumps into the sea, presumably to her own death. The coat protects Ilse and she survives, just. A newly-married naval auxiliary, Ruth Fleischer, is literally flung onto a lifeboat by a burly seaman who thrusts aside others who are fighting for a place. Fleischer too survives, although her new husband – the communications officer on a nearby cruiser – is convinced for some days that she is dead.

The *Damned Don't Drown* isn't a history book and doesn't pretend to be. There's no index, and nothing is referenced; presumably it was all from survivor interviews but the author does not state whether he carried these out himself, or drew on other accounts. The book is also quite brief (the US edition is 160 pages). A better-referenced, and more recent, book is Cathryn J. Prince's *Death in the Baltic* (2013). It contains some excellent research; the author has consulted a wide range of sources, some quite obscure. She has also interviewed survivors and obtained some outstanding eyewitness accounts – no mean feat given that Prince is writing nearly 70 years after the event. The book lacks the rigour of *The Cruellest Night*; there are signs of careless editing, and also an odd omission (of which more below). But Prince conveys a remarkable sense of who the victims really were, their diversity, and the shades of grey that surround the sinking.

Death in the Baltic's main strength is the testimony of the survivors. Their accounts are very alive, even after 70 years. Horst Woit, then 10 years old, today living in Canada, tells Prince how he and his mother had fled their home in Elbling, East Prussia, a few days earlier; on impulse, as they leave, the boy grabs his uncle's eight-inch jackknife. Later, he and his mother will be among the few who get into a lifeboat, but the crew will be unable to sever the icy rope holding it to the ship; then he produces the knife. "The knife," he tells Prince, "saved 70 lives." Eva Dorn, later Eva Dorn Rothschild, is a naval auxiliary, and should have been billeted with the rest of them in the drained swimming-pool below decks, but realises it's an overcrowded death-trap. She goes up to help the doctors, who are delivering children and treating the wounded. When the torpedo strikes, a skeleton in a glass case falls over in front of her. She steps over it, and tells herself: "You have stepped over death. Nothing will happen to you." She *has* stepped over death; the second torpedo strikes the swimming-pool where she is supposed to be, and some 300 young women are blown to pieces.

Besides capturing testimony of the actual sinking, Prince has done very well to tell us who the civilians aboard really were. Eva Dorn, the naval auxiliary, was not some stereotyped Nazi but the daughter of an improvident unemployed opera singer and a viola player. A rebellious young woman, she had been delighted to be thrown out of what Prince calls the Hitler Youth (actually it will have been the female equivalent, the *Bund Deutscher Mädel*, or BDM). Even more interesting are the Tschinkur family, who don't seem really to have been German at all. They were from Riga, but when the Nazi-Soviet Pact was signed, the Baltic States (soon to be swallowed up by Stalin) were pressurized into repatriating anyone who was vaguely German. Their mother was Russian but their father had been German some generations back, so they were classi-fied as *Volkdeutsch* and forcibly "repatriated" to the Reich. Reset-tled in Gotenhafen, one of the children is caned at school because, asked to recite a poem, she does so in Russian. It is a strength of Prince's book that she helps us see the passengers on the *Gustloff* not simply as a bunch of Germans who had started a war and whose lives were thus forfeit, but as thousands of individuals, each with their own story, and some surely deserving of something bet-ter.

Two things do let *Death in the Baltic* down. One is a certain care-lessness in the editing. Friedrich Petersen, the captain of the *Gustloff*, is 63 in both 1938 and 1945 (both wrong; he was 67 in 1945). The Polish name for what was formerly the German city of Thorn is Toruń, not Turin. More strangely, the book claims to break new ground in covering the sinking; Prince says that "The most infor-mation I found consisted of footnotes in World War Two histo-ries... I had no explanation for the lack of news articles." But both the two earlier books had had American editions. It may be that Prince simply did not know about them and besides, she doesn't quote from or rely on them, so is not obliged to cite either title. But it is odd that she does not at least reference them as general sources. Still, nothing can detract from Prince's achievement in teasing out the stories of the survivors and obtaining their testimony – the more so as, 75 years on, few others will now do so.

*

While Prince's book and Sellwood's are well worth reading, any-one who wants to read only one book should stick with *The Cruel-lest Night*. It is a book that combines journalism and history, both to a high standard. Besides, while the *Gustloff* sank on January 30

1945, *Hannibal* continued pretty much until the end of the war; and whereas Prince and Sellwood end their accounts with the *Gustloff*, Dobson, Miller and Payne do not.

Farther east from Gdynia, many refugees had made their way to the port of Pillau in East Prussia, not far from the major city of Königsberg (now Kaliningrad); the area was now surrounded by the Red Army. The authors recount that evacuees who had made it on board a ship: "Threw their babies to relations on the quayside, who used them as boarding vouchers. Sometimes the infants fell into the water between ship and quay."

On February 8 one of the former North Atlantic liners, the *General Steuben*, arrived in Pillau. The authors state that the defensive perimeter around Königsberg was thought to have given way. In fact, Königsberg would hold out for another two months. But there was widespread panic in the port. In the chaos, it was not possible to record exactly how many people boarded the *Steuben* for her westward voyage, but the authors quote contemporary estimates that there were about two thousand wounded, a thousand refugees, about 350 medical staff and a hundred crew – so, about 3,450 all told. Once again, the ship was escorted only by an old torpedo boat (this time the authors are right – the *T196* was from the first war), and an equally ancient torpedo recovery vessel.

It was the latter that would be the *Steuben*'s undoing. Marinesko was still at sea in the *S13*. Around midnight, one of his lookouts spotted a curious pattern of lights low on the horizon. They were sparks from the ancient coal-burning vessel, which was struggling to keep up. They led Marinesko to the *Steuben*, which he later said he mistook for a cruiser (the authors say this could have been true). Marinesko's torpedoes hit the ship just before 1 am. The authors say she sank in just seven minutes. Other sources say about 20, but it doesn't matter. Few got out; some wounded soldiers shot

themselves on their stretchers. "As the *General Steuben* went under," say the authors, "a great scream issued from the people
trapped aboard. It was something the men on the escorting warships never forgot."

Once again, no-one really knows how many people died. The
authors say about 3,000, but in fact 659 people are now known to
have been rescued, which would make their estimate a little high.
On the other hand, the authors probably underestimated the number aboard, perhaps by quite some number. The wreck of the
Steuben was found some 60 years later, and the *National Geographic*
published a feature on it (titled *Ghost Ship Found*, by Marcin Jamkowski). In an accompanying piece, a researcher for the magazine,
David W. Wooddell, reported that a surviving German officer
claimed to have counted 5,200 people on board. He said they had
deliberately underreported the numbers because they were not
meant to have carried so many. If this is correct, the death toll was
about 4,500. However, Heinz Schön eventually put the number at
4,267, of which 3,608 died. It seems hard to be that accurate, given
the circumstances. But Schön's research is respected, and it is the
best estimate anyone is likely to get.

There was worse to come. On April 16 a smaller ship, the 5,000-
ton troopship *Goya*, left the Hela Peninsula off Gdynia after taking
on members of the 35th Tank Regiment. The number of refugees is
again uncertain, but the total number of people on board is thought
to have been about 7,000. The ship stood off Hela and loaded by
lighter, but there was still a fight to board. Dobson, Miller and
Payne recount the testimony of a German officer who heard a
young man, who had only one arm, screaming at his parents that
they should stay behind because they were old and useless,
whereas he and his wife had a lifetime to live. "He and his wife
climbed the scrambling nets up the side of the Goya, and never

looked back at those they left behind," they write.

The *Goya* left, again with an inadequate escort; she was a modern ship and could outrun a submarine, but was slowed by a breakdown of one of the ships accompanying her. Just before midnight, she was hit by two torpedoes from a Soviet submarine (not the *S13* this time). She split in two and sank, according to the authors, in just four minutes. Of the estimated 7,000 people aboard, just 183 survived.

*

Good though it is, *The Cruellest Night* cannot cover everything. There is only a page or so on the sinking of the Hamburg-Amerika liner *Cap Arcona*, which was set on fire off Lübeck on May 3 by rockets from Typhoons of the Royal Air Force. The RAF apparently thought the vessel carried members of the SS who were escaping to Norway. There were indeed SS on board, but they were guarding thousands of concentration-camp inmates brought from the East who they may have planned to kill by scuttling the ship at sea. The British had occupied Lübeck the previous day and seem to have known that the ships lying off the port contained prisoners, but this information was not passed to the RAF. Thousands of prisoners died.

The authors could also have mentioned, at least in passing, that the Hannibal sinkings were matched by the death of several thousand (possibly 7,000) refugees and wounded on the Soviet hospital ship *Armenia*, sunk by the Luftwaffe off the Crimea in 1941. But again, they may just not have known of it. In any case, *The Cruellest Night* generally avoids moral judgments of the "well, they started it" variety. It is surely right to do so. This is not a book about who started the war.

Although *The Cruellest Night* has the odd quirk, it is extremely well researched. The *S13*'s captain, the flamboyant and headstrong Sasha Marinesko, had died in 1963; he had been disgraced and was a partial "unperson", and questions about him were discouraged in the Soviet Union, which still existed when the book was written. Yet the authors managed to find out a great deal about him, and appear to have interviewed friends and comrades, although they naturally did not feel able to name their sources.

Better still, in a considerable coup, one of the authors, Ronald Payne, secured an interview with Dönitz himself. The former commander-in-chief of the German navy, and briefly Hitler's successor, was 87 and rather deaf (he died two years later). But he seems to have received Payne kindly, if formally, and was ready and able to talk. He clearly believed that his evacuation of hundreds of thousands of soldiers and refugees from the east was one of his greatest achievements. He had even managed to negotiate a surrender with the British two days before the other Allies. This must have irked Eisenhower but allowed Dönitz to bring hundreds of thousands more evacuees west into the British zone. Dönitz was also the architect of the U-boat offensive, and was convicted at Nuremberg of waging aggressive war. There is no free pass for him. One doubts he would have sought one. But from December 1944, knowing Germany had lost the war, he did try to rescue at least some of its people. Few of Hitler's other commanders really did this.

Moreover, while the sinkings of the *Gustloff*, *Steuben*, and *Goya* were appalling human tragedies, Hannibal as a whole was a success. Between January 23 1945 and the end of the war, the German navy lifted a staggering 1.2 million people out of the path of the Red Army, 900,000 of them civilians. Just 1% of the evacuees were lost. In fact, Dobson, Miller and Payne credit Dönitz's operations of May 1945 with nothing less than the rebuilding of Germany:

"Without it the post-war German miracle might never have been achieved, for the revival of West Germany needed," they say. "The country had been drained of millions of men, and... absorbed the newcomers with ease."

Is this true? Many of the soldiers arriving in the British zone went straight into prisoner-of-war camps and stayed for several years in Britain, due to a debatable decision by the Attlee government to make them help in British reconstruction – a story well told in Matthew Barry Sullivan's excellent *Thresholds of Peace*. They would indeed help rebuild Germany, but not until later. As to Western Germany feeding and housing the refugees "with ease", it didn't; it struggled terribly, at least in the first two or three years. Yet it is true that many hundreds of thousands of Germans escaped the Iron Curtain because of Hannibal. By 1948, when the Deutschmark and Marshall Aid began the economic miracle, most of those held in Western countries had been released. The authors are probably not right to credit Operation Hannibal with West Germany's postwar prosperity. But it will have played a part.

There are some strange codas to Hannibal. One is that the *Cap Arcona* had been used, earlier in the war, as a stand-in for the *Titanic* in a Nazi propaganda film about that ship. Another is the fate of Marinesko; always suspect politically, he was drummed out of the Navy after the war, found a job on a building site and was then deported to Siberia. He survived and was released, but died in 1963 at the age of just 46. As stated earlier, at the time *The Cruellest Night* was written, he was still in partial disgrace. In fact, Gorbachev was to make him a posthumous Hero of the Soviet Union in 1990.

There is a further, stranger coda. The authors do not mention the last of the big North Atlantic liners involved in Hannibal. This was the *Berlin III*, the ship that had rescued the passengers of the British liner *Vestris* in 1928. The day after the *Gustloff* sinking, the

Berlin III left for a new trip eastwards but hit a mine and was beached near Kiel. In 1949 the Soviets salvaged her and converted her to a Black Sea cruise liner, and renamed her *Admiral Nakhimov*. Although used briefly as a troop transport to Cuba during the Cuban missile crisis, she remained in her Black Sea role for many years. Just after 11pm on August 31 1986, the 61-year-old ship was rammed by a bulk carrier while on passage to Sochi. She sank in just a few minutes, and over 400 of the 1,200-odd Soviet passengers and crew died. Was there an ancient curse?

*

Although few English speakers know of the *Wilhelm Gustloff*, Germans do remember. The late Günter Grass claimed that it had become a political football, with right-wing revisionists claiming the disaster as a war crime. That, he said, was why it became the subject of what turned out to be his last novel, *Crabwalk* – to wrest the *Gustloff* from the hands of the Right. In fact, the book appeared during a period of debate in Germany after W.G. Sebald's warning that Germans' silence about their own suffering had given the Right free rein to use it for its own purposes. Grass clearly agreed.

Crabwalk is the story of a fictional German teenager, Tulla, who gives birth to a boy on the ship that has rescued her from the sea. After the war she settles in East Germany, and becomes an enthusiastic Stalinist. But son Paul goes to the West and becomes a journalist. He is pressed by his mother to write the story of the sinking, although he does not want to. In the meantime, he marries and has a son of his own; the marriage fails, and the son, Konrad, grows up to become an awkward, geeky teenager with neo-Nazi tendencies. He starts a revisionist website dedicated to the *Gustloff* and the Nazi "hero" after whom it was named. But a Jewish boy enters his chatroom, and starts to argue with him.

Who this Jewish boy turns out really to be, and how their dispute ends, shouldn't be revealed here. But this book is a fascinating allegory for Grass's view of postwar German history. The wartime generation (Tulla) appears to repent (but does it? – or does it simply adopt new orthodoxies?); the next generation (Paul) is so appalled by their country's history that they barely speak of it, and so do little to help the third generation (Konrad) come to terms with it. The book ends against a backdrop of skinhead hate crimes in the late 1990s, forging a link between fascists past and present.

If I were German, I'm not sure how I would view this book. If I liked Grass, I might see it as a shrewd warning of time-bombs from the past. If I didn't, I might see it as a contrived vehicle for Grass's own view of postwar Germany. Either way, my view would likely be coloured by where I lay to the left or right. I honestly don't know. Let Germans decide. In any case, it isn't seen as Grass's best book. The characters, though well-drawn, are unattractive and don't engage you. The structure is complex and confusing. Neither is it especially vivid; there's nothing like the haunting horse's head scene in *The Tin Drum*. The critical reception for the English translation was mixed (the *Observer*, in particular, gave it a good kicking). Nonetheless it's a sharp, shrewd sideways look at history, by a man who, at 75, was still profoundly engaged with the past and future of his country.

*

Still, it isn't *Crabwalk* that brings the disasters in the Baltic alive. It's the other three books, which show how wars are not historical events in which X beat Y. Rather, they are accretions of individual agonies. Seen in the mass, they are beyond comprehension.

They become easier to grasp when A.V. Sellwood describes passengers trying to escape from the *Gustloff's* sun deck and being held back at gunpoint, or the marine auxiliaries settling down cheerfully in the swimming pool where they will soon be blown apart. In *Death in the Baltic*, Cathryn J. Prince describes how many of the children drowned because their lifejackets were too big, and they were seen floating with only their legs above the water. *The Cruellest Night* includes an ID picture of one of the auxiliaries before the sinking, pretty and smiling with a saucy cap on her curly hair (she was to be one of the very few survivors). The same book describes refugees waiting at Pillau, from which the ill-fated *General Steuben* would leave on February 9. "They queued before the wrecked buildings where the authorities boiled cauldrons of porridge to feed the helpless... A soldier reported that the most pathetic sight was that of the children who had lost their parents. 'Even their tears froze'."

Why have we known so little of the *Gustloff* and the other Hannibal disasters? After all, they have never been a secret, at least not in the West (the Eastern bloc did discourage their discussion). Perhaps it's not a mystery. The Germans had started a war that no-one else had wanted, and killed an untold number of people; there was little sympathy for them. Meanwhile the Allied occupiers in the three western zones of Germany had their hands full with literally millions of German refugees from the east; there was little time to ask how they had got there, and what they had seen on the way. In any case, 1945 was the worst year in history. When everyone has a story, no-one does.

Nearly seventy years later, survivors would tell Cathryn Prince that they had never felt able to discuss the wreck. Ellen Tschinkur, who emigrated to Canada, mentioned it tentatively years later to a Canadian workmate. "One of her colleagues interrupted her. 'Oh the war. That was hard, we had to use margarine'," she says. Tschinkur did not speak of it again. Instead, says Prince, some of the remaining survivors talk to each other each January 30; sharing, in Prince's poignant phrase, their "lifeboat of shared memory".

It is a phrase that Heinz Schön might have understood. He was the young assistant purser who survived, but devoted much of the rest of his life to researching, and writing about, the *Gustloff* and other losses during the evacuation. When he died in April 2013 at the age of 86, the urn with his ashes was placed on the stern of the wreck that he had survived, but not escaped, as an 18-year-old nearly 70 years before.

Since this chapter was written (in 2015), a brief but interesting account of the Gustloff *sinking,* Ship of Fate *by Roger Moorhouse, has been published. Besides the sinking, Moorhouse adds some detail on the ship's origins and its Strength through Joy cruises before 1939.*

Being Beastly to the Germans

On January 17 1947, a book review by George Orwell appeared in *Tribune*. "I hope everyone who can get access to a copy will take at least a glance at Victor Gollancz's recently published book, *In Darkest Germany*," he wrote, and continued: "It is not a literary book, but a piece of brilliant journalism intended to shock the public of this country into some kind of consciousness of the hunger, disease, chaos and lunatic mismanagement prevailing in the British Zone. "

The British themselves, Orwell conceded, were not having a great time either (and they were just about to have a much worse one, as some of the worst winter weather in history was just ahead). Even so, Orwell thought it remarkable how unaware the British were of what was happening in Germany. With *In Darkest Germany*, Gollancz aimed to tell them.

Victor Gollancz is remembered today as a publisher, and was a significant one. He had produced Orwell's first books among others. In the later 1930s they had political differences, and Gollancz had not taken *Homage to Catalonia*, which cast doubt on the account of the 'official' Left – but Gollancz himself would split with them over the Nazi-Soviet pact. Henceforth he was to be as much an activist and polemicist as a publisher. The Nazi regime was an early target. As early as 1933, the year Hitler came to power, he produced a pamphlet by Labour peer Dudley Marley, *The Brown Book of the Hitler Terror*. In 1942 he published one of his own, *Let My People Go*, in which he argued that "a million or two" Jews had already been murdered in Europe, and that six million would die. Yet in the postwar years Gollancz, who was Jewish, would devote considerable energy to call for better treatment for German (and other

European) people.

In October and November 1946 Gollancz made a six-week visit to the British Zone. The resulting book, *In Darkest Germany*, was based on the letters, public and private, that he wrote during the visit. It could therefore be rushed out quickly on his return. Nonetheless one is impressed at the speed with which it was done, at a time when books were set in hot metal and there were also austerity regulations for book production. The book is 128 pages, plus 144 photographs – the latter would each have required an individual block to be made. Despite this, the book was out in January 1947. Moreover, my own copy shows it to be a second impression in the same month – suggesting that sales had been brisk.

The pictures are stark. Plates 4 and 5 are the heads of men lying on hospital beds. Plate 8 is a full-length picture of a naked man from the back; it is captioned, "Emaciation, not oedema. 56, looked 70. Was clearing rubble and got half heavy worker's ration." Plates 14 and 15 show boys of about 10 or 11, though they may be older. They are stripped to the waist (according to the caption, at the author's request). They are thin; their ribs show, and they are clearly undernourished.

Neither is the text easy reading, although the facts have long passed away. In Hamburg, Gollancz reports, about 100,000 people were suffering "from hunger oedema or the equivalent". In the same city, he stated, "active lung tuberculosis is at least five times as prevalent as before the war, and may even be 10 times as prevalent." The reasons for the growth in TB, he argued, were twofold – malnutrition and overcrowding: "In the British zone 12,000 people with open, infectious tuberculosis live in the same room with others – sometimes in the same bed with children."

He does not quote a source for these figures, and they should be approached with caution. The 100,000 for hunger oedema was questioned at the time by doctors working with the UN Relief and Rehabilitation Administration (UNRRA). Historian John Farquharson, writing in the 1980s (*'Emotional but Influential': Victor Gollancz, Richard Stokes and the British Zone of Germany, 1945-1949*), has also said that it was not credible, and has pointed out that the overall death rate did not reflect such a number. He has also challenged other statements by Gollancz in the book, including the allegation that prevalence of TB had risen fivefold. In general, Gollancz's numbers are open to question.

But there was clearly hunger. Gollancz cites a survey under British auspices of around 1,000 Hamburg postal employees in which the incidence of hunger oedema was found to be 17% amongst males and 9% amongst females. Reproducing one of his own letters, he also gives a figure of 13,000 hospitalized cases of hunger oedema for Düsseldorf in September; this apparently was also challenged, so he goes on to point out that the British colonel in command of the Düsseldorf district had said that the number of non-hospitalized cases was nearly double that.

The reason for this was not hard to see, according to Gollancz. The standard ration (that is, for people not doing heavy work) had recently been increased but was still just 1,550 calories, in contrast to the 2,650 that UNRRA had stated as necessary for "full health and efficiency" in a normal population. (Today Britain's NHS says men need about 2,500 to maintain body weight, women about 2,000.) However, most people in Düsseldorf were not even getting 1,550 calories a day as most basic foodstuffs were in short supply. Gollancz went so far as to say that those who could not or would not supplement their rations on the black market were managing on 400-1,000 calories a day. Once again, it is not clear where he got these numbers; he is perhaps giving his own observations – but sometimes he is able to quote more official figures:

*In the Control Commission's information room at Bünde there is a chart
...showing a graph of seven diseases with March 30 1946 as the first date
and September 14 as the last. Scarlet fever is about the same... diptheria
is a trifle higher, gonorrhea considerably higher, syphillis much higher,
tuberculosis about a third higher, and typhoid nearly double. But what
really matters is a more generalised degeneration in the health and
strength of the whole community.*

A British health official, thinking Gollancz to be a visiting politi-
cian, let fly at him in a mess in Hamburg one afternoon. "What on
earth are you politicians up to? ...Do you realise what's going on
here?" he asked. "An epidemic of any kind would sweep everything before it. ...If you...don't do something about it two problems
that seem to have been worrying you will be solved. The size of the
German population and manure."

*

There can be no doubt that the refugees from the east worsened the
situation. Gollancz recounts being shown a list of the clothing
needs for those in Schleswig-Holstein. He calls them "expellees"
and they will have included some who were literally expelled from
what had been eastern Germany, but one suspects that many will
have arrived earlier as part of Operation Hannibal, the German
navy's mass evacuation of the Eastern regions in the last few
months of the war (see previous chapter). However they had arrived, they numbered 1.2 million out of Schleswig-Holstein's 3 million population and needed 200,000 men's overcoats, a million
pairs of shoes, 800,000 undergarments and half a million blankets.
Gollancz visits a ship and a camp in which expellees are housed,

and sees "mostly stretchers, wooden bunks, and bundles of sordid beclothes on the floor: indeed ...I don't recollect seeing a single bed."

Not that the people of Hamburg were doing much better; Gollancz enters one building and finds a woman and her four children living in a single room. The husband is a prisoner in Russia. Nearby, a couple, their seven children and a dog are living in a two-room makeshift shelter totalling 200 sq. ft.

Rebuilding was clearly urgent. According to Gollancz, the cement works in the British Zone had a capacity of 7.7 million tons. But 25 cement works, accounting for about half of this total, were threatened with closure as reparations. This was an iniquitous facet of the 1945 Potsdam four-power agreement under which plant and assets were not only to be seized as reparations, but also destroyed if they could be used in the future to make war. Cement could be used to construct docks for U-boats, fortifications etc., so must not be allowed – although it was not clear how ordinary Germans were to be housed without it.

This lunacy extended right across large parts of the economy, affecting even food production. Thus 13 fishing vessels at Bremerhaven had been used during the war as minelayers; the Germans wished to return them to their real purpose, but the British would not permit it. In another case, a fishing vessel was a metre longer than the permitted length. The Germans offered to reduce the vessel's size, but the British refused and blew it up instead. "Meanwhile, the wretched German fish ration has been reduced," writes Gollancz, "and we complain that the cost of feeding Germany is almost more than we can bear." He quotes other examples of this crass stupidity, and others were raised in a Commons debate on the occupation on November 27 1946, in which his reports were debated.

Gollancz regarded the destruction as wholly irrational – including the shipyards. He would, he said, be asked whether he had forgotten the weapons that Blohm & Voss had built. No, he said, and indeed he had warned of the dangers of fascism in the 1930s (as we've seen, this was true). "But I say that if there is one absolutely certain way of making a repetition of the last few years inevitable, it is to acquiesce in this godless destruction, and to drive a whole people, with whom we have to live, into hatred and despair."

Why had the British Zone, with its 23 million inhabitants, got into such a state? Was this an act of revenge by the British for a war that they had not wanted? Many British people were deeply angry with Germany well into my own lifetime (I was born in 1957). Was this a mass punishment-beating?

*

The evidence, at least for the British Zone, strongly suggests otherwise. To be sure, the Germans were not the flavour of the month. But there was genuine public concern in Britain about their conditions; much of it was humanitarian, and it was reflected in Parliament and in the Press. It is especially evident from the support Gollancz had for his campaign, which had begun in earnest only a few months after the war had ended. It focused initially on the mass expulsions of Germans from Poland and Czechoslovakia. The campaign was driven by vivid descriptions in the *Daily Herald* and the *News Chronicle* of the scenes around Berlin's Stettiner Bahnhof, where refugees were arriving from the east.

The skill and energy with which Gollancz latched onto these events as a humanitarian cause has been recounted in an interesting and engaging 2006 article by Matthew Frank, *The New Morality*.

Frank describes the startling extent to which Gollancz managed to mobilise the chattering classes, and a big chunk of the political establishment on both right and left. Gollancz asked people to send in a postcard pledging their willingness to give up ration points in support of German refugees. Within just over a week he had received 20,000. One wonders how many signatures would have been received had one been able to respond online.

By mid-September 1945, according to Frank, the issue was receiving extensive coverage right across the British press, even the right-wing dailies (apart from the Beaverbrook group. And one newspaper that did support the campaign headed its leader "Feed the Brutes"). On the left, supporters included J. B. Priestley, not an obvious enthusiast for the Germans; in fact he was so sympathetic to the USSR that Orwell later fingered him as a fellow-traveller. Nonetheless Priestley wrote a dispatch from Berlin for the *News Chronicle*. "Whatever happens to the German people this winter ...the world conscience must see to it that the children of Germany do not starve," he rumbled.

To be sure, not all of this was compassion. Frank makes it clear that much of it was based on the argument that an epidemic or disorder in the British Zone meant trouble for Britain, for it would spread. Nonetheless there was a strong humanitarian undertone. The wave of sympathy and/or self-interest reached a peak at the end of November 1945, when Gollancz's Save Europe Now (SEN) held its inaugural meeting at the Albert Hall. The crush was so great that there were two overflow meetings in the nearby church of the Holy Trinity, Brompton. The speakers included such diverse figures as the former Conservative minister Bob Boothby and the young left-wing MP and journalist Michael Foot. Matthew Frank is unimpressed, seeing the moral crusade less as a humanitarian movement than as an affirmation of Britain's image of itself. This is not entirely fair – but there is truth in it. However, what the SEN episode does suggest is that the British establishment, and for the most part the people, did not want unnecessary suffering for the Germans, however self-inflicted it might be. Their attitude was probably summed up in Noel Coward's flippant satire from 1943:

Don't let's be beastly to the Germans
When our victory is ultimately won...
Let's be meek to them
And turn the other cheek to them
And try to bring out their latent sense of fun
... don't let's be beastly to the Hun.

*

The British, then, had no wish to make the Germans in their Zone miserable. So why the shambles?

Surprisingly little has been written about the British occupation of north-west Germany, an area of 23 million people. This is beginning to change as interest grows in the entire post-war era, and modern scholars of the occupation, such as Christopher Knowles, are not always so bleak about it. But Gollancz was right that the Germans under British occupation faced terrible hardship (though conditions elsewhere in Germany were scarcely better). There were several reasons. Perhaps the Attlee government simply did not pay enough attention to Germany. It was extremely busy – not just with Germany but with the crisis in India, which looked likely to explode at any minute if no agreed path to independence could be found. Britain was still fighting in both Greece and Palestine. She was also broke; much of her gold reserves had been spent on the war, and the US had insisted, as part of its postwar loan agreement, that sterling be convertible within a few years. This was a huge financial bomb waiting to go off, and the occupation of north-west Germany was costly (in the end, reparations would cover just 2% of its cost). At home, labour shortages in the mines restricted coal supplies and would immiserate everyone in the winter of 1946-47, still one of the worst in Britain in living memory.

Moreover, the British found the Zone in a terrible state, not least because of their own bombing. In a 2014 article in *History and Policy (Germany 1945-1949: a case study in post-conflict reconstruction)*, Knowles – who is one of the few modern researchers to have published widely on the occupation – states that 66% of the houses in Cologne were destroyed, and in Düsseldorf 93% were uninhabitable – figures that confirm Gollancz's own impressions. The housing shortage was exacerbated by German refugees from what had been eastern Germany and from other parts of central and eastern Europe where Germans were no longer welcome. Meanwhile, the country was full of displaced persons, often former forced or slave labour brought forcibly to Germany by the Nazi regime. All were walking somewhere. Knowles quotes Ivone Kirkpatrick, a British diplomat who later became head of the Foreign Office, describe his first impressions of Germany in 1945; there were "hundreds of thousands of Germans on foot, trekking in all directions … as if a giant ant-heap had suddenly been disturbed."

The British authorities were also hamstrung by the Potsdam agreement in the summer of 1945, under which the four-power occupation had been agreed in detail. Potsdam had decreed the "orderly" transfer of populations (it was anything but orderly) but also had clauses on reparations and demilitarization. Clause 3(i) called for: "The complete disarmament and demilitarization of Germany and the elimination or control of all German industry that could be used for military production." It was this clause that had led to the orgy of bureaucratic destruction that Gollancz had described. In fact, the agreement stated that Germany could retain industries essential for war to the extent that it needed them for its prewar peacetime economy. However, there was also a provision for reparations that was effectively a license to loot. Moreover it was specified that 10-15% of industrial plant from all three Western zones should be dismantled and sent to the USSR, meaning that even if the British had decided to remove nothing as reparations for themselves, they would still have had to dismantle some plant that the Germans really needed to keep.

There were other constraints. The Potsdam Agreement stated that occupied Germany should be treated as a single economic unit, but not everyone cooperated. Eventually, frustrated, the British and Americans would merge their zones. In 1948, failure to agree with the USSR on currency reform, among other things, would lead the Western allies to clear the way for the creation of the Deutschmark in the three western zones. At the time of Gollancz's visit, however, the British zone was effectively an economy on its own. An industrial region, it could not import sufficient food from areas further east that had supplied it, even those that were still part of Germany – which they were often not. In fact, according to John Farquharson, Attlee responded to Gollancz's criticism of food shortages by blaming the USSR, saying that the regions under their occupation were not sending food to the industrial Ruhr as they always had. The Foreign Secretary, Ernest Bevin, apparently agreed. Moreover all of this should be seen in the context of the sheer size of the British Zone. It was the largest of the four. The Russian and US zones had 17 million inhabitants each against the British zones 23 million; the French zone, just five million. It must also have been the hardest-hit by the RAF's own bombing, containing as it did Cologne, Hanover and the Ruhr as well as Hamburg.

In fact, the British occupation deserves a more nuanced examination. It gets one from Christopher Knowles, in his 2017 book on the British zone (*Winning the Peace: The British in Occupied Germany, 1945-1948*). Knowles's approach is to look at the occupation through the experience of a number of British soldiers and civilians who took part in it – a method known as 'collective biography'. The danger of this is that one's choice of witnesses may colour one's assessment. In this case, however, it seems to work well. And Knowles makes a good case for a more balanced view.

Field-Marshal Montgomery's mandate when he took control of the British Zone was that agreed between the allies at Potsdam – to demilitarize, denazify, deindustrialize and democratize Germany. It is hard to see how the third aim was compatible with the others, given that (as Gollancz noted) Germans needed to feed and house themselves. But Montgomery's policy quickly changed to one of reconciliation and reconstruction. As Knowles notes, this was in part pragmatism; the British could not afford to run the zone and needed the Germans to start exporting and earning so that they could do so themselves. But Knowles's account shows that there were also more generous impulses at work. This is clearly evident with men like Sir Henry Vaughan Berry, the civilian Commissioner for Hamburg from 1946 to 1949, who forged an excellent working relationship with a new elected city council. British officials also opposed the merger of the German social-democratic party, the SPD, with the Communist Party, and promoted the development of a free press (Knowles recounts how one junior officer, John Chaloner, founded what went on to become *Der Spiegel*).

But Knowles does not ignore the food and housing shortages, the tensions that sometimes arose between the British and the Germans, or the neocolonial attitude the British sometimes showed to the occupied. In fact he points out that some of the British administrators were from a colonial background, and had a tendency to impose their idea of how things should be done on the natives. Neither were some of the British, including the odd senior officer, above a little light looting.

*

In any case, although the British administration in Germany faced a difficult situation, some of its problems were of its own making.

For a start, not everyone was as punctilious on Potsdam as the British, who (as Gollancz saw) could have taken it a little less literally. As the Conservative Bob Boothby put it in the Commons debate in November: "Are we going to continue to sabotage industrial production in the British zone in Germany... by carrying out the terms of an Agreement which most of us believe the other signatories are making not the slightest attempt to carry out?"

Besides, the British administration was not always up to it. This has been discussed in a 1993 paper in the journal *German History* by John Farquharson (*The British Occupation of Germany 1945-6: A Badly Managed Disaster Area?*). Farquharson describes how authority was vested, after some confusion, with the Control Office for Germany and Austria, or COGA, which was based in London. (There was also a British Zone of Occupation in Austria, centred around Klagenfurt in Carinthia.) Not only was COGA not in Germany; it was headed by the Chancellor of the Duchy of Lancaster, John Burns Hynd, who almost never went there, did not have Cabinet rank, and did not impress his contemporaries. According to Farquharson, British staff in the Zone itself referred to COGA as "Hyndquarters". (Hynd was later succeeded by Lord Longford, but in practice much of the authority was to remain with the military governors of the Zone – initially Montgomery – succeeded later by Marshal of the RAF Sholto Douglas).

The quality of the British control commission staff in Germany itself was mixed. They had no future when the occupation came to an end, and they would have to return to Britain, where the best jobs would already have been taken. So it was hard to get the best people. Farquharson quotes a London civil servant as saying in 1946 that they were mainly "a highly-paid army of retired drain inspectors, unsuccessful businessmen and idle ex-policemen." Farquharson also refers to heavy drinking after wartime abstinence, and corruption ("Officials were making hay while the sun shone, as there was no real future in Germany"). Some of this may have been unfair. Some of it may have been all too fair. One staff member was the former star record-breaking pilot of the early 1930s, C.W.A. Scott; unable to handle loss of fame as the war approached, he struggled in later years, and eventually joined the control commission staff in 1946, perhaps for want of something better. Soon after arriving, he blew his brains out.

Gollancz himself encountered attitudes amongst the control commission staff that he did not like. "Though there are many fine exceptions, the general attitude varies from a disgusting offensiveness, through indifference... to that humane and almost unconsciously superior paternalism which is characteristic of the "white" attitude to "natives" at its best." He quotes examples of misuse of privilege: a hairdresser keeps a British wife waiting for 20 minutes, and the next day is warned that her premises may be requisitioned; there are separate queues at the cinema. The building of a new headquarters and facilities in Hamburg, when the materials and labour were desperately needed to rehouse Germans, was especially iniquitous – the more so in that it was to require eviction of numerous Germans. (In *Winning the Peace*, Knowles quotes an esti-mate that it was expected to require the eviction of some 6,000 fam-ilies.) The Hamburg Project, as it was called, was later much downscaled. But Gollancz may not have been wrong about some of the attitudes amongst the occupation forces. Knowles records how one NCO, asked his commanding officer for permission to marry his German girlfriend and was told, "Look, I'd rather you married a wog." One remembers the remark, quoted in an earlier chapter, that Benn Levy MP made in the November 1946 Com-mons debate: "It is not good for a nation to be conquered. But it is also not good for people to be conquerors."

*

In Darkest Germany was not the end of Gollancz's campaign. In Au-gust 1947 he was back in Germany; on his return to London he penned a 40-page pamphlet, *Germany Revisited*, in which he re-ported that, "during the Spring and Summer... rations for the nor-mal consumer of about 1,000 calories or even considerably less were common...". "For 25 percent," he added, the diet is a daily experience of dull and devitalising misery." He once again ex-pounded on shortages of underwear, shocking housing, wanton acts of destruction under the guise of reparations or demilitarisa-tion, and the lunatic bureaucracy of denazification. One wonders how the British administrators in the Zone saw him; probably as a pompous pain in the arse.

But in the end, of course, Gollancz and the British administra-tion were both moot. Most Germans would have known that they had got themselves into this situation and would have to get them-selves out, and they did. In 1948 a currency reform ushered in the Deutschmark in the three Western zones, and the next year saw assumption of power by the new republic. From then on, the British army was only nominally an army of occupation; in reality, it became part of Germany's defences. It finally left in 2019, and will now likely be remembered chiefly as a traffic hazard. Meanwhile the Germans rebuilt their country with lightning speed. Many individual Germans may have had another, longer, private journey, summed up perhaps in Heinrich Böll's novella, *The Bread of Those Early Years.* But that journey they took alone.

What should we make of Gollancz's extraordinary crusade, 70 years on? Like Orwell, he should not be seen as some sort of secular saint. (One remembers Orwell's own comment in *Reflections on Gandhi*: "Saints should always be judged guilty until they are proved innocent.") Although Gollancz split with the Communists after the Nazi-Soviet Pact, he had hitherto supported them, despite mounting evidence of their real nature from the war in Spain. His April 1945 pamphlet *What Buchenwald Really Means*, which appeared to pin as much blame for Hitler on the British as on the Germans, was premature and ill-judged, and drew a stinging rebuke from an Austrian former prisoner, Franz Burger. Some of his statements in *In Darkest Germany* were exaggerated and were from unreliable sources; as we have seen, his estimates of hunger oedema and TB prevalence were likely simply wrong. Gollancz may also have been something of a gadfly, flying from one fight to another. By 1948 he had moved on to other causes, including relief for the Middle East and eventually the abolition of capital punishment. In *The New Morality*, Matthew Frank quotes him thus: "'There is nothing so depressing', Gollancz once told a veteran of one of his many campaigns, 'as a movement which has attained its aims'."

As for *In Darkest Germany*, it is a museum piece; it was not reprinted after 1947, and is today very hard to find. Victor Gollancz Ltd is now part of Orion, and publishes science fiction and fantasy.

There is a Victor Gollancz elementary school in Berlin, but one wonders if the pupils, or residents of the Gollanczstraße in which it stands, know who he was.

But perhaps that would not have bothered him greatly. One can view him as a gadfly or polemicist, but his actions were underpinned by a profound morality. In *What Buchenwald Really Means* he argues that the Judaeo-Christian tradition cannot compromise with fascism: "For the one the ultimate reality is the human soul, individual, unique, responsible to God and man," he wrote, "while for the other this ultimate reality is some abstraction – a State, Folk or Collective which men have created out of nothing, and which has no existence except in their vain imagination. ...This Judaeo-Christian tradition is our inner citadel." In the end, Gollancz was at least touched by greatness – something the British state finally acknowledged with a knighthood in 1965, a year or so before his death at the age of 73. It was a recognition already given in Germany. Postwar Chancellor Konrad Adenauer would write in his memoirs that "Germany owes Victor Gollancz a great debt of gratitude, a debt which is all the greater in view of his Jewish descent."

One of the many, often upsetting, photographs in *In Darkest Germany* is taken in a hospital. It is a high-key print lit by a window that is just out of shot to the right; soft light catches the white blanket and sheets on the iron bed, on which there is a young boy. The caption reads: "Child of 10 dying from TB in the Town Hospital, Düsseldorf." Above the bed stands a balding man with a moustache, round dark-rimmed glasses and a professorial air; he is dressed in a dark winter coat and scarf. It is hard to read his expression, but his distress seems real. One wonders who his successors are today, and how many figures there are in modern British life who have made so clear a decision to serve good over evil.

Rear-View Mirror

I do not sleep well. I never have. Early memories link sleeplessness to childhood fevers, some of which came close to delirium. As an adult I have never been able to get comfortable in bed and fidget constantly. For years I have lived in a brownstone in Manhattan; I love the building but in the summer I am bombarded by cold air from the air-conditioner and wake very early, sometimes to the calls of a raccoon family in the garden. In the winter, too, I often wake in the small hours to the gurgling of the central-heating pipes and know that I shan't sleep again. Then I use the radio for company.

A week or two ago, waking at four, I decided to listen to a back number of BBC Radio 3's *Through the Night*. Lying back and letting my thoughts drift, I found myself thinking, for no obvious reason, of TV programmes I remembered from the 1970s, when I was in my teens. There seemed to be many more from then than from recent years. By the time my alarm went off a few hours later, I had drifted off, and it was not until the evening that I found that I had, half-asleep, written the programme titles on the notepad by my bed.

Now, people do this. Back in the 1970s a British Liberal peer, gravely ill in hospital, was given narcotics to dull the pain. He was convinced that the resulting drug-fuelled dreams held the key to the universe, but could not quite recall them later. So he asked for a notepad. One night he jerked awake, aware that he had been given the answer to existence, and scrawled it rapidly upon the pad, then went straight back to sleep. It wasn't until the afternoon that he remembered, looked at the pad and saw scrawled upon it the words: "It's Henry V! It's Henry V! *He's taking his horse to*

France!!"

My own notepad contained no such revelation. Instead, there were the following words:

BLOXHAM TAPES
MANY HAPPY RETURNS
BLAIR CASTLE
WE ARE ALL GUILTY
THROUGH THE NIGHT

There is no *Rising Damp* here, no *Pennies from Heaven* or *Fawlty Towers*, and no *Reginald Perrin* (apart from the last-named, I don't think I saw any of these at the time). The programmes I had written down were half-remembered mysteries. The next weekend, I searched my memory, and then the internet; and I know, now, what all these programmes were and when they were shown. They had nothing in common with each other, except that they were broadcast in 1974-1977; and they have stayed alive in my memory for 40 years, although I have seen none of them since. I wondered whether my memories of them were correct.

I also wondered whether TV leaves us, as a society, with shared memories. If others also remembered these programmes, then perhaps it does. Had they left some impact on the collective memory? And did they still exist, or had they vanished without trace, the creativity that went into them completely lost?

First, *The Bloxham Tapes*.

*

Arnall Bloxham was a Cardiff hypnotherapist. In 1976 he startled

the British public with a programme in which he appeared to re-
gress three apparently quite normal subjects into past lives. One
had been a sailor in Nelson's navy; another had been a Jewish
woman murdered in a pogrom in medieval York. Their recollec-
tions were striking and vivid, and appeared to be backed by such
evidence as was available. The programme had a significant impact at the time, the more so since Bloxham – an avuncular, white-
haired gentleman – said nothing during the programme, letting the
tapes speak for themselves. However, presenter Magnus Magnusson interviewed the subjects when they were awake, and they
claimed to have had startling, vivid recall.

Some doubt was cast on the story of the pogrom victim, who
claimed to have sheltered in a vault beneath York's St Mary's in
Castlegate, which was not thought to have one. A few months
later, however, workmen stumbled upon it, bringing the programme back into the public eye. Certainly Jeffrey Iverson, the
BBC producer who initiated the programme, remained convinced,
and later wrote a book called *More Lives Than One? Evidence of the
Remarkable Bloxham Tapes* (1977).

The evidence has since been challenged. In particular, Melvin
Harris, in his 1986 book *Sorry, You've Been Duped* (later republished
as *Investigating the Unexplained*), argued that the alleged sailor, Graham Huxtable, could have absorbed the details he gave under hyp-
nosis from popular literature and other sources. In particular, he
had named the ship on board which he was severely injured as the
Aggie, forcing researchers to conclude that it had been the *Agamem-
non*, a far more powerful ship than Huxtable said it was. A 1982
book by Ian Wilson, *Reincarnation?*, was similarly skeptical. It has
been suggested that what was actually happening was cryptomnesia, a phenomenon where the subject remembers something without recognizing its origin; thus a story from one subject of having

lived in Roman Britain was actually taken from a 1947 novel that she had read but forgotten.

Not having read Harris's or Wilson's books, I can't judge. Without looking at their evidence, it would not be sensible to take *The Bloxham Tapes* at face value, and as an individual I dislike the mystical. But I was intrigued at the time, and still am. Nearly 40 years later the programme inspired my novella *Dog!* (2015), in which reincarnation is central to the story. Even if – as is probably the case – the Bloxham episodes can be ascribed to cryptomnesia, that surely says something about the human brain that is interesting in itself.

I have found it hard to find much about Bloxham the man, apart from the fact that he was a former president of the British Society of Hypnotherapists and was the author of a book, *Who Was Ann Ockenden?* (1958), in which he presented evidence from an earlier case. He seems to have started experimenting with hypnotherapy in the 1940s. He was already elderly at the time the programme was made. One source says he was born in 1881, which would have made him 95 in 1976. It then contradicts itself and says that he was 18 in 1914, which would have made him 80. This seems to be correct; Anthony Holden, who interviewed him for *The Sunday Times Magazine* in 1971 (*This Was Your Life*, May 2), gave his age then as 75. So he would no longer be with us. But the programme inspired at least three books (four, if you count mine), and has never quite been forgotten. TV does not – quite – always eat its young.

*

I could initially find nothing on the next title on the list, *Many Happy Returns*, although I remembered it very well. It made no appearance in the BBC Genome Project listings or the IMDb site; but

I was sure of the title, and probably the year – about 1975.

I was slightly out on both counts. *Happy Returns* was part of the ITV series *Sunday Night Drama* and was screened on 5 June 1977. The series had some distinguished contributors, including Ken Russell. This one was by Brian Clarke and was directed by an experienced Granada TV insider, Brian Gilmour. The lead character is a tax inspector, chasing a Yorkshire businessman who he is sure is misreporting his income. The inspector raises his suspicions with his superior. "Who's his accountant?" asks the boss. "Mr X," he is told. He frowns. "That's funny, he's not one of the bent ones, is he?" he asks.

We meet the accountant, who is indeed not bent and is very embarrassed. He convenes a meeting between the Revenue and his client, at which the latter thumps the table and complains he is being harassed. The Revenue doesn't buy it and sticks him with an assessment for some £20,000 in back taxes. It is clearly less than he really owes. (To put this in perspective, I earned £1,495 in the mid-seventies; a Mini cost less than £1,000). Meanwhile at the businessman's home, his wife hears their temporary cleaner, Mrs Y, complain that she can barely manage.

In the final scene, the businessman sits at his dining table doing his sums. "It'll be all right," he calls out to his wife. "'Fraid we'll have to sell the boat. But we'll get a new one for next season." His wife expresses her relief. She then reads an item from the paper. "That Mrs Y has just got six months in prison," she says, surprised. "What for?" asks the businessman. "She fiddled her social security," says the wife, naming the sum (it is pathetic).

"I dunno," says the businessman. "Why do they do it, eh." Roll credits.

It's a little jewel of a play, a mere 30 minutes, with not a scene out of place. It's lost now, and no-one remembers it. But you could remake it today. The world hasn't changed in 40 years; if anything, the plotline would seem more up-to-date than ever.

*

The next programme on the list is not forgotten. The man who inspired it, Yehudi Menuhin, never will be. What I had written down as BLAIR CASTLE was *Mr Menuhin's Welcome to Blair Castle*, and it went out on BBC1 on November 30 1974. It was again fronted by Magnusson, then ubiquitous; a popular Icelandic-born presenter, he was also a scholar and translator of Norse sagas and author of a history of the Vikings.

In the programme Yehudi Menuhin met Hector MacAndrew, a distinguished Scottish fiddler who endeavoured to teach Menuhin the fast, resonant technique of Strathspey bowing. Menuhin couldn't do it. As an article in *The Scotsman* would recall nearly 30 years later: "Menuhin just couldn't get a hold of the famous Scottish up-stroke, and he got more and more frustrated and eventually said to Hector, 'Oh, I cannot play *The Marquis of Huntly's Farewell*.' But Hector looked at him and said, 'Ah, but you can play the Beethoven [violin concerto] and I can't.'"

I cannot say I remember that exchange word-for-word. I do remember the programme clearly, though, in part for the vigour of the music, much of which likely came from that Strathspey style. I had not seen or heard it before. (This was many years before the wonderful Ally Bain series *Down Home*, which was also to stick in my mind.) MacAndrew, 71 at the time, died only a few years later but left a legacy of compositions of his own that have now been recorded.

As for Menuhin, he had first performed in public when just six or seven years old. In 1932, Elgar recorded his own Violin Concerto for HMV; the soloist was to have been Kreisler, but he was not available. Instead he used Menuhin, a 16-year-old kid from New York City. I often fall asleep (when I do) to this astonishing recording, made on a late spring morning nearly 90 years ago but sounding like yesterday. Later Menuhin would tour the battlefronts during the war and would, with Benjamin Britten, play for the survivors at Belsen. In later life he remained firmly committed to liberal causes; he could for example not abide apartheid. In 1974 he was already Sir Yehudi Menuhin (though he was not yet a British national, so did not use the title). Eventually he was Lord Menuhin.

He was a colossus, and yet there was no hint in *Blair Castle* that he knew that, or cared. Another fiddler, Michael Welch, in a memoir of Hector MacAndrew, has written of Menuhin's appearance in the programme: "It was a measure of the pupil that he recognised the gift of his teacher and was willing to listen to and be guided by an undoubted master of his own particular form." *Mr Menuhin's Welcome to Blair Castle* is memorable for the music, but also for the charm and modesty of one the greatest musicians of the time.

*

The next title scrawled on my pad was WE ARE ALL GUILTY.

I remembered this play as having been shown in the summer of 1975, and this time I was right; the IMDb Movie Database says it was on August 17. It also gives a cast list, and records that it was part of a series of stand-alone dramas made by a British company, Associated Television (ATV). The series was called *Against the Crowd* but I can find little information about it, except that one of the other episodes was written by a well-known science fiction writer, Nigel Kneale, and another by Fay Weldon. No-one seems to remember *We Are All Guilty*. But IMDb does name the writer; it

205

was Kingsley – later Sir Kingsley – Amis.

Amis was only 53 in 1975, but had long ceased to be the *enfant terrible* of *Lucky Jim* (in fact son Martin was already emerging as *terrible* in his own right). His personal life was complex, and he drank. But he was far from finished as a writer, and several of his best books were still to come. (*The Old Devils*, which would win the Booker, wasn't to be published until 1986.) He had also changed his politics. A Communist Party member as a young man, by 1975 he had been moving to the right for years, and *We Are All Guilty* was a snapshot of the way Amis *père* now saw his world.

The plot is thus: A teenage layabout and his friend break into a warehouse. The security guard chases them, and in so doing he crashes through a faulty safety rail to the floor below, incurring injuries that look permanent. The teenager, Clive, finds himself in the criminal justice system. The trouble is, it's full of social workers and vicars who see crime as a social disease and want to see him, not the guard, as the victim. The play ends with Clive wishing that someone would blame or punish him for the mess he's made. It sounds like a right-wing rant about the state of society. Indeed that is how I remembered it. But Amis was more subtle than that.

Searching for *We Are All Guilty* online, I was surprised to find that Amis had turned it into a novella, which was published many years later, in 1991 – not long, in fact, before he died. I don't know why he did this; perhaps he wanted to put it in a less ephemeral form so that it would be part of his body of work. It is mainly cited as having been written for young people (though I wonder about this), and was in fact published by Penguin's imprint for younger readers, Puffin.

Although some of Amis senior's books are still well-remembered, this one seems to be largely forgotten. At the time, Kirkus Reviews were not impressed with it. Amis, it wrote, "seems as oblivious to the real roots of Clive's antisocial behavior as his adult characters are; he even gives Clive the (unlikely) option of easily finding a job, and depicts him as bored with the girls he hangs out with. It all smells of the establishment believing that the lower classes would be all right if they'd just shape up."

Kirkus might have missed something. To be sure, Amis *didn't* think that We Are All Guilty; this book is about personal responsibility. But the book is not a rant – it's satire, which should be no surprise from Amis. There may even have been satire in his rightward shift. As David Lodge wrote in the *Independent* after Amis's death, that shift was sincere, but: "There was always an element of deliberate provocation and self-parody in this stance... As soon as left-wing attitudes became trendy, as they did in the late 1960s, Amis's innate scepticism was turned upon them and their proponents." In any case, what comes strongly from the book is not that Clive gets off nearly scot-free. It is that he himself does not understand why he has, and feels the need to expiate his guilt – but is not allowed to. By being forgiven, he is denied absolution. That is something that Kirkus (and probably others) missed.

Moreover both the book and the original TV play had some nice touches. In the play, a social worker offers Clive a cigarette; he takes it and leans forward to light hers, but she hasn't got one – she doesn't smoke. In the book, Clive and three of his friends eat in an Indian; they are plainly bored, with the place and each other, and you sense that Clive's problem is not that he is evil or stupid, but that there is just not enough in his head. The book is not Amis's best; some of the dialogue is stilted – one senses he knew very few Clives – and he could have done more with the plot than this slim novella; Martin Amis would have, I am sure. Yet, reading it 40 years after seeing the TV play, I found it oddly satisfying.

*

Once in a blue moon, something shown on TV changes the way people think and, maybe, act. The classic example from British TV is the BBC's 1966 episode of its Wednesday Play, *Cathy Come Home*, in which a decent couple's descent into homelessness is charted to the point where their children are taken from them – the latter in a disturbing scene that was filmed "live" in a Tube station. *Cathy Come Home* had mixed results. It is said to have led to the foundation of the homelessness charity, Shelter – but in fact this was coincidental, and the film's director, Ken Loach, has apparently since said that the film made little impact on homelessness. Still, no-one who has ever seen this film will have forgotten it.

I didn't see it in 1966 (I have since). But the last of the titles scrawled on my pad was part of the same series, although by then it had been renamed *Play for Today*. For it, the BBC commissioned some of the best playwrights and directors ever to work in Britain, including Loach himself, Jack Rosenthal, David Hare, Howard Brenton, Trevor Griffiths, Mike Leigh (whose contribution *Abigail's Party* is still revered) and Dennis Potter (one of whose episodes was initially banned). It's an A-team, and I hadn't understood to what extent until I started researching this chapter. But I did remember Trevor Griffiths's *Through the Night*. While writing this, I found the British Film Institute (BFI) page on the programme, and saw that I had seen it 40 years ago to the day – on December 2 1975.

Through the Night concerns a young woman, played by Alison Steadman (then 29). Admitted to hospital for an investigation into a lump in her breast, she is asked by a nurse to sign a consent form "just in case". She wakes the next morning to find that her breast has been removed, something that she in no way expected or thought she had agreed to. The play follows her shock, the insensitivity of some of the hospital staff, and the arid coldness of her stay in hospital.

Some of the play can now be seen online, but I have tried to reconstruct in my memory the scenes that impressed me so much 40 years ago. They include the casual presentation of the consent form, Steadman waking up on the ward, and the confusion and distress of her husband when he visits her with the children. But there are two scenes that loom especially large in my mind after not much less than half a century. One is when the surgeon emerges from theatre (Steadman, presumably, has been wheeled back to her ward). Another doctor appears and reminds the surgeon that he is seeking cancerous tissue for his research. The surgeon replies that he has as much as his colleague could possibly want. The savagery of his reply leaves us in no doubt of what he found.

The second of these scenes is still the most powerful thing I have seen on TV. Steadman's character is taking a bath; we see her sitting in an old-fashioned portable tin tub, in the middle of a bare room flooded with sunlight. A cleaner is washing the floor, paying no attention to the young woman who sits stiffly upright in the tin bath, dressings drawn across her torso where her breast used to be. The light streams through the window, and is bleak.

According to the BFI, the play drew little critical response; I wonder if that is true – I do not remember. But it was seen by a large audience of about 11 million, and struck a chord with the viewers. The BFI's piece adds that author Trevor Griffiths himself was "swamped" with letters about the play. I do remember that a besuited senior consultant was wheeled on straight after it ended, and insisted that Steadman's character had had a rare "bad trip" in which everything that could go wrong had done; and that few patients would endure such an experience. Griffiths himself was in the studio, in a simple sports-jacket and tie, but I have the impression that he said very little. Perhaps he was content to let his play speak for itself. I did not know then that the play was a response to Griffiths' own wife's experience of breast cancer.

Although I remembered the author's name clearly, I knew nothing about him, and researching this story has been a revelation. His credits include a long list of plays for TV and the stage, and he also wrote the original screenplay for the film *Reds*, a project he left after disagreements with Warren Beatty (but he has since said that the eventual screenplay was about 45% his). A fascinating 2011 interview with Robert Chalmers in the *Independent* (*Putting the World to Rights*, October 23) recounts how his screenplay on the great revolutionary Thomas Paine struggled to get made, despite support from Richard Attenborough and Kurt Vonnegut; it was eventually produced on stage in London.

Chalmers writes that: "Like *Bicycle Thieves*, *Through the Night* is a classic work so intense that you wouldn't want to watch it twice. That play generated a greater public response than any one-off piece in the history of British television, apart from Ken Loach's *Cathy Come Home*. The *Daily Mirror* alone received 1,800 letters after its broadcast."

So *Through the Night* is not forgotten then, and neither is its author – and Steadman of course is not. The play's director, too, is still around; Michael Lindsay-Hogg, a distinguished figure who had worked with some of the music giants of the 1960s, later directed *Brideshead Revisited*, and has had a string of BAFTA nominations. He too should surely take some of the credit for the play's impact. (I did not know that Lindsay-Hogg was a baronet, and may

be the illegitimate son of Orson Welles. It is amazing what you discover when you dig back into the half-remembered.)

*

What has that dig back revealed, if anything? Maybe nothing; just
myself, a middle-aged man, looking back – which is nothing to anyone else.

But I asked two questions at the start of this chapter. One was
whether TV left us, as a society, with shared memories. The other
was whether TV sucked up the creativity of people like Amis and
Griffiths, then threw it away, lost to those who follow.

The answer to the first question is yes. My search found that at
least two of these programmes (*Blair Castle, Through the Night*) were
widely remembered, and I suspect at least one other (*The Bloxham
Tapes*) is too. This is at least partly about their excellence. But it is
also about a glue that then stuck a society together. The BBC and
ITV chains still exist, but there are far more choices now; many
younger people may not watch conventional TV at all. As stated
earlier, *Through the Night* got 11 million viewers, then about one in
five of the population. I don't suppose anything would today. Does
this mean that, in another 40 years, there will be no shared memories? Does that mean we will be fragmented, with nothing in common? And if so, should we worry about it?

In a 2015 article for *The Spectator*, Ed West argued that "The
BBC was a product of a strong national culture, but it also helped
to further cement it, making events like the Proms or FA Cup final
part of our collective experience...

"Yet the world in which Lord Reith established the BBC has
gone... The fact that the Beeb is attacked by everyone, whether it's

the left or right, Scots or English, reflects the fact that we have become a far more diverse country." In short, there is nothing left to
glue us together.

Or is there? I am writing this a few minutes after British MPs
voted to authorise air strikes on Syria. This decision is itself divisive, but the brouhaha around it appears to have involved much of
the country. I am far from sure that there is now no national conversation, even if it takes a different form and is in different, and
more diverse, fora.

However, something subtler may be at stake. The mainstream
broadcasters in Britain have been bound by the rule that they
should have "balance" in their reporting and they have, very im-
perfectly, observed it. But what if they were *not* to do so? Abandonment of this rule in the US in the 1980s allowed the media to
fragment into partisan cable channels such as Fox News, and saw
the rise of the talk-radio "shock-jock", with the late Rush
Limbaugh prototypical of the latter. This has surely been divisive.
The effect of the Nazi media in Germany or Radio Mille Collines in
Rwanda is a yet grimmer warning.

On the other hand, so is Welles's 1938 radio drama *The War of
the Worlds*, which allegedly sparked mass panic. So this fragmenta-
tion may not be wholly bad. Today, the rumour of a Martian invasion would soon be dispelled on Twitter. If there is a corollary, it is
that *Through the Night* would not have the impact that it had in
1975. But I wonder if even that is true. If work of that quality appeared online, or on Netflix, it would be shared and tweeted far
and wide. We are in a different world from 1975, and the audience
for a play like that would now be self-selecting. But the national
conversation has not quite gone.

*

What of the other charge – that TV was and is a monster that sucks up creativity, uses it once and throws it away, leaving no trace of the blood, sweat and tears it has taken? This is harder to disprove.

While searching for these programmes, I also tried to establish whether copies survived. In the case of *Happy Returns*, I could not even find evidence that it ever *had* existed. I eventually identified it from a very brief entry on the British Film Institute (BFI) site; they do not seem to have a recording. As for *We Are All Guilty*, not long before his death in 1995 Amis said he would love to know if it still existed in any form. It appears not, although the script is held at an American university (but at least we have the novella). *The Bloxham Tapes* does exist, in four places; according to the global bibliographic database, WorldCat, three copies are in libraries in the US and the fourth is at Monash University in Melbourne. In all cases, however, they are VHS tapes and one wonders how well they have survived.

I had better luck with the others. The Royal Scottish Country Dance Society in Edinburgh holds the original 16mm film of *Mr Menuhin's Welcome to Blair Castle*; moreover it has been carefully digitalised and transferred to DVD. Sadly it is only available as a loan to branches and members of the Society, and only for private use. But this is likely for copyright reasons, so is fair enough; in fact, it is wonderful that the RSCDS has ensured the film's survival.

Last but not least, *Through the Night* has been preserved by the BFI, which has it in multiple formats, including digital. Clips are available online. The complete play is not, but can be viewed at any of the BFI's "Mediatheques", as it calls them; there are nine of these, in Glasgow, Wrexham and seven locations in England.

We may be lucky that any of these programmes have survived at all. The first official TV broadcasts, in Britain and Germany, were in 1936 and were live; they were usually not recorded. This remained the case for some programmes into the 1960s. Videotape arrived from the late 1950s onward, but in the 1970s it was still expensive and some programmes were, incredibly, simply recorded over so the tapes could be reused. Much TV from earlier decades has simply gone.

Digital technology mean that TV is easier to preserve. Today, a broadcast can easily be recorded in simple binary sequences of 1s and 0s; the results are unambiguous, unfaded and unstreaked, and need never be lost. However, this does not assure us that all will be preserved. The volume of media produced expands exponentially year by year, and much of it is cat videos. The challenge now is to know what we have, where it is, how to find it again, and why we might wish to.

I suppose that is up to all of us. When something grabs your attention, stop, and store it away; you won't pass this way again. It will always be our own job to remember the things that we feel we should, and to write them down when the raccoons wake us in the morning.

Being Beastly in Fleet Street

Sometime in the 1970s *Punch* published a cartoon strip in which a downtrodden journalist walks into his editor's office.

Editor: *Now, about that nun who was raped by the International Red Cross.*
Journalist: *But that was last week.*
Editor: *It sold six million, so we're having her raped again. Dammit, do I have to do everything round here myself?*

The cartoon was, I think, by the great J.B. Handelsman, whose work graced not only *Punch* but also *The New Yorker*. I found myself thinking of this strip while reading Alexander Starritt's 2017 novel *The Beast*, a savage and funny satire set on the sub-editors' desk of a British tabloid.

Starritt's *Beast* resembles the *Daily Mail*. Apart from anything else, its HQ definitely sounds like that of the *Mail*, in the old Biba building in Kensington; I visited it a couple of times when, as a young man, I had an abortive try-out as a feature writer. In fact, I bet its lawyers have given the book the once-over. If they have, they've likely told management to draw as little attention to the book as possible. I would, if I were them.

The story in *The Beast* is simple enough. Jeremy Underwood is a sub-editor; subs are the link between the reporter and the finished paper, taking the stories, hacking them into shape, headlining them and getting them ready for the page. Returning from holiday, Underwood walks past two women in burqas apparently hanging around near the building. Feeling he should tell someone, in case it's a story, he tells the reporters. They do see a story and

215

quickly "confirm" that there is a credible threat to the *Beast*. In fact, the two young women in burqas were tourists looking for a branch of Wholefoods. But nothing can now stop the mayhem that starts to unfold, as the *Beast* embarks upon a string of stories about an alleged Muslim plot to destroy it. This starts a chain of events that has violent results in the country. The book ends with a slightly bathetic tragedy that you don't see coming, but is entirely logical. In between, tabloid journalists scream and growl at each other and seethe with casual racism while people get killed in the world outside.

Scratch the surface of this book and you will find much more than satire. You'll find a vivid picture of how a story comes together once it hits the sub's desk, and it all has a ring of truth. Boring facts relayed by some reporter drudge in a county court can be quickly reassembled to support whatever theory the paper is pushing that week, whether it be on health foods or Muslim terrorists. It's all done under a tyrannical, unstable editor who sees himself as the embodiment of British values. (In a neat touch, Starritt calls him Brython, which is a Welsh-derived word sometimes used to refer to pre-Roman Britons.)

The Beast is a shrewd depiction of who tabloid journalists are, and how their sub-culture has survived, insulated against a changing world. The older ones remember the world of Fleet Street as it was. It's a world that I myself saw briefly, just before it ended; the hot-metal typesetters, the clatter of machinery, the great rolls of newsprint being winched from lorries in the narrow streets that ran from Fleet Street down to the Embankment. The subs also remember the legends who worked in the Street of Shame; the long liquid lunches, the tradition of boozy contempt for morality. And they proudly pass this tradition on to the young recruits who join them.

Yet it's not a world that anyone should be proud of preserving. Lord Northcliffe, who founded the *Mail*, is alleged to have said "Give them something to hate every day"; in fact this is apocryphal, but that is certainly how the tabloids have been sold. The *Mail* whipped up alarm about Jewish refugees in the 1930s, and disseminated the awful Zinoviev Letter hoax in the 1920s in order to discredit the Labour Party. As for the *Daily Express*, one remembers what Max Hastings wrote about a famous prewar journalist, H. V. Morton – that he had "the qualities of an outstanding Beaverbrook journalist of his period: masterly understanding of public taste, deployed in a moral void." Starritt's characters clearly do function in a complete moral void, and bad things happen as a result.

*

But the *Beast*, of course, predates Starritt. It first appeared in Evelyn Waugh's 1938 novel, *Scoop*, in which it is widely assumed to have been not the *Mail* but the *Express*. Robert McCrum once wrote that *Scoop* was "the supreme novel of the 20th-century English newspaper world, fast, light, entertaining and lethal." I can't completely agree. I think Starritt gets closer to the mark, and there's a third book that I think is better than either – more of that in a minute. But *Scoop* certainly has its points.

It begins with a fashionable but bored writer, John Boot, persuading an aristocratic patroness, Lady Stitch, to use her influence and get him sent abroad on a newspaper job. Milady obliges by badgering press magnate Lord Copper, who issues the appropriate instructions to his staff. Unfortunately they misidentify Boot as their own William Boot, their countryside correspondent, who comes from an eccentric family of impoverished gentlefolk in the West Country. This Boot is duly dispatched to cover an incipient crisis in an African country called Ishmaelia. This is clearly Abyssinia (now Ethiopia), where Waugh had just covered the brutal Italian invasion of 1935-36. Boot is widely supposed to be based on one of Waugh's fellow correspondents, Bill Deedes, then a very young correspondent for the *Morning Post*.

Some of *Scoop* is funny, and acute. Boot has a long and uncomfortable trip down the Red Sea on a second-class ship (the era of sea travel was not always glamorous). In the capital, he joins a foreign press corps whose coverage of the war quickly declines into farce. When one correspondent is rumoured to have got a lead, excitement reaches fever pitch. Eventually, most of the press disappear into the country on a wild goose chase while Boot is smoothly swindled by Kätchen, the attractive mistress of the Fascist agent. It all ends with Boot being praised to the skies for a dispatch that he did not write. Meanwhile in London no-one notices that the wrong Boot has been sent; all are too scared of the tyrannical press baron, Lord Copper, so do not question why he has sent a countryside correspondent to cover a war.

There are some nice moments in *Scoop*. Boot's non-romance with Kätchen is well done (there is a charming scene when they sit in a collapsible canoe together). Boot's family seat in Somerset is lovingly described at night, white in the moonlight. The old Fleet Street and the *Express* building come nicely to life. Also, as critic Thomas Jones has pointed out, *Scoop* is a keen satire on patronage networks – the writer Boot can get an assignment because he knows a powerful society hostess; the paper gets its tips from the police; in Ishmaelia, William Boot is at an advantage over other correspondents because he has been to school with a senior staff member at the Embassy. As Jones reminds us, the media still works that way.

In some ways, however, *Scoop* has not aged so well. It lays on the satire heavily; *The Beast* also does that, but is near enough reality to get away with it. *Scoop* may have been too when first written, but somehow it doesn't feel like it. Lady Stitch is too eccentric, Boot is too naive, and Lord Copper never quite takes shape. Boot's rural relatives seem to have escaped from *Cold Comfort Farm*.

Bill Deedes, the supposed model for William Boot, was not impressed. Deedes went on to long careers in both politics (as a Minister under both Churchill and Macmillan) and journalism (he was a successful editor of the *Telegraph*, a role he filled as late as 1986). A few years before his death in 2007, he refuted his supposed role as Boot in a long piece for the *Telegraph* in which he claimed that few good novelists really caricature anyone; their characters, he argued, are composites (*The Real* Scoop: *Who was in Waugh's Cast List and Why*, May 28 2003). He also gave Waugh a kicking:

> *To some readers,* Scoop *confirms the impression that Waugh was a successful novelist but a failed newspaper reporter. Behind the banter, they reason, we find a man poking fun at a profession that humiliated him. He takes his revenge on those who outclassed him in the newspaper business by lampooning them and with a storyline that has them all outwitted by a country hick. It is not an unreasonable interpretation...*

It isn't. Waugh had, on graduation, had a trial in Fleet Street, and had failed. It was not the first time he had taken revenge on those who had found him wanting. He had not been a huge academic success at Oxford either and on that institution, too, he had sought revenge, through a series of attacks on the Dean and later Principal of Hertford College, C.R.M.F. Cruttwell. Waugh's attacks on Cruttwell probably hastened the latter's mental illness and death. Waugh may have forgotten this in later life, but Oxford didn't. My father, who was an undergraduate at Hertford during Cruttwell's final illness and was later a Fellow, had never read a book by Waugh and did not like to hear him mentioned.

That, then, was what drove *Scoop* – not genuine anger at the newspaper world and its venality or the patronage networks it depicts. They don't anger Waugh; they afford him a certain malicious amusement at a world that had rejected him. Starritt, by contrast, does seem angry.

So was J.B. Priestley.

*

Priestley's *Wonder Hero* was published in 1933. It concerns Charlie Habble, a modest young night worker in a chemical works whose actions one night appear to have prevented a fire and an explosion that might have blown his drab Midlands town to smithereens. In fact, they were the actions of another man whose role Habble cannot, for honourable reasons, reveal. Meanwhile a feature writer for the *Daily Tribune* happens to be in the town, having come to chase an important story. Having failed to secure it, he is anxious not to return to London empty-handed, and fastens onto Habble's story instead.

The hapless Habble is hailed as a hero. He is dragged to London, suited and booted, recorded on newsreel, given a substantial cash award by the paper and lionised in its pages. Moreover the *Tribune* gives him a taste of the high life, housing him in a luxury hotel, and insisting that he make an appearance at the theatre and at a fashionable nightclub in the company of another newspaper protégé, a beauty queen also from the Midlands, Ida Chatwick. They clearly wish to hint at a romance between their two creations.

Habble is a straightforward provincial working man but is neither stupid nor dishonest, and these events trouble him. His qualms increase when the proprietor of the *Tribune*, the tyrannical Sir Gregory Hatchland, decides that Habble is the sort of fine upstanding young man he needs to parade before his pet political party, the vaguely fascist League of Imperial Yeomen. As the League's rally progresses, Charlie, waiting backstage, feels a distinct lack of enthusiasm. As he waits, he hears from his uncle; his aunt, who lives in a Northern industrial city called Slakeby, is very ill. He abandons the *Tribune* and the League without making his appearance, and goes north to see if he can help.

It's a chance for Priestley to confront us with a terrible contrast. One moment Habble's being wheeled from luxury hotel to nightclub to theatre, shown off like a prize pig to London's glitterati. The next he is right in the very worst of the Great Depression – or as it was also called at one time, the Slump. He uses the award from the *Tribune* to get his aunt the help she needs. When he returns to London, the paper has lost interest in him. Ida Chatwick, too, has been tossed aside. They are yesterday's fish-and-chip paper and they know it.

Wonder Hero is an angry book. The slump, the unemployment, the arbitrary behaviour of Hatchland and the press, all are there. When Habble decides he must go to Slakeby, he takes leave of the cynical but friendly young journalist who has escorted him for the *Tribune*. The journalist warns him that he won't be a story any more if he goes. "Perhaps they'll send me up to see you at wherever it is – perhaps. Not much chance, though; we don't like putting the spotlight on that part of the country. Your uncle could hardly have lived in a worse place. He's taking you right out of the news."

A few hours later Habble stands on the bridge across Slakeby's river:

Where were the shipyards and ships he remembered all along the banks?

221

The sheds were there and a crane or two, and that was all. Everything else
– finished, gone. ...Some of the towns in the Midlands had been knocked
sideways by the depression, but this place had been knocked flat.

But that is not news.

There is no doubt that this did anger Priestley. The following
year, 1934, he would publish his *English Journey*, in which he described his progress through a country in which the ravages of the
Great Depression were all too evident. In a memorable scene, he
describes a Northern reunion with members of his former regiment, who he has not seen since he was badly wounded in 1916.
He is affronted that some cannot afford the clothes to attend the
event. (He did not forget this incident, and mentioned it again in
his much later book *Margin Released*.) It would be easy to conclude
that *Wonder Hero* was a product of the same journey. In fact it
wasn't; it was published in September 1933 and Priestley set off on
his travels a month or so later. But it's clear that his two books were
driven by the same anger.

It is this anger that makes *Wonder Hero* memorable and I believe that is also true of *The Beast*. It is also why both books are
superior to *Scoop*. Waugh may have been angry with the Fleet
Street that rejected him, or with his friends, or with Cruttwell, but
he seems to have felt little real anger at the abuses he was supposed
to be satirising. *Scoop* is a good yarn, but as satire it is vapid.

*

There is no doubt that all this matters. It did in the 1930s, when
Priestley's fictional *Tribune* showed no interest in the state of the
country, and when the real *Mail* was busy printing scare stories
about Jewish refugees pouring into Britain; one wonders how

many failed to obtain asylum as a result, and in due course died.

The press still distorts the agenda today. In a much-admired feature in the *The New Yorker* in 2012 (*Mail Supremacy: The Newspaper That Rules Britain*, March 26), Lauren Collins described how in 2000 Tony Blair ordered his advisors to focus on several issues that, as it happened, the *Mail* had highlighted that morning. Collins also quotes a story that illustrates why the treatment of Muslims in *The Beast* is so important. She describes a story the *Mail* ran of a "hard-working café owner" who had to get rid of an extractor fan because the smell of bacon was offending Muslims. But if one read carefully to the bottom of the story, one found that complaint had been made by a neighbour who said "Muslim friends" had not liked the smells when they visited. No Muslim had complained. It also turned out that the café owner's husband was Muslim. Still, one should never let the facts take the edge off a good headline, and in Starritt's book the subs make sure they don't. And this does have consequences. As the distinguished journalist Ian Jack has said in a warm review of *The Beast*: "The real achievement of the popular press is to have played a part in making Britain, particularly England, the strange, febrile country we now know."

Does all this matter as much as it did? The newspaper world Starritt describes is a dying one. Print newspapers have nothing like the circulation they did in the 1930s, or even 20 years ago. Starritt's characters know that; they look over their shoulder at the online editions that they know will soon replace them. But what Starritt nowhere mentions is fake news; the bizarre websites that spread rumours – for example that the Sandy Hook shooting was a hoax, or that the liberal establishment was running a child-abuse ring in restaurants. The latter rumour, 2016's Pizzagate "scandal", which led to a shooting, was apparently spread (though not invented) by a site called YourNewsWire.com – the stories for which are allegedly made up by the site's owner's mum. I've written elsewhere about this assault on truth, which bloody petrifies me.

Neither is this a solely Anglophone problem. In October 2017 the *New York Times* Rome bureau chief Jason Horowitz reported that in Italy, the Ministry of Education had been sufficiently alarmed to launch a pilot project in 8,000 high schools, teaching pupils how to tell fake news from real. It quotes Laura Boldrini, President of Italy's lower house, as saying that fake news "drips drops of poison into our daily web diet and we end up infected without even realizing it." Compared to the damage these "fake news" sites may do, tabloids are mild stuff. British newspapers are vicious and mendacious. But they always were, and we may soon miss them as we are hit with something much worse.

Does this mean that Starritt's, Waugh's and Priestley's books are no longer relevant?

I don't think it does. The message that we can draw from these books is that every news outlet has its agenda, and that whenever we see anything inflammatory, we should ask the lawyer's question: *Cui bono*? Who benefits? What was the story meant to make you believe, and to what end? Why is that news outlet in business anyway – what is its business model, and why is it there? The rise of fake news sites hasn't made books like Starritt's, or Priestley's, irrelevant. On the contrary, it has invested them with more meaning than ever before.

It's the Science, Stupid. Or Is It?

Science is under attack. From the right, sceptics attack climate science; for the left, molecular biology and its products inspire deep suspicion. Science no longer seems to inspire the young or the progressive, who espouse mysticism or retreat into homespun philosophy. Meanwhile both Left and Right cherry-pick from science's conclusions; they accept or reject climate science or advances in biotechnology according to their prejudices, and examine the evidence on neither.

This is dangerous, especially now. As Al Gore wrote in his modestly titled book *The Future* (2013): "The… multiple revolutions in biotechnology and the life sciences will soon require us to make almost godlike [decisions]… Are we ready to make such decisions? The available evidence would suggest that the answer is not really, but we are going to make them anyway."

There are several areas in which science has been disrespected. Health is one; we are fed with endless reports of "research", or arguments that we should/should not eat this or that, often with little basis in real knowledge. However, the worst example is climate change. The basic science has been understood for a long time; it was propounded by Jean-Baptiste Fournier as long ago as the 1820s. The radiative forcing capacity of various gases was demonstrated by John Tyndall in 1859. Its probable impact on the climate was quantified by Svante Arrhenius in 1896. Yet for many, warnings of what may be coming are a dishonest dirge of the "liberal elite", a mean trick. Why they should be, is not clear; but the issue has got tangled up with the "culture wars", and has become a touchstone for what sort of people you do and don't believe. This is very dangerous.

Climate change is not the only example of this willful ignorance. In her book *Honourable Friends?* (2015), British Green MP
Caroline Lucas has described the controversy in Britain over the
killing of badgers because they are a vector for bovine TB. Lucas
accepts that they are – but as she points out, all the research suggests that shooting them is not the answer, not least because it
makes infected animals more mobile. Yet Owen Paterson, Britain's
Secretary of State for Environment, Food and Rural Affairs in 2012-
2014, continued to insist that badgers should be shot, although the
evidence – while somewhat inconclusive – suggested this was the
wrong thing to do. It had become a totemic policy both for Paterson
and for farmers, who were his political allies. So he stuck to it. On
one occasion, he was asked why a pilot cull had failed. To the delight of the *twitterati*, he said that "the badgers moved the goal-
posts". Crafty little blighters. As to his views on climate change,
Lucas described them as "the ramblings of a bloke in the pub." No-
toriously, as Secretary of State, Paterson refused an offer to be
briefed on climate change by the chief science adviser to the Department of Energy and Climate Change. What the hell is the point
in a free market in knowledge, if that knowledge is simply rejected
by those in power?

Why do voters and even ministers take pride in their own ignorance?

In the US, this is sometimes about science *vs.* religion. For
some, to teach evolution in a school is to deny the role of the Creator. Others use the cudgel of rationality to attack religion. It is a
false dichotomy. Both sides would do well to remember the words
of Andalusian scientist and philosopher Ibn Rushd (1126-1198),
known in the West as Averroës: "The more perfect becomes the
knowledge of creation, the more perfect becomes the knowledge of
the Creator. ...the Law urges us to observe creation by means of

reason and demands the knowledge thereof through reason." The deeply religious, and strongly irreligious, should both think hard about that quote. They won't.

But the real issue is not religion (especially in irreligious Britain). It is about the way we see science and interpret its findings; what it tells us, and what it doesn't; and where it should stand in public discourse.

Part of the problem is the oversimplified view of science as a magic thing that delivers only truths, and whose findings cannot be disputed. Somebody who believes this will demand that the link between emissions and climate change be visible to their own eyes. But science does not work like that. Science is inductive; that is to say, I observe an object or phenomenon, and decide that my observation allows me to infer something about other, similar or connected objects or phenomena.

An induction is therefore different from a deduction, in which I observe a number of objects or phenomena and know that a certain fact applies to each one; from this, I can infer that another fact does too. The most reliable form of inference is the syllogism. A syllogism is, in effect, deductive logic. I will say, A working bicycle must have wheels; my bicycle works; it therefore must have wheels. Change this proposition to: A working bicycle has wheels; other bicycles have wheels; therefore they work too. This is not a syllogism, because we don't know it to be true; all the other bikes might have some other broken part, so might not work. However, we know from observation (of other bikes) that it is *probably* true, so we may infer that they work. This is an induction.

Modern science depends on this extrapolation of the general from the particular. As Bertrand Russell explains, an induction "has less cogency than a deduction, and yields only a probability, not a certainty; but on the other hand it gives new knowledge, which deduction does not" (*A History of Western Philosophy*, 1945). This is demonstrated by modern advances in astrophysics; we cannot (yet) test for dark matter, but its existence is a rational probability – one that we would not discover through a purely deductive process.

The problem with this inductive process is that it excludes the unknown; you cannot include in your reasoning a factor that you do not know to exist. One can argue, in the case of climate change, that the causal mechanism is clear, but what if there is some unknown factor acting upon it, or about to do so? The philosopher Moritz Schlick, of whom more later, wrote that in any such situation there were "infinitely many circumstances that might possibly enter into consideration as the cause, since, theoretically, every process in the universe could make a contribution" (*General Theory of Knowledge*, 1925).

Thus we do not know, in a literal sense, that human activity is changing the climate. We have inferred it from the fact that we are releasing a certain tonnage of greenhouses gases and know that some of it is accumulating in the atmosphere. We also know that that accumulation will make the atmosphere retain more heat. Neither of these facts are in themselves inference – we know them to be true; we can (for example) measure the concentration of CO_2 in the atmosphere and know that it has increased from 280 to nearly 400 parts per million since the Industrial Revolution began in the 18th century. We also know the extent to which these gases will increase the propensity of the atmosphere to retain heat; this was demonstrated by Tyndall in his 1859 experiment. What *is* inference, is that this process will lead to climate change. It is inference because we cannot be sure there is no third factor that would cancel out the interaction between the two.

The history of science and technology is littered with failures due to such a "third factor" that was not predicted. A famous example of the unexpected comes from aviation history. The first jet airliner, the De Havilland Comet, entered passenger service in 1952. Very soon, several aircraft exploded in flight. The Royal Aircraft Establishment at Farnborough put an intact Comet in a water tank and pressurized and depressurized it until it suffered the same failure. Pressurization of the cabin had searched out a point weakened by metal fatigue. As the aircraft had been tested to twice its maximum cabin pressure in trials, this should not have happened. In fact it was the cycle of pressurization and depressurization that was the agent of failure, not the cabin pressure itself. As Geoffrey De Havilland was to admit in an autobiography published after his death (*Sky Fever*, 1979), the Comet was so close to the frontiers of technology that there was nothing in existing experience to predict this. The cause could never have been hypothesized.

The failure of an inductive process to apprehend an unknown factor can also arise because that process's evidential base is limited in time or space. The social-science theorist R. Andrew Sayer cites one of the Paradoxes of the ancient Greek philosopher Zeno of Elea. If one conceives of time as consisting of discretely distinct points (he says), movement cannot exist. "If an arrow can only be at a single distinct point in space and at no other discrete point in time, then it cannot move" (*Method in Social Science: A Realist Approach*, 1984.) Again, this seems theoretical; but it has implications for the modelling of environmental processes. Conclusions drawn from observations of natural phenomena are especially suspect in this respect.

Sayer cites the example of plant growth: "If we [describe] the growth of a plant [in] distinct stages occurring at discretely distinct times we can hardly expect to learn how it happens." An example quoted to me during my own research on agriculture and climate change was that of the naturalist E.P. Stebbing, who observed environmental degradation in northern Nigeria in 1934 and concluded that the desert was moving southward. In a sense it was, but Stebbing might not have known that it had also moved *north* in recent times, because his observations were temporally inadequate. However, Stebbing's views started an ongoing narrative on the desertification menace that at one stage tended to oversimplify land-management issues in Africa.

The problems of the inductive approach become acute in the case of climate modelling, where the number of different phenomena that would be material is so great that they cannot all be known; so great, indeed, that some may be simplified or excluded even when their existence *is* known. Thus at least one major climate model was drawn up in the past on the basis of single rate of decay for soil carbon – although it is highly variable and non-linear.

Does this mean we should ignore the outputs of climate science? No. It is based on an induction, but as we have seen, all good science is. There can always be new evidence coming from left field, but we have yet to hear of anything that would really invalidate the climate models that we have so far.

In any case, as the historian of science Naomi Oreskes pointed out in a 2004 paper (*Science and public policy: what's proof got to do with it?*), science rarely provides absolute proofs; rather, a consensus arises between scientists based on what *is* known, and provided that consensus is wide enough, the majority will ignore the doubters and move on. This is where climate science now stands. If we always insisted that science offer up those absolute proofs from the outset, we would have no powered flight, no vaccines, nothing; they all started as hypotheses based on what *was* known so far, and so did climate science.

What I am trying to do, however, is to make a deeper point about the rights and obligations of science, the limitations on what it demonstrates, the need for evidence, and the need for humility when its conclusions are questioned. Failure to find that humility will itself politicise science and throw its objectivity into doubt. It may even bring it into disrepute.

Roger Pielke of the University of Colorado, who has written widely on the links between science and politics, demonstrated this in a 2004 paper in *Environmental Science and Policy*, in which he discussed the furore that erupted over Bjørn Lomborg's book *The Skeptical Environmentalist* (2001). Lomborg had argued that environmental threats were exaggerated and that proposed measures to address them were uneconomic. He was subjected to intense and often savage criticism, with one critic going so far as to compare him, by implication, to a Holocaust denier. A more reasoned attack came from Harvard scientist John Holdren; Pielke quotes him as saying that Bjorn Lomborg's book had "wasted immense amounts of the time of capable people who have had to take on the task of rebutting him. And he has done so at the particular intersection of science with public policy... where public and policymaker confusion about the realities is more dangerous than on any other science-and-policy question excepting, possibly, ...weapons of mass destruction."

This frustration with Lomborg is understandable (and Holdren is in fact a scientist of distinction; he has served as senior science advisor to the White House). However, Pielke's point is that by taking this view, scientists are themselves politicising science. This is a wise observation in itself, but there is surely a deeper danger. The critics (many far ruder than Holdren) were, in effect, saying to Lomborg: Science says you are wrong, so shut up. The implications of this will be obvious to anyone familiar with the abuses committed in the 20th century in the name of "scientific socialism", and the revolutionary doctrine that because we are right, we may behave as we see fit. The fact that Lomborg *was* wrong is not the point. As we have seen, science is a flawed instrument, and is not in a position to claim absolute truth. One is reminded of John Stuart Mill's contention that no opinion should be suppressed "lest it aught be true".

*

However, there are also dangers in questioning the scientific method.

Science has always had its enemies. When I lived in Rome some years ago I would often visit the Campo de' Fiori; it had the best bars. In its centre stands the rather threatening statue of Giordano Bruno. (Not to be confused with Bruno Giordano. One was burned at the stake; the other played for Lazio – though, for Roma supporters, that may mean he should burn too.) Bruno was burned on that spot in 1600. His quarrel with the Inquisition was basically theological, but also concerned his science; like his younger contemporary, Galileo Galilei, he believed the earth revolved around the sun. Further, he posited the existence of other life in other worlds, which challenged the Church's view of creation. Bruno was, by all accounts, a disputatious pain in the arse; yet he led a life of principled intellectual endeavour. His fate reminds us of what might then have befallen Christopher Hitchens or Richard Dawkins.

It would be easy to see Bruno's fate as something of another time, but attacks on science are with us still. The arguments about creationism, and the teaching of evolution *vs.* intelligent design, are an example; so is the funding by lobbyists of research to discredit the consensus on climate science. However, there have been other, subtler attempts to undermine the rational, sometimes with good intentions. The best example is the "Science Wars" that began in the 1960s and ran on into the late 1990s.

The "Science Wars" can trace their origin back to a seminal 1962 work by Thomas Kuhn, *The Structure of Scientific Revolutions*. Very crudely stated, Kuhn's argument was that what we accept as "scientific truth" is the result of a consensus that is in part a product of society and its preoccupations at any given time, and that certain conditions must occur for that consensus to be reformed (a process he referred to as a "paradigm shift"). Kuhn's arguments are interesting and complex. A physicist by training, he did not so much question the value of science as try to illuminate how it proceeds, and under what circumstances a scientific consensus will admit of major revisions. However, some have since interpreted his work as meaning that what we take for scientific knowledge is actually moderated by a society's culture and history.

This has led to science being weakened by the academic establishment itself. Some have gone so far as to make statements that seem to imply there is no "scientific" method of inquiry. Thus in 1986 the philosopher Sandra Harding could define the radical feminist position as a claim that science is "not only sexist, but also racist, classist, and culturally coercive". This should be taken in context; from a feminist viewpoint, there are real questions as to how science is organized. Even so, this statement could be read, rightly or wrongly, as saying that the products of science are in themselves relative. That view does not help the rational to prevail.

It is especially worrying that some of what academics have written in the past has been, or at least seemed, quite meaningless. Richard Dawkins has quoted, with glee, such statements as the late

Jean Baudrillard's (in *The Illusion of the End*, 1994): "Perhaps history itself has to be regarded as a chaotic formation, in which acceleration puts an end to linearity and the turbulence created by acceleration deflects history definitively from its end, just as such turbulence distances effects from their causes." In fact the argument as to whether history is linear, or to some extent predefined, or subject to an endpoint, is a legitimate one, and the above words should be seen in the context of Baudrillard's work in this area. But the best thought is marked by its simplicity and if a meaning cannot be clearly conveyed (and for most people it won't have been here), it has not been defined.

In 1994 the physicist Alan Sokal was sufficiently irritated to write a spoof paper that he titled *Transgressing the Boundaries: Toward a Transformative Hermeneutics Of Quantum Gravity*. Dawkins later described the paper as "a carefully crafted parody of postmodern metatwaddle." Sokal submitted the paper to the journal *Social Text*, which published it as part of a "Science Wars" special issue. Sokal then admitted that it was a hoax. What Sokal, and others, were in effect saying was, look, it's not all right to just talk complete rubbish.

They were not the first to make this point. The classic example was that of the logical positivists and their leader Moritz Schlick, mentioned earlier. In principle, logical positivism held that a statement is only meaningful if it could, at least in theory, be verified.

This sprang in part from a distrust of metaphysical philosophy. The Vienna Circle – a group of thinkers centred on Schlick who met between the mid-1920s and mid-1930s – argued that philosophy could only be a part of science. If it wasn't, then it wasn't knowledge. In arguing for this essential unity of science, Schlick and the logical positivists were undermining the metaphysical claims of philosophy, theology and the humanities, which in early-

20th century Germany and Austria had, as Schlick's colleague Eugene Gadol put it much later: "Alleged that there were special ways of enquiry (hermeneutics) and special ways of understanding (intuiting, *Verstehen*) which transcend the ordinary operations of the human mind as it manifests itself in the natural sciences" (Gadol, *Rationality and Science*, 1982). In other words, the theory of the unity of science propounded by the Vienna Circle challenged the right to claim these "special ways of understanding" and write anything that did not make sense.

On the morning of June 22 1936, as he climbed the stairs to his lecture room at the University of Vienna, Schlick was shot and fatally wounded by a former student, Johan Nelböck. This has often been presented as a political act, but Nelböck was simply deranged. However, Nelböck defended himself in court by arguing that Schlick's rejection of metaphysics had somehow deranged him. In the weeks that followed, Nelböck received increasing press support as someone who had rid Vienna of a pernicious left-leaning foreign Jewish philosopher, who had sought to destroy the nation's moral compass. He used these arguments to secure a pardon after the Nazis took power in Austria (his sentence had in any case been only 10 years).

An enlightened, West-leaning philosopher murdered by gloomy irrational Central Europeans untouched by the Enlightenment? Indeed Schlick fits the role; a German aristocrat (and not in fact Jewish), he was married to an American and spoke good English. The British philosopher A. J. Ayer, who met him in Vienna in 1932, said that he "made on me above all an impression of urbanity – like an American senator in a pre-war film." It's exactly the gulf expressed by the characters Settembrini and Naphta in Mann's *The Magic Mountain*.

Arguably this conflict was resolved by the defeat of fascism:

the rational won. But this is not so clear. The "Science Wars" showed that the validity of science is still under attack from those who do not wish to be bound by its conclusions. Meanwhile, politicians seem to think it is fine to play fast and loose with the facts.

Our public lives must be the realm of disciplined, secular, rational thought. Both Sokal and Schlick – in their very different ways – were insisting that it is not all right to make meaningless statements and offer them up as knowledge. Both were right. As Moritz Schlick's assassination showed, it is sometimes a short step from talking shit to doing it to other people.

Diana Athill: Self-Scrutiny, and the Writer's World

Those who can, write; those who can't, edit. Or is that unfair? I hope so, as I do both. In Diana Athill's case, however, there was no doubt; she wrote with grace and concision.

Athill, who died in January 2019 at the age of 101, helped found the firm of André Deutsch in the early 1950s and built up a formidable list, making it a leading English-language publisher for 40 years. Following her retirement in 1993, she turned to writing, with astonishing success; her account of aging, *Somewhere Towards the End*, has been widely admired, and her most recent book of memoirs and reflections, *Alive, Alive Oh!*, was published as recently as 2016. In fact, to those in the know, she had long been a writer as well as an editor; she won the *The Observer's* short-story prize in 1958 when she was in her early 40s, and published a short-story collection in 1962. This was followed soon afterwards by a remarkable memoir, *Instead of a Letter* – of which more below. But the most widespread acclaim came for books she had written since her retirement.

I must admit I was late to the Athill party. In recent years she has been fashionable, and I have an aversion to writers I have been told to like. Moreover I was nonplussed by the first of her books that I read, *Stet: An Editor's Life* (2002), her account of her publishing career. I was irritated by Athill's privileged background and was disappointed that she highlighted authors I had not read and, in several cases, had never heard of. But I sensed I was missing something. Rereading *Stet* after several years, I saw that I was.

*

Athill was born in Norfolk and brought up as part of the "county" set; she went to Oxford, and spent the war in the BBC – a job she got through a personal contact in its recruitment office; class was as powerful then as now. Disappointed in love, she fell into a series of relationships, one with a young refugee met at a party. ("He sat on the floor and sang 'The Foggy Foggy Dew', which was unexpected in a Hungarian.") This was André Deutsch. The affair did not last long; the friendship, however, did, and at the end of the war he asked her to join him in the publishing company he was founding. She was to work as an editor for the next 50 years, all but the last few with Deutsch himself. She says little in this book of her personal life, but she has written of that elsewhere (again, more of that below). *Stet* – the word is a proofreader's instruction, used to cancel a correction – is about Athill's life in publishing.

Stet is in two pretty much equal parts. The first is a narrative account of her career, mostly with Deutsch. The second recalls her work with a series of writers, the best-known of which are Jean Rhys and V.S. Naipaul; the others – Alfred Chester, Molly Keane, and one or two more – are not forgotten, but are not household names.

The first part of the book is a fascinating picture of postwar publishing in all its amateurish glory. When André Deutsch was founded in the 1950s, it worked out of a converted house; books were dispatched from a packing bench that was a plank over the bath. This doesn't surprise me; my first job, in 1974, was in publishing, and I sometimes ran the packing bench. Things hadn't changed much. But there is nothing amateur about Athill's shrewd insight into book buyers: "There are those who buy because they love books and what they can get from them, and those to whom books are one form of entertainment among several. The first group, which is by far the smaller, will go on reading ...The second group has to be courted." In Athill's view, by the 1980s the second group had been seduced away by more visual media, leaving little space for literary publishing. She may have been right – then. But electronic publishing has now made books good value again, at least when sold by independents or small publishers whose over-heads are low. So that second audience is being reclaimed (albeit mainly with genre books). Although Athill retired in the 1990s, she will clearly have been aware of these developments, and one won-ders what she thought of them. She says little in *Stet* about techno-logical change in general, although photosetting and on-screen page design arrived in her time.

When it comes to editing, though, Athill clearly had rigorous judgement. If a book didn't quite work, she didn't want it, whoever had written it; and she rejected one of Philip Roth's – a decision that caused her some pain later, but was surely right at the time. She had felt that he was writing about a different type of character than usual simply to prove that he could, and it did not ring true.

This is, in fact, the key to the second half of *Stet* itself; it does ring true. This is because Athill has chosen to recall not the writers who would be best known today, but those about whom she feels she has something to say. The result is a series of character sketches that do have impact, and draw you in whether you are interested in the writer or not. V.S. Naipaul is the only modern "superstar" covered here. Of the others, I had heard of Jean Rhys and Molly Keane, but knew little about them; I knew nothing of Alfred Ches-ter at all. But I was fascinated. These three, and the other, sketches suggest that Athill was not just a good editor; she was a generous friend to her writers as well. (And to Deutsch himself, despite his apparent self-absorption.)

Of these sketches, it is that of Jean Rhys that stands out. "No-one who has read Jean Rhys's first four novels can suppose that she was good at life," writes Athill, "but no-one who never met her could know how very bad at it she was." The later stages of Rhys's life and the mess she had made of it, and her struggle with alcohol, are there – but so is her gift as a writer, and the strange early life that Athill felt explained much about her. Athill's thumbnail sketch of V.S. Naipaul, too, is vivid, with this shrewd insight: that those whose cultural or national background is unclear must define themselves, and the personal resources needed for this can be great. Not everyone has them, and one can become lost, and stumble. As someone who has spent much of their life in an international environment, I understand this all too well.

I am glad I read this again. Athill was, to be sure, a member of a privileged group – she used the word caste – with an iron grip on the publishing world; but she knew that. This caste was "the mostly London-dwelling, university-educated, upper-middle-class English people [who] loved books and genuinely tried to understand the differences between good and bad writing; but I suspect... our 'good' was good only according to the notions of the caste." She puts this in the past tense but one wonders if that caste and its prejudices have really quite gone yet. However, Athill's judgment as an editor clearly transcended it. So did her empathetic and subtle understanding of those she met.

This is a charming book.

*

But what of Athill herself? From *Stet*, it is clear that she was someone of substance, but she says little of her own affairs. In her other books, however, she does. Her private life was colourful and she was frank about it. It included the suicide of a lover and an affair with an American revolutionary, Hakim Jamal, a cousin of Michael

X. Jamal and his associates inspired a later novel by V.S. Naipaul, *Guerillas*; Athill, then his editor, did not like it. She eventually wrote a memoir of her own about her friendship with Jamal, *Make Believe: A True Story*.

However, her first volume of autobiography, *Instead of a Letter* (1962), contains nothing so lurid (though it is quite frank about sex). What it does contain, is acute self-analysis. I rarely admire introspection in autobiography; too often it comes over as solipsism, and in any case, it is a poor substitute for narrative. So I should not have liked this book. But I did.

It is, in sum, a meditation on why one can be bothered to live; and why, in effect, she decided that she *could* be bothered. She starts with her grandmother, who, not long before death, "turned her beautiful speckled eyes towards me one afternoon and said in so many words: 'What have I lived for?'" Athill's answer was that her grandmother had lived for what her life had been, that she had "created a world" for the family, in which they lived and functioned as human beings. But what of Athill herself? Why was she to live? "That," she writes, "was a question to whistle up an icy wind."

Athill proceeds to take us through her early life at the Norfolk manor, including her realisation that her mother did not really love her father. Her grandmother has an absolute belief in a secure and transparent world, but Athill does not: "I shocked her once. I was about ten years old and had thought of an image for life. I thought that it was as though people were confined in a bowl which was floating on a sea." Every now and then someone might be tossed upwards by the sea and would see, over the rim, the "endless chaos" of the waters and would find it intolerable. That view of the sea, she thinks, is the origin of madness. Her grandmother is appalled.

But in her early 20s Athill does look over the rim of the bowl. Since her mid-teens she has been in love with a man who, as an undergraduate, was brought in to tutor her brother; she calls him Paul. She grows to adulthood in her love for him, and they become engaged. He joins the RAF and goes to Egypt and she intends to join him as soon as she finishes at Oxford, which she soon will. But then he is transferred to Transjordan and his warm, intimate letters cease, with no explanation; two years later a curt note arrives asking to be released from the engagement, as he wishes to marry someone else. It appears, she thinks, to be the sort of formal note one might send to a fiancé one is jilting, in order to avoid a breach-of-promise suit.

It seems to destroy her. She spends the war working for the BBC, but feels little interest in the job, or in life; she does not say so, but her 20s seem to be overshadowed by what we would now call depression. "I was not even affected by whatever feverish gaiety there may have been about (people speak of it in memoirs); it did not come my way. Years of emptiness. Years leprous with boredom..."

And yet it is her, not Paul, who survives. He – his real name was Tony Irvine – does marry, but flies into a mountain in northern Greece soon afterwards and never meets his unborn son. (Oddly, Athill herself eventually does, some 60 years later.) Athill, meanwhile, has been set adrift, and her capacity for close relationships will never recover. But she rebuilds herself as something else. First comes her successful collaboration with Deutsch, which will make her one of the most powerful and respected editors in Britain. And then, in 1958, a chance meeting in Regent's Park causes her to write a short story that, to her surprise, wins the *Observer* prize. The happiness this brings her is wonderfully described in the book.

Instead of a Letter could have been very dull. After all, one's life may be interesting; one's soul is usually not, at least to those not close to us. What lifts the book is its descriptive power and delightful asides. At Oxford: "On the river at night, moving silently through the darkness under trees: suddenly the man punting whispers 'Look!' ...Three naked boys are dancing wildly but without a sound in the moonlight." She writes, too, of sailing with Irvine in the years before the war, something he very much liked to do, and there is "the sound of a jetty underfoot", seaweed and the iron rings to which boats are moored. There is a gift here for using few words to invoke a scene in the reader. Moreover her language has clean, spare lines, and yet it flows; always concise, but never abrupt. One feels that she could have drawn one in had she written of a blade of grass, or a crack in the pavement. Athill has since said that *Instead of a Letter* came to her quite naturally; there was no plan; she could not wait to return home in the evenings and write, and it simply came out the way it did. Perhaps the best books often do.

Instead of a Letter takes Athill's life to 1962, when it was written. It seems to strip her bare, and later books have been even franker. Yet one wonders if something is hidden, deep down. She is English after all. John Preston, who interviewed her for *The Telegraph* in 2011, commented that "while she is very welcoming, there's a natural reserve to her. Something both distant and scrutinising. ...Behind the affability, one suspects, she would be as unsparing in her judgments of other people as she is of herself." There are hints of this in *Instead of a Letter*; now and then some prevailing hypocrisy or the prejudices of her family are coldly skewered. Portraits show a strong chin and steely blue-grey eyes. Athill has, it seemed, hidden nothing from her readers; yet I wonder if we really know who she is.

Or maybe we do. She tells Preston that she has always been a watcher. "Even at times of acute unhappiness I've watched myself being unhappy. I also think I'm one of those people who has never been wholly involved in an emotion, but then I think a lot of writers are like that."

And she, of all people, would know.

Of Pagford and Bradford

In 2012 J. K. Rowling published her first non-Harry Potter book. It was a major publishing event.

First there was the hype. The *Guardian's* correspondent, Decca Aitkenhead, was "required to sign more legal documents than [when] buying a house" before reading *The Casual Vacancy;* as for the author interview: "Its prospect begins to assume the mystique of an audience with Her Majesty – except, of course, that Rowling is famously much, much richer." She was in fact then worth about £620m, according to Sky News.

Then the book came out. In its first week, it sold 124,000 copies in the UK and three times that in the USA. To put that in perspective, the initial print run for a novel is rarely more than 3,000-5,000 copies.

The book divided the critics. But for me, as an Englishman, what mattered is what it told us about ourselves. Those 500,000-odd buyers were confronted with a picture of modern England that many English people could have done without.

The Casual Vacancy is a portrait of Pagford, a small town in the West of England, said to be based on the one in which Ms Rowling grew up, although she has never confirmed this. It begins with the death of a likeable parish councillor who has opposed attempts to shut down the town's methadone clinic and to rid the town of responsibility of the local sink estate – "project", in American parlance – called the Fields. The election that follows for the dead man's council seat is the frame upon which Rowling has hung her portrait of the town's people.

They fall into three basic categories: smug, ineffectual, and disgusting.

The smug include the "first citizen" of Pagford, Council chairman Howard, a shop and cafe owner, 65 years old, of mighty girth and opinions; and his wife Shirley. Like others in the town, they hanker after the company of the local posh family, although the latter are clearly bored by them, and indeed sold the land for the sink estate Howard wants to be rid of so much. The smug also include Parminder, the doctor, who holds liberal views but makes no effort to communicate with her awkward teenage daughter and is unaware that the latter is quietly mutilating herself with a razorblade in the night.

The ineffectual include Colin, a deputy headmaster who lacks social skills and is mentally ill; and Ruth, a nurse who tries to be bright and jolly in a home dominated by a violent inadequate of a husband. The disgusting, besides her husband, include Colin's vile teenage son, who despises his parents and uses his wit and popularity to inflict cruelties on others. Last but not least there's Terri, a middle-aged junkie who lives on the sink estate and has messed up her life, but whose daughter Krystal could maybe be something better. Rowling uses Krystal as a dramatic cipher in a battle between good and evil.

Rowling serves up many characters – in fact, too many too quickly, sometimes. Yet she has taken trouble to try to get inside their heads and to show us who they really are. Thus Howard dreams of the Pagford of his youth, where the poor grew runner beans and potatoes, and hates the Fields with its boarded-up windows, graffiti and satellite dishes. Parminder does not communicate with her daughter but half-knows it, and keeps meaning to try. Colin's horrible teenage son is determined to be "authentic" and does not know that he is actually pretentious. Neither does he really know that he is vicious; in class, he mutters savage insults at Parminder's miserable daughter, wanting to impress the friend next to him. He is unaware that his friend finds the girl's pain discomfiting. Not every character works so well; for example Terri the tragic junkie might have seemed more real, and sympathetic, had she been one of those people who do manage their addiction better. Even so, Rowling's given us some very real characters.

The book ends with a tragedy that a number of them might have prevented, either earlier in the book or – in several cases – in the hour or so before it happened. Several people get their comeuppance, for this or other reasons. In fact, the book is, for all its satirical modernity, a very old-fashioned morality play that, with a slight change of characters and messages, could have come from someone on the right as much as the left.

That's a point that clearly didn't strike the *Daily Mail*'s Jan Moir, who called it "500 pages of relentless socialist manifesto masquerading as literature". The council chairman, Howard, is "middle class, so, of course, he is a racist, pompous twit". Ms Rowling is, says Moir, "on a mission to portray the poor underclasses as plucky but blighted, and the British middle classes as a lumpen mass of the mad and the bad." Actually, Rowling could just as easily have been slammed for failing to include more normal balanced working-class characters rather than the awful Terri. But the charge is not totally unfounded. Even Doug Johnstone in the progressive *Independent* said: "The snobbishness and hypocrisy of the Pagford residents is held up for mild satire throughout, while the deprivation of the Fields is played with a straight bat, and that unevenness of tone rankles."

Other reviews were far more generous (*Time, The Wall Street Journal, The Scotsman* and *The Economist* all gave the book a warm welcome). Yet there was food for thought in one of the hostile reviews, by Michiko Kakutani in *The New York Times*. The book, she said, showed us nothing of people at their best; instead, "we are left with a dismaying sense of human weakness, selfishness and gossipy stupidity."

None of this is entirely fair. So Rowling has some prejudices; well, she is scarcely alone in that. She could have shut up and enjoyed her considerable wealth. Or she could have trotted out any old trash, knowing that, with her name on it, it would at least sell a few copies. She could, like many British novelists of the last half-century, have written genteel novels about middle-class marital difficulties. Or books about food for people who already spend too much time cooking; or she could have restored a farmhouse in some fashionably unfashionable part of France or Spain and then written an amusing book patronising the local peasants. Instead, she is, as one says nowadays, "engaged"; she has painted a vivid, well-written warts-and-all portrait of modern Britain. To be sure, she has majored on the warts; but, well, there *are* a few, aren't there? Some of the characters, it's true, don't come off – but others do, and the book is a genuine page-turner. *The Casual Vacancy* is a flawed but courageous attempt to write about the way we English are in 2013.

If it does not quite work, is it because the characters are cynically drawn to order, as some of these reviews implied? Or Is it, as Kakutani implied, because the novel's view of humans is so cruel? If so, is that Rowling's fault – or could it be because the modern Brit is not much to write about?

Actually the answer to this might be messier than the reviewers would have you believe.

*

After finishing *The Casual Vacancy*, I wanted to return to a book that I had read before, and have long loved. Whereas *The Casual Vacancy* is a caustic view of England in 2013, J. B. Priestley's *Bright Day* is a thoughtful portrait of 1913, recalled 30 years later by a man in middle age. Although now rediscovered and republished, the book, like many of Priestley's, was forgotten for years. I should not myself have known of it had I not found an ancient copy some 20 years ago in a secondhand bookshop in the Middle East, and bought it purely because I had little to read.

The book opens in an expensive but bleak cliff-top hotel in Cornwall. It is the spring of 1946 and a successful but jaded middle-aged screenwriter, Gregory Dawson, has been sent there by a producer to finish an urgent script. Dawson is English, but spent many years in Hollywood, then returned at the start of the Second World War. At the hotel, he works; there is not much else to do; the weather is mixed, the (rationed) food mean and dull, the other guests old, wealthy and sclerotic. However, one older couple catch his eye. Discreet enquiry tells him they are a wealthy and titled couple, Lord and Lady Harndean; the husband, a businessman, received a lordship for services rendered to the prewar Chamberlain government. Dawson is sure they have met, yet he cannot place them. Then a day or two later the band in the lounge play a Schubert trio that jogs his memory, and he remembers who they are.

Dawson is back in in 1912. His father, who is in the Indian Civil Service, and his mother both die suddenly of a fever in India just as he, an only child of 17 or so at school in England, is preparing to take his entrance examination for Cambridge. Too shocked to sit the exam, he finishes the school year and is then taken in by an aunt and uncle in Bruddersford (a thinly disguised Bradford); and instead of attending Oxford or Cambridge, as befits the son of an ICS officer, he finds himself working for – in effect, apprenticed to – a wool merchant in a Northern city.

This does not trouble him, for the sudden loss of his parents has rendered everything meaningless. In any case, he already knows that he wants to write. He reads widely, especially poetry; and in Bruddersford he discovers some of the magic of being young as well as its oppression.

At the time when verse becomes magical to us, there is also another sorcery, created by glimpses, brief and tantalizing, of people we do not know... Later in life we merely see interesting strangers ...the mystery, the magic, the sense and promise of unexplored bright worlds, no longer haunts us.

On the tram he often notices a group, probably a family, with lively young people; they fascinate him. And then he starts work, and finds that Alington, the local head of the wool merchant for which he is working, is the father of that family. Bit by bit he comes to meet them all, including the three attractive daughters; and there is an air of adolescent magic discovery. In the winter and spring of 1912-1913 the young Dawson accompanies this magical family to the pantomime, to classical concerts, and finally out to the high moors beyond the city limits, where long days are spent in bright sunshine.

It is after one such day on the high, bright Pennine moors that the Alington family, with Dawson, return to Bruddersford on a May evening in 1913, and decide to have some music. Three of them are playing the Schubert trio when a youngish couple enter unannounced: "And then there were two strangers standing in the doorway, among the splinters of the Schubert."

They are the Nixeys. Malcolm Nixey has been sent by the London office, ostensibly to learn the business, but actually to force Alington out. His wife, meanwhile, will stray, and in so doing will wreck the life of one of Alington's daughters. Together they will destroy the family, and, indirectly, they will cause a terrible death. Then, just over a year later Dawson will leave for the Western Front, leaving the Alingtons among the splinters of their lives.

Dawson never returns to Bruddersford. But when on a cold spring day in 1946 he hears the Schubert and sees Lord and Lady Harndean at the same time, he knows that they were, before ennobling, the Nixeys. Over the next few days he tries to recall, for the first time in years, his life in the last two years before the first war, and in so doing, tries to make sense of the life he has led since. The story switches between 1946 and 1912-1914 as memory leads Dawson to change his life, absorbing hard but decent lessons from a past that he had thought he had understood.

The Casual Vacancy, set in 2013, is well-paced, well-constructed and has real insight. Yet it is oddly unsatisfying. *Bright Day*, set in 1913, is one of the best novels in the English language. What separates them?

To some extent, it is Rowling's partisan approach noted by one or two of the reviews; they are not being entirely fair, but she does seem to have an agenda. In 1940 George Orwell, in his essay *Inside the Whale*, praised Henry Miller's *Tropic of Cancer* precisely because it was completely amoral and therefore flowed completely from experience. Books with an agenda, Orwell contended, did not communicate with the reader. Those that did, were by authors simply overwhelmed by experience, for we could better identify with their feelings. To support his argument he compared the literature of the First World War with that of the Spanish war just ended:

The immediately striking thing about the Spanish war books, at any rate those written in English, is their shocking dullness and badness. ...[They are] by cocksure partisans telling you what to think, whereas the books about the Great War were written by common soldiers or junior officers who did not even pretend to understand what the whole thing was about. Books like All Quiet on the Western Front, Le Feu, A Farewell to Arms... ...*are saying in effect, "What the hell is all this about? God knows. All we can do is to endure."*

Rowling does seem to have a picture that she wants to present of Pagford. The characters must fit the role she has determined for them and now and then one does feel that their strings are pulled in pursuit of an argument. (Orwell, in *Inside the Whale*, actually goes so far as to use the word "marionette" of the everyday literature to which he feels Miller is superior.) Priestley, by contrast, in this book (although not in some others), simply expresses the force of the past and the challenge of the future as he feels them. This contrast is evident in *The Casual Vacancy*, good though it is (and it really is).

But Rowling faces a challenge. I suggested earlier that the fault could also lie with us – that we are, in effect, now a sorry lot to write *about*. How did we get this way?

*

In *Bright Day*, Dawson's friend Jock has a very strange sister, who communicates with the dead and perceives other worlds. (This was not unusual in 1913, although spiritualism really peaked a few years later, after the losses of the First World War.) One night Dawson dines with them; her otherworldliness irritates and unsettles him. She remarks, in her vague way, that: "It's all... quite different ... from what you imagine ... Like the dead and the living ... some people you think are alive are really dead ... and others you think are dead are really alive. ..."

Encountering the Nixeys, now the Harndeans, 32 years later,

Dawson is struck that they had "always lacked something essential and vital"; in essence, they are in some way not quite alive. They had succeeded, he says, in "everything they had attempted, [but] it was only in Flatland, among triumphs cut out of the thinnest cardboard." This is driven home, in different ways, at several points in the book. A night out with Nixey in prewar Bradford (well, all right, Bruddersford) is notable for the lack of enjoyment, or otherwise, that Nixey derives from it. In his bleak cliff-top hotel in the wake of another war, Dawson feels this has become typical. He reflects that there are now far more "rootless, parasitic and acquisitive people about"; and that "what had once been a tiny fifth column was now a settled and familiar army of occupation."

Is that it? Did the Nixeys take over, leaving Ms Rowling with no-one real to write about?

Priestley might have understood that argument. As Dawson, he bitterly describes a night at the music hall in 1919, "chorus girls swarming over gangways into the auditorium, and half-tight fat profiteers in the stalls waving rattles. ...This ...greedy rabble didn't seem worth the life of one stammering lance-corporal. We'd thrown away the best, only to keep and to fatten the worst." That is, in part, what happened to us; and people like my parents, born in 1920 and 1922, would have found it credible enough, for there persisted into my own lifetime a feeling that the best young men had gone to Flanders and that what was left was not quite the same. In 1914, and 1939, the best *were* full of passionate intensity, and were butchered for their pains. The rest remained to infest Pagford a century or so later, and there is not much that Rowling can do for them.

But there is something else here, and again Priestley has seen it; Nixey has no trade. Quite late in the book, when it is clear that Nixey will destroy Alington, the hard, kind Yorkshireman who works for him, and to whom Dawson has been apprenticed, re-signs in disgust. As he prepares to go, he tells Dawson: "If a chap learns a trade he won't do so much 'arm. ...But these smart chaps who know nowt... only thing they've a respect for is money."

Is that us too? As I come to the end of my own working life, I find myself surrounded by people with vaguely-defined profes-sions, management consultants and the like – people who do not make anything, but are often unleashed upon those who do in the name of efficiency or lean production. The people of Pagford, too, seem short of skills. True, two are solicitors, and one is a doctor – and one works for a printer, though we are not told in what capac-ity. One is a nurse. For the rest, nobody really makes anything; there are no welders, no master builders, no draughtsmen or dress-makers, no pride. Who are they? Who are we? One is reminded of a Khalil Gibran poem, the title of which, *Pity the Nation*, was bor-rowed by the late Robert Fisk for his magisterial account of the Leb-anese civil war:

Pity the nation that wears a cloth it does not weave,
eats a bread it does not harvest,
and drinks a wine that flows not from its own wine-press.

*

This, then, is part of Rowling's challenge; we are less to write about than we were in Priestley's time. Yet even this does not explain why *Bright Day* is such a good book.

Bright Day is a novel of remembrance and the richer for it. It must be partly autobiographical; Priestley, who was from Brad-ford, went to work for a wool merchant at 16, and left aged 20 to fight in the First World War – an experience that marked him, as it did the fictional Dawson. Priestley too never moved back to Bradford (though, unlike Dawson, he never cut his links with the city). Although more a novelist and playwright than a screenwriter, he did have contacts in Hollywood and visited the US a number of times in the 1930s, spending many months there. However, he spent the Second World War in Britain, and was very active in the media and in public life. He was more or less the same age as his Gregory Dawson and the book was published in the year it was set, 1946.

Priestley wrote several books about parts of his life, but never wrote a proper autobiography. The closest he got was *Margin Released* (1962), a series of three autobiographical sketches, each of 100 pages or so. The first concerns his time as a very young man at the wool merchant's in the years just before the First World War, and there is a clear sense of a time when the world was new. *Bright Day* itself drips with the remembrance of things past; seen from the bleakness of 1946, Christmas 1912 is "a vast Flemish still-life of turkeys, geese, hams, puddings, candied fruit, dark purple bottles, figs, dates, chocolates, holly... It was Cockaigne and ...there has been nothing like it since and perhaps there never will be anything like it again." A concert in the city's main hall, Dawson's first and thrilling night out with the glamorous Alingtons, is lit by gaslight, so the hall is steeped in a golden October-like light. A bright spring day on the moorlands begins "in an almost empty little train, chuff-chuffing towards the Dales through the vacant and golden Sunday morning. (There don't seem to be any trains like that any more... All transport now seems to be fuss, crowds, rain and anger.)"

This is the key to *Bright Day*: remembrance. It is not mere nostalgia; there is no weird yearning for a country that never existed. In 1914 Britain and Europe were heaving with social unrest. It was a tense world with rotten underpinnings, brought wonderfully to life by the late Barbara Tuchman, herself born in 1912, in *The Proud Tower*; and recently by Michael Portillo in the radio series *1913: The Year Before*. There was no Cockaigne. Priestley was not so daft as not to realise this. He was on the Left, and was a fierce social critic, most notably in his 1934 travelogue *English Journey*. At about the same time, in his satirical novel about the Press, *Wonder Hero*, he hinted he had no great love of Empire either. His work was rarely divorced from reality, and *Bright Day* is not a paean to some pre-lapsarian Edwardian heaven stolen from us by the Great War. Rather, it is a very personal journey back through that time of one's life when everything glittered with the unexplained and undiscovered.

Priestley died in 1984, when Rowling was at university. By that time he was not as widely read as he had been. He was not a perfect writer; as a technician, he was inferior to many of his contemporaries, including Orwell, Evelyn Waugh, or Graham Greene. He could be pompous and wordy. He could certainly write for the gallery and could, if he wished, serve up more ham than a wholesale butcher. But at his best he was superb. And *Bright Day* is one of the great English novels of the 20th century. I wanted to write about it because I thought it told us how we got, God help us, to Pagford. But the real gift of this book is that it is deeply personal, a far-off place of bellowing Yorkshiremen and enormous lamb chops and cricket and bright sunlit moorlands, tinged by the magic of youth and remembered by a tired man in a pinched, bleak postwar world. It is not really Rowling's fault, yet somehow we see Pagford in 2013 in a snapshot from Google Earth; Flatland, seen from above. Bradford in 1913 is remembered in relief, at length, from a seat on a high fell as the bright day turns into late afternoon and then to dusk, the shadows climbing slowly towards us across the fields and the bracken and the drystone walls.

The Endgame in the Age of Stupid

Consider this as the plot of a science-fiction novel. A scientist discovers the secret of eternal life and produces Juvenex, a pill that rejuvenates. Its results are miraculous. It can reverse the aging process; one's hair recovers its cover, the skin its elasticity, the breasts their firmness. The British government wonders whether this is a good idea, knowing that the old, young forever, will block and frustrate the young, and that there will be more and more mouths to feed. But the secret is out; the people clamour for Juvenex; and the government must fight an election against a Conservative opposition that promises to make the drug available. Of course the opposition win, and everyone starts popping the pill like there is no tomorrow. Before long the rest of the Western world follows suit.

Then a Chinese government hostile to the West discovers that those who have taken the pill are sensitive to radioactivity, which reverses its effects and causes its users to age so rapidly that they become hideous. It starts an extended round of nuclear "testing". The West spins downward to collapse.

This novel was real enough. It was called *Not With a Bang* (1965), and was by the British writer Chapman Pincher. who died in 2014 aged 100. Pincher was famous in the 1960s and 1970s as a journalist with a particular interest in defence and intelligence, and several of his books had quite an impact on the security world – especially *Their Trade is Treachery* (1981), in which he fingered a former director of MI5 as a Soviet spy. It is less well known that he wrote five or six novels; I don't think many people read them today. *Not With a Bang* is pretty much forgotten now, and appears to be out of print – a pity, for it is rather good.

The title itself is drawn from the closing stanza of T. S. Eliot's *The Hollow Men* (1925):

This is the way the world ends
This is the way the world ends
This is the way the world ends
Not with a bang but a whimper.

Was Eliot right? Pincher clearly thought so; in the closing scenes of *Not With a Bang*, thousands of people, grotesquely aged, bent and deformed, shuffle together into the sea. But Robert Frost, writing like Eliot in the wake of the First World War, was not so sure:

Some say the world will end in fire,
Some say in ice. From what I've tasted of desire
I hold with those who favor fire.

Eliot himself would say in old age that that the hydrogen bomb had negated that closing stanza of *The Hollow Men*, and that he would not have written it again. But of course we do not know how our world ends – with fire or ice, a bang or a whimper.

Or do we?

When the Soviet bloc collapsed in 1989 there was a tendency to believe that the capitalist, liberal democracy had triumphed and would now prevail everywhere; that this was, in Francis Fukuyama's famous phrase, the end of history. At least one philosopher realised early on that this was pernicious nonsense and that, far from being freed from history, we might soon have a surfeit of it. This was John Gray, then Professor of European Thought at LSE. In 2007 he published his book *Black Mass: Apocalyptic Religion and the Death of Utopia*.

The book propounds the thesis that our thought, at least in the West, has been shaped by religions – chiefly Christianity and Islam – that foresee some final apocalypse, an endpoint toward which human affairs progress. In Gray's view, this has made Western thought teleological – that is to say, everything has a purpose that is defined by its ultimate end; and this perspective has pervaded not only religion, but the secular thought that has succeeded it. In this respect, he sees Marxism and Nazism as direct descendants of Christian thought. Teleology, in this view, is as likely to cause us to believe in a coming paradise as in an apocalypse.

One does not have to accept Gray's theory wholesale to note the warning for us all in *Black Mass*: that if we are too sure that we are progressing towards a given endpoint, we may give history a little push in that direction – and then find out it was the wrong one. But also, those in control may feel, as Fascists and some revolutionary socialists have done, that their theory of history justifies violence against others. The implication is that the pragmatist, with no such theory, is the ultimate humanitarian.

But for me there is an even more important implication: History is not fated to progress. It can go backwards.

Which brings us to Joseph Tainter.

*

Tainter is a Professor in the Department of Environment and Society at Utah State University. He trained as an anthropologist at Berkeley, obtaining his PhD in 1975. He has published widely; the publications list on his CV goes on for several pages. But he is best known for his landmark book *The Collapse of Complex Societies* (1988).

There have been plenty of books on the collapse of civilization.

259

There is no mystery as to why, according to Tainter. "The image of lost civilizations is compelling," he writes in *Collapse*. "Cities buried by drifting sands or tangled jungle ...The image is troublesome to all, , not only for the vast human endeavors that have mysteriously failed, but also for the enduring implications of these failures ...civilizations are fragile, impermanent things."

And yet, argues Tainter, there has been relatively little study of how complex societies collapse. There has been a "seemingly inexorable" trend towards complexity, the growth of ever-larger settlements, and technology. We now understand more and more about the way this happens. "Yet the instances when this almost universal trend has been disrupted by collapse have not received a corresponding level of attention."

In fact, on the evidence of Tainter's own literature review in *Collapse*, it has had quite a bit of attention. But that review does show how fragmented and, at times, subjective that study has been. Tainter's aim is to present a dispassionate theory of collapse based on the evidence, and that he has done. Tainter's theory, put crudely, is that the more complex a society becomes, the more that complexity costs in relation to its benefits. And at some point, it is no longer worthwhile.

Tainter begins by telling us what collapse looks like. He describes several such events, from the Western Chou Empire to the Chacoans and Hohokam of New Mexico and Arizona respectively. He avoids hyperbole, but he is not dry. At times he adds detail that the archaeologists have found; thus the end of the Casa Grande society in Mexico: "The dead were buried in city water canals and plaza drains." The collapse of the lowland Maya seems to have resulted in a population drop from around 3 million to about 450,000 in just 75 years; in the last years, according to archaeologists who have examined the bones, the population was increasingly stressed and weak. Tainter does not say so, but this must have involved terrible suffering. He also quotes Stanley Casson's 1937 book, *Progress and Catastrophe: An Anatomy of Human Adventure,* in which the author talks of the sudden desolation in what had been Roman Britain after 400 AD.

Tainter defines the collapse of a complex society. It occurs when there is "a rapid, significant loss of an established level of sociopolitical complexity." This includes the loss of specialization – of individuals, but also of geographical entities. The loss of distinct occupations is important. Tainter states that a hunter-gatherer society may contain only a few dozen "distinct social personalities" (in fact one suspects it is less). But a modern European census will, he says, recognize 10-20,000. What will happen when individuals with specialized functions cease to perform them?

Tainter makes a distinction between complexity and civilization; he insists that he is discussing the first and not the second. Indeed he regards the very word 'civilization' as a value-judgment and, as a rationalist, he does not like those. He is particularly rough on the historians Arnold Toynbee (*A Study of History*) and Oswald Spengler (*The Decline of the West*). "Such biases have no place in objective social sciences, and a concept [civilization] that is so laden with this problem is better abandoned or rethought." In any case, he points out, the collapse of complexity need not be followed by the immediate disappearance of all cultural phenomena. But his own discussion of societal collapse suggests that it often is (in particular, in the case of the lowland Maya, which he discusses in detail).

In any case, even if one accepts his statement at face value, the concept of 'civilization' – what constitutes, in a sense, almost the whole of our non-mechanical life outside the family unit – is widely accepted, even if badly defined. To most of us, a wholesale collapse in complexity does equate to a collapse of our civilization, however we may define it; everything meaningful will be lost, and this explains our fear of dystopia. Stanley Casson, mentioned earlier, had witnessed Istanbul after the collapse of Ottoman authority in 1918, with intermittent electricity, abandoned trams littering the streets, corpses at street corners, dead horses, no drains, unsafe water, and (as quoted by Tainter): "a police force which had largely become bandit, living on blackmail from citizens in lieu of pay ...All this was the result of only about three weeks' abandonment by the civil authorities of their duties." This last example, especially, encapsulates the fear we all feel about a sudden breakdown. Tainter clearly understands this. But he is determined to be completely objective, and that does explain why his theory of collapse commands as much respect as it did when *The Collapse of Complex Societies* was first published over 30 years ago.

That theory, as stated earlier, is that as a society grows more complex, the cost of that complexity will rise. It is not hard to see why. Everyone who moves away from the land and into a specialized role (let us say, from peasant to stablehand, or from stablehand to clerk) moves farther from primary production, and is producing nothing directly. (Tainter defines that production, including food, as energy.) Moreover their training will become more specialized and thus more expensive. Meanwhile the cost of their subsistence falls upon those still producing that energy in the form of bread, pulses, whatever.

Of course the specialized roles do contribute to primary production; that clerk may be helping to maintain an irrigation system, or a doctor may cure maladies that would otherwise need palliative care, the cost of which would fall on everybody. This is because societies become complex in order to solve problems (such as irrigation or healthcare). But at some point the return on this specialization will fall relative to its cost. "Investment in sociopolitical complexity as a problem-solving response," says Tainter, "often reaches a point of declining marginal returns."

He explains why in terms of what he refers to as an "energy subsidy"; as societies grow in complexity, the surplus production this requires will be gained through conquest of new land or through new sources of energy. These will be acquired in order of their ease of acquisition. The Romans naturally occupied the nearest and most fertile lands first; it was easier to bring grain from North Africa by boat than by land from inland Europe.

It is not hard to find other examples. The English turned to coal when they had cut down the forests; as they dug deeper to get it, the steam engine became necessary to pump water out of the deep workings. And so to fracking and to nuclear energy, with the specialized roles they require; all are more complicated, and require more effort and training, per joule released than burning wood.

The energy subsidy becomes harder to obtain. Complexity grows. The rate of return is falling. At some point society will cease to support its own complexity, because its costs have weakened the population (as in the case of the Maya) or because the state demands so much taxation from its people that they find its dissolution a rational choice. In fact the latter is Tainter's view of the Roman Empire; the barbarians were not resisted, in Tainter's view, because doing so had become so costly in taxes that the peasants thought their rule a better option; and they were, at the time, right. Civilization (or, for Tainter, complexity) does not "become decadent". It simply fails to provide the return on investment that it needs to survive.

The Collapse of Complex Societies is an impressive book. It is a masterclass in clear thinking and expression, the collection and presentation of evidence, and the ordering of facts so that they become knowledge. It should probably be compulsory reading for anyone about to embark on a Masters dissertation.

But that does not mean we can't pick holes in it if we choose. For one thing, to me Tainter is too dismissive of the environment as a cause of collapse. He does not ignore it, but says that environmental challenges are problems and complexity is a problem-solving strategy; in effect, of complexity can't deal with (say) climate change, it has failed to provide that marginal rate of return on investment. It is true that the environment is one of many challenges that complexity is supposed to meet and a society may be judged by the extent to which it does so, a point well made in Jared Diamond's more recent and also excellent book, *Collapse*. Even so, to treat the environment as one more challenge may be too simple. Biophysical factors – desiccation, a vile winter, disease – can appear suddenly in forms that a society had no reason to expect.

Another point that Tainter does not address – and in this case, he does not raise it – is that a society's complexity may yield sufficient returns and yet not be *perceived* as doing so. It's with that in mind that we should park Tainter for now and move on to the second of these three books.

*

Tom Nichols is a lecturer in international and strategic affairs who taught for some years at two of America's most exclusive institutions, Dartmouth College and later Georgetown University. He is now Professor of National Security Affairs at the U.S. Naval War College, a venerable institution in Newport, Rhode Island. He is a conservative, but with a small C; he never bought into Trump and finally left the Republican Party after the Kavanaugh confirmation hearings. In 2017 he published *The Death of Expertise: The Campaign Against Established Knowledge and Why It Matters*. It's just been re-published in a new paperback edition.

The Death of Expertise is, in some respects, a good old-fashioned rant. The possession of facts does not, says Nichols, equate to knowledge, but too many people do not understand the difference. The Internet has driven some of this, making everyone an instant expert. It offers an "apparent shortcut to expertise", but actually just a limitless supply of facts, which does not constitute knowledge. "The Internet," says Nichols, "lets a billion flowers bloom, and most of them stink."

Ignorance, says Nichols, has become hip. He cites the raw milk movement – people who demand untreated dairy products. He quotes the *New Yorker* (Dana Goodyear, April 2012) saying that untreated milk, which is often from pasture animals, is sometimes "richer and sweeter, and, sometimes, to retain a whiff of the farm – the slightly discomfiting flavor known to connoisseurs as 'cow butt'." As Nichols points out, the Centers for Disease Control reckon unpasteurized products are 150 times more likely to cause food-borne illnesses. Still, says Nichols, it's a free country, and if adults wish to risk a trip to hospital for a whiff of cow's arse, that's up to them. He also describes how Gwyneth Paltrow has encouraged people to steam their vaginas, which she claims (says Nichols; I haven't checked) cleans your uterus and helps balance your hormones. Nichols blames the Internet for much of this nonsense. "In an earlier time," he rumbles, "a sensible American woman would have had to exert a great deal of initiative to find out how a Hollywood actress parboils her plumbing."

True. But people do not need the Internet to be daft. I remember, a few years before it arrived, there was a fad for colonic irrigation, which some very fashionable people did in London in about

1990. I asked a doctor friend what the health benefits were likely to be. "Peritonitis," she said crisply. The following year I was travelling in Ecuador and found a craze for a wrist ornament that was supposed to deliver energy and equilibrium. It was, of course, tosh. In an earlier era the travel writer Norman Lewis and his brother-in law, passing through Madrid in 1934, decided to investigate a reported mania amongst *madrileños* for drinking animal blood. They visited a slaughterhouse, but were "deterred by a woman on her way out, made terrible by the smile painted by the blood on her lips." We have never needed the Internet to be bizarre.

However, Nichols is not simply being (or at least, not *only* being) a grumpy old man. There is a serious point here. An expert would quickly tell you that unpasteurized milk is not as safe and that steaming, or flooding, one's insides is best not done unsupervised. In ceasing to respect expertise, people no longer acknowledge that the world is now too complicated to be run without it. This was directly reflected in the 2016 election result, according to Nichols. Trump's election was, in his view, partly achieved by sneering at experts – which tapped into a long-standing American prejudice. Why is this happening?

Nichols has more than one explanation; the Internet, to be sure, but he also cites a decline in academia. He opines that universities are not teaching critical thinking; that they are instead just peddling the "college experience", part of the "commodification of education". Given the mountain of debt with which students emerge from college, it is not surprising that they see themselves, sometimes, as customers, rather than realise they are there to learn intellectual rigour. This is also a problem in the UK, where the introduction of tuition fees means that students are, increasingly, being sold a product, and that they expect to get concrete promised returns afterwards, having paid for it.

Are universities really commodifying education and abandon-ing the obligation to make people think? A £65,000 settlement won in 2019 by a student in England, Pok Wong, who felt her degree had not been meaningful, could be seen as a demonstration of this. However, objective data on this is hard to find, and universities have always varied in quality. Still, Nichols may have a point – he talks, for example, about lecturers being evaluated the way a Yelp review is done of a restaurant, and it is by definition absurd to have situations where all the students are above average.

Academic research gets a battering as well. Nichols devotes a chapter to saying that experts themselves have been producing re-search that cannot be replicated (there is a "replicability crisis" go-ing on, especially in some areas of the social sciences). There is great pressure on academics to publish, which does not help. Nei-ther are research journals always so rigorous as they should be. I cannot help wondering how Andrew Wakefield's notorious MMR-and-autism study was published by the The Lancet, but it would at least not have published it had it suspected that data had been fal-sified (and it eventually retracted it). Other journals might not have been so scrupulous.

Nichols also blames the media for failing to check facts and for spreading disinformation through sheer laziness. The classic case he describes is a story that claimed new research had found that chocolate helps weight loss. There is of course no real evidence for anything of the kind. The story had been cooked up by a science writer, John Bohannon, to demonstrate bad science and how easily its "results" could be accepted. The institute that was claimed to have done the research did not exist. But the journalists who spread the story did nothing to check. Journalists, like all of us, are sometimes lazy and want a ready-made story. Not all journalists are like this, of course – one could cite for example Will Saletan of slate.com, who wrote in depth about genetically modified organisms. There are others. But Nichols is right; the media are part of the problem. All of this has helped build public distrust of "experts".

But perhaps the most important factor in this distrust is one that Nichols mentions only briefly. He quotes political scientist Richard Hofstadter, writing in *Anti-Intellectualism in American Life* (1963), as follows: "In the original American dream, the omnicompetence of the common man was fundamental and indispensable ...Today he reads about a whole range of issues and acknowledges, if he is candid with himself, that he has not acquired competence to judge most of them." Hofstadter said that this complexity induced feelings of helplessness and anger among a people that knew they were at the mercy of smarter elites. "Once," says Hofstadter, "the intellectual was gently ridiculed because he was not needed; now he is fiercely resented because he is needed too much."

This is a rich vein that Nichols could have mined much more deeply than he does. If people seek to abandon complexity, could it be as much because of this as for any objective reason, such as its declining rate of return? As Nichols himself says, Trump's election was partly achieved by sneering at experts. But as he also says: "It is ...ignorant narcissism for laypeople to believe that they can maintain a large and advanced nation without listening to the voices of those more educated and experienced than themselves ....The celebration of ignorance cannot launch communications satellites ...or provide for effective medications."

Which brings us to Michael Lewis.

*

Lewis is a successful writer and journalist with 18 non-fiction books to his credit. Originally from New Orleans, he graduated in art history and wanted to pursue it as a career, but found there was no money in it so became a bond salesman in the City of London instead. After a few years he returned to the States and became a financial journalist. Now in his late fifties, he has written widely on Wall Street, the roots of the financial crisis and subjects as diverse as technology and baseball. He has a particular interest in risk.

In 2017, he wrote a series of pieces for *Vanity Fair* on the transition to the Trump administration, highlighting the Department of Energy, the US Department of Agriculture (USDA) and the Department of Commerce. In 2018 these pieces matured into a book, *The Fifth Risk*. It looks at the experiences of the civil servants in those departments as Trump took over. This sounds like a rather dull book. It isn't. Lewis has a clear, deadpan approach; he nowhere tells the reader what to think – but you are left in no doubt, at the end, of what you have learned.

In essence, Lewis describes an administration with no interest whatever in the government machine and no understanding of what it does. Normally, a candidate recruits a transition team that will base itself in Washington in the later stages of a campaign, preparing policy and choosing and screening the 4,000-odd political appointees that will need to be put into the various departments during the period between the election and the inauguration. Of Trump's team, only Governor Chris Christie understood how important this would be, and how much work would be involved. Trump himself did not, and only reluctantly permitted Christie to set up such a team.

Three days after the election, Christie and much of his team were fired, and the files and references they had collected were junked. The appointments were not made. Over the next two months, the senior civil servants at the three departments waited for the Trump transition teams to arrive. Almost none of them did, leaving the machinery of government rudderless.

The staff at Energy were taken aback when, quite simply, no-one turned up. Two weeks after the election, they read in the papers that one Thomas Pyle, an energy-company lobbyist who had worked for the Koch brothers, was to lead the transition team at Energy. Pyle visited once, briefly, but then stayed away. He eventually sent a request for a list of officials who had been involved in climate meetings. He then disappeared. Meanwhile the Chief Financial Officer of the Environmental Protection Agency under Obama, Joe Hezir, received no instructions as to whether he should go or stay. "Not knowing what to do, but without anyone to replace him, the CFO of a $30 billion operation just up and left," says Lewis. Even six months after Trump took office, there was still no-one to run the federal disasters management agency, FEMA; the Transportation Security Administration (TSA); the Centers for Disease Control; or the Patent Office. When the senior appointees finally did appear, they seemed mainly chosen to dismantle their departments and had little interest in understanding their work.

Having told us all this, Lewis then briefs us on the wide range of things these department actually do. It is far more than we suppose. The US Government's two million employees manage a portfolio of risks that no smaller entity could manage. They include the obvious ones, such as financial crises, terrorist attacks and hurricanes. But they also include those we are less likely to think of, such as a prescription drug suddenly proving to have been addictive and dangerous, and killing thousands of people a year (Lewis does not say so, but he is clearly thinking of the opioid crisis). Other risks, Lewis adds, feel unreal – a virus that kills millions (that is easier to imagine now!), economic inequality that causes violence, and so on. "Maybe the least visible risks," he adds, are "of things *not* happening that, with better government, might have happened. A cure for cancer, for instance."

What Lewis is describing is complexity, and the many skills on which it draws. As we've seen, Tainter pointed out that a modern European census will recognize 10-20,000 distinct roles. I also quoted above Nichols's statement that: "The celebration of ignorance cannot launch communications satellites ...or provide for effective medications." But what this complexity also does is manage risk.

Lewis interviews the former Chief Risk Officer of the Department of Energy and is told that there are five key risks that the Department must manage. The first four are nuclear weapons, loss of or accident with; the nuclear threat from North Korea; likewise from Iran; and threats to the electric grid.

The fifth risk, which gives the book its title, is project management.

Lewis does not explain the latter; he is a show-not-tell writer and takes us instead to one of the DoE's biggest projects, the Hanford nuclear facility in the Pacific Northwest. In 1943 the US army evicted the population of a large area in eastern Washington State and transformed it into a nuclear facility. Between 1943 and 1987, when it closed, Hanford created two-thirds of the US's plutonium and supplied the material for 70,000 nuclear weapons. It is now being cleaned up. According to Lewis, the DoE pours $3 billion, or 10% of its budget, into the place. Asked what it would take to clean it up, the former Chief Risk Officer tells Lewis: "A century and a hundred billion dollars."

"The people who created the plutonium for the first bombs, in the 1940s and early 1950s, were understandably in too much of a rush to worry about what might happen afterward," says Lewis.

"They simply dumped 120 million gallons of high-level waste, and another *444 billion* gallons of contaminated liquid, into the ground. ...Beneath Hanford, a massive underground glacier of radioactive sludge is moving slowly but relentlessly toward the Columbia River."

In short, complexity still generates that rate of return, for its loss would be a catastrophe. There would be nobody and nothing to manage this risk. But how well is that understood?

What has changed is not the rate of return on complexity but our perception of it. Joe Klein, reviewing *The Fifth Risk* in *The New York Times* in October 2018, asked whether we have: "Grown too lazy and silly and poorly educated to sustain a working democracy? We live in a moment when tribal bumper stickers — both left and right — pass for politics, when ignorance and grievance drive policy. The federal government exists at a level of complexity most people just can't be bothered to understand."

Richard Hofstadter was right; we resent our lack of control of the human machine. But we cannot do without it, and if resentment and willful ignorance make us try, we will find out why. Especially if we live near Hanford. That underground glacier of radioactive sludge could be our future; this is the way the world ends – not with a bang but with a peevish, agonised, long-drawn-out whimper.

But it hasn't happened yet, and I do not believe in any form of predestination. I began this piece with a quotation from T.S. Eliot's *The Hollow Men*. Let's end with one from his *Little Gidding* (1942):

Sin is Behovely, but
All shall be well, and
All manner of thing shall be well …

The words are not Eliot's; they are those of the 14th-century Julian of Norwich, a woman who witnessed a savage age (she lived through the Black Death), but in whose teachings God is seen as ultimately loving and merciful. These words tell us that sin – by which, it seems, she meant all bad things – is necessary ('behovely') for our self-knowledge, but that God will forgive all. So perhaps that radioactive sludge, or some other avoidable disaster – maybe the COVID pandemic – will be our wake-up call; we will understand the benefits of expertise, and of complexity; and "all manner of thing" may yet be well. After all, Tainter is describing a mechanism; he at no point says that it is our certain fate. It is for us to create our future, and we must do so.

A Life in the Saddle

It is November, and a cold morning in in New York. I walk two blocks down to Central Park North, where a line of blue CitiBikes wait in a stand. It's just before eight and there are still plenty there, so I choose carefully; one of the latest ones, with the infinitely-variable gears, a lovely smooth twistgrip, and a seat post that is not so worn that one can't see the seat-height markers.

My bag goes in the basket at the front, then it's time for some quick pre-flight routines. Check the brakes and tyres; you don't want to take the bike out if it has a problem – you'll only have to put it back and report the fault before the stand will let you take another. Adjust the seat-post; after much trial and error, I now put it between four and five. Then the key with the barcode goes in the slot; there's a clicking and whirring, a flash of amber lights, then a green one, and the bike slides backwards onto the sidewalk. Time to go.

*

The bike's been with us a while. Its ancestor was the Velocipede, a sort of weird wheeled hobby-horse that appeared in Germany in the 1810s. Pedals arrived much later, but there was, as yet, no way of gearing them; they had to be attached to the hub of the front wheel, and the only way to get gearing high enough for progress was to make that wheel enormous.

The result was the lethal penny-farthing, with its huge front wheel and tiny rear one and its rider sitting some feet above the rocky roadway onto which he would, all too often, be ejected by

274

some emergency, vagary of the surface, or his own lack of adroit-ness when mounting or dismounting. Nonetheless, as BikeSnob-NYC (of whom more later) puts it: "for the first time people could move themselves quickly without the aid of steam, wind, or hairy, flatulent animals."

And it wasn't long before, for the first but not the last time, some idiot decided to ride round the world. His name was Thomas Stevens; born into a poor family England, he had moved to the US at 17. He made it round the world in less than two years, via Con-stantinople, Delhi and Hong Kong, arriving home at the end of 1886. The tradition of the eccentric cyclist had begun.

But by the time Stevens got home, the roller chain had been invented and in England J. K. Starley had invented the safety bi-cycle, which had (in general) two wheels of more or less equal size, a diamond frame and a saddle not far from the road so there was less far to fall.

And it's a safety bicycle that, in all essentials, I'm riding today. It's a Bixi bike, first built for the Bixi bike-sharing scheme in Mon-treal. They're now the mainstay of New York's CitiBike scheme, while in London they're painted red and called Boris bikes after the mayor who helped introduce them. They weigh 20 kg, about 43lb, and going up the Great Hill of Central Park, you can feel every ounce. I don't care. Bikes are freedom. And it beats the rush-hour subway train on which you breathe in someone's armpit.

The Central Park perimeter road is traffic-free and takes me up through the North Woods. The trees have shed their leaves now; it's late in the month. (In New York City the trees retain their colour well into November.) Every morning ride through the wood marks the calendar. In winter the trees are bare but for the brownish rem-nants of the year's foliage, and patches of snow linger on the verge.

Then as February rolls into March the daffodils appear, buds poking through the remaining snow, though the road still bears a grey film from the salt of winter. The seasons are changing but your hands are still frozen as you sweep down the far side of the Great Hill, past the Pool and across the Glenn Span Arch, a masterpiece of fitted stone. Later, in April, a green fuzz appears on the branches and then spring takes you by surprise in a blaze of white, blue and green. You do not see this if you take the subway. I am sure Thomas Stevens felt a sense of wonder as he rode into Constantinople on his penny-farthing. I feel one crossing the Great Hill on my way to work.

I felt that sense of wonder from the beginning. Sometime in the early 1960s my parents removed my beloved dark-blue tricycle with the little luggage boot on the back; it went, I suppose, to another family (or maybe ended up in the canal). I was taken to a shop to choose my first real bike. There was not much of a choice. I could have a red and white bike, or a light and dark blue one. I chose the blue. It was wheeled into the back garden and I was mounted on it and told to pedal. Of course I kept swaying in different directions. Then the day came when I rode down the garden for the first time without falling off. I was six; I am now over sixty, but nothing has entranced me the way that moment did. There was a sense of autonomy, of something achieved, of a barrier not so much broken as smashed to a thousand pieces.

My elder sister tried to knock me off my bike. We played a game called Nine Lives; we rode side by side and tried to steer each other into my father's rose bushes. I can see us doing that now, some 55 years ago, and the lawn and the sky and the trees and the roses are as bright as a restored Kodachrome.

*

There's some pedalling to do now. Once past the Pool, the ground rises and I twist the grip to get a lower gear. The North Meadow drifts past on the left; it's quiet now but in the spring there'll be basketball there, and brightly-coloured caps and vests. On my right looms the twin towers of 300 Central Park West, one of my favourite buildings in the city, and once home to Sinclair Lewis. More recent residents include Alec Baldwin, Faye Dunaway and Moby. Good luck to them; Irving Berlin once lived opposite me. New York's like that. The building's two huge Art Deco towers pass by framed by bare branches; in the spring they will be masked by vibrant white blossoms and in the fall by the flames of the dying year.

I know I'll see traffic here. There'll be the odd person who overtakes me on another CitiBike – of course they do, when you're in your 60s; once I would have raced them. And there's a man on a tandem who sweeps along with his six or seven-year-old on the back, a trailer behind for the groceries. He'll curve gracefully onto an exit somewhere on the Upper West Side near 96th St and drop his son off at kindergarten, and rejoin us on the Central Park circuit going south, overtaking me again somewhere near the Dakota Building. One or two Lycra louts also pass me by, heads down, ass-in-the-air, on custom-made road bikes built of the finest unobtainium.

When I see them, I think of my sister's bike. That was red and white, with a single gear when that wasn't fashionable, just cheaper and simpler to maintain. It had rod brakes. The brown plastic saddle was surprisingly comfortable. One day when my sister was in her teens, my parents bought her a better bike, a maroon Elswick Hopper with three speeds. The red-and-white bike was relegated to a country cottage on the moors in the West of England.

She still rode it sometimes, when we were on the moors in the spring or summer. One day when I was about 10, and she 15, she sat me on the saddle and I clung on behind her, legs spread wide to avoid the spokes, and we careered off down the narrow vertiginous country lanes on a late spring morning with the sun lancing through the fresh, bright new leaves. It was a Sunday and the church bells chimed as we shot through a village, and later we splashed through a ford near a chapel where people were preparing to worship, and they looked at us daggers drawn for our godlessness. Later, as I grew into my teens, I took over the red-and-white bike and darted through the lanes with their gravelled crowns and their high hedges that fell away now and then to reveal a valley of steep, bright-green fields and bracken-coated hills crowned with granite outcrops called tors, standing out against against blue skies lined with clean white clouds. Now and then one swept round a blind bend to find a car (the rod brakes worked surprisingly well, when one was frightened). More often one encountered the rumps of cattle on their way to milking, packed tight into the narrow lane, the sweet smell of their dung filling the air.

*

As I approach Columbus Circle the perimeter road sweeps round to the left, and just for a while there are cars with me in the park. I start paying attention, and prepare to cross the traffic stream for my exit into Seventh Avenue. The latter is wide and straight, and heads down to Times Square, which I can see in the distance. I'm headed for 46th St, which I will take across to Second Avenue. I go carefully here; three miles through Central Park has relaxed me but now I must remember than I am an infantryman in a tank battle. But I shan't let that stop me trying to catch every light. Once, just once, I got every single set on green and sailed down to Times Square in three or four minutes. But I mustn't forget the bitter lesson that every New York cyclist has learned at one time or another: Don't run a red unless you are very, very sure.

There are more bikes now, and I'm enjoying spotting the two-wheeled tribes of the city. There are a few of these. For definitions, I recommend Bike Snob's. Or, to give the official author's name, BikeSnobNYC. (It's his website. He does have a real name – it's Eben Weiss – but Bike Snob will do fine.) His book's title is *Bike Snob: Systematically & Mercilessly Realigning the World of Cycling*. Which he doesn't really because he has too much sense of humour.

Anyway, Bike Snob's classification is a masterpiece of Linnaean taxonomy. Let's start with the Urban Cyclist. S/he (it's usually a he) is a devotee of single-speed, fixed-wheel bikes, preferably with no brakes; large, impractical messenger bags; relentlessly casual clothing; and (though Bike Snob does not say this) a sort of sod-you mien which assures the rider that he is a rebel even if his destination is actually a merchant bank where he will shower, don a tie and defer to the senior analyst.

Am I an Urban Cyclist? I do worry about this.

"Urban Cyclists endlessly seek 'authenticity,' and are often fond of 'vintage' bicycle frames," rasps Bike Snob. However, he says, they're clearly not the original owners. So they're actually less authentic. Hang on though, Bike Snob, I ride a 45-year-old bike, and I'm authentic. Mind you, I actually am old enough to have ridden it new. One day an Urban Cyclist past me in Central Park, not far from Columbus Circle. "You're doing all right on that old bike," he said kindly. I explained that the combined age of bike and ride was 104. Still, I'm not an Urban Cyclist, because I don't ride a fixed-gear single-speed bike with narrow bars or carry a messenger bag. Neither do I have the ghastly road manners of the Urban Cyclist, who seems to consider all other traffic an excrescence and road rules an affront. Maybe I'm what Bike Snob calls a Retro-Grouch ("the Retro-Grouch always dwells approximately fifteen to twenty years in the past. This is because the Retro-Grouch has a passionate respect for the tried and true...".) This may fit me. I do prefer steel frames. I loathe integrated shifters and dislike indexed gears, both being a pain in the arse to repair and adjust.

The absolute limit, for me, are electric dérailleurs. I mean, just get a bloody car.

*

Today my CitiBike is taking me to work. But once upon a time a bike was an escape from hell.

At 13 I was packed off to a boarding school in North Oxford-shire, in the heart of England. Built in the 1850s, the school was basically a cut-price Hogwarts, without the magic. The dormitories were cold and the food indifferent. One of the vilest things about the school was the cadet force. As a young elite, we were being trained to run the Empire (which even then had slipped away). So we were expected to emerge from school with a basic military training. Every Thursday we would parade in full uniform in a windy playground and learn drill, and in the summer months we would bump through country lanes in the back of army Land Rov-ers to a firing range where we would learn to shoot with .303 rifles that had been obsolete in 1939 and whose recoil smashed back into your shoulder. Meanwhile the parades were the occasion for near constant screeching as some empowered 16-year-old, made an "NCO", would find fault with your webbing straps. I hated the place.

On Sunday morning there were two chapel services. You could

go at seven or you could go at nine. If you went at seven and had breakfast afterwards, you would get butter. If you went at nine and ate after that, you got margarine. A nasty, cheap value judgement on those who chose to get some sleep on a Sunday; God knew we got little of it for the rest of the week. But I went to early chapel, had my butter – and then slipped out of the school on my racing bike and hit the country lanes around the school.

In those years I acquired a love of the Middle English country-side; the gentle hills, hedgerows, woods and soft light, the hazy clouds drifting across the horizon, the winding roads and the sudden vistas, the ancient pre-Roman fort that rose above the fields near Banbury, the long quiet roads between sleepy country towns. Nearly 50 years on, I have random images. Riding across the Oxfordshire-Warwickshire border and feeling that the quality of the light had changed, that it was softer; an old man in a Mini, likely on his way to market, with collarless shirt, watch-chain and pork-pie hat; Land Rovers so well-used that they seemed to have merged with the countryside.

I had an Ordnance Survey map that became crinkled and creased with use. I would search it for the strange diagrams that told of an abandoned airfield, for there were still many of them then, a legacy of a war that had ended really not that long before. They will be gone now. Even then, some had been ploughed up; at others, a farmer's gate lay across the entrance. But sometimes you could ride onto the main runway and feel the ghosts all around you. At other times I would sweep up and down the rolling South Midland hills, through stone-built villages, past abandoned quarries or huge churches whose bells tolled on Sundays and whose sound lingered from village to village. For a few hours, the bleak aggression of school was forgotten.

I learned then that the bike has a special purpose. You need no

281

fuel, no-one's permission; you are gone. It is a way of saying, fuck you.

*

I rattle south down Seventh Avenue. I'm quite lucky with the lights today, but there's an Urban Cyclist who thinks I'm in his way. (I'm not. He seems to think I should ride into the back of a parked car rather than ride around it and make him do so too.) It's the usual obstacle course of yellow cabs pulling in, yellow cabs pulling out, beer trucks, somnambulent pedestrians staring at their phones, and people darting out between parked cars. (The beer trucks I do not mind. They do God's work.)

Bike Snob has plenty of other stereotypes for us besides Urban Cyclist and Retro-Grouch. I rather like what he calls the Beautiful Godzilla ("generally young, good-looking ...She's on her cell phone at all times..."). I give her a wide berth. In fact, I give a few things a wide berth. As Bike Snob says, all that's needed for you to be knocked flying is a driver trying "for half a second to retrieve a dropped McNugget."

I was reckless once. One day in the early 1980s a friend from Birmingham was staying with me in London and I spent the night drinking with him in the Ship and Shovel below Hungerford Bridge. Tossed out at closing time, we decided he should not take the Tube alone (my part of London was then dodgy at night). "Get on the saddle," I told him. He did so, and it promptly tipped back-wards; I kept the saddle loose so I could tip it forward when I stopped at the lights. Finally he got his balance and I drove us south across Waterloo Bridge and around the big roundabout at its base, along the South Bank, through the Vauxhall Cross and down South Lambeth Road without serious incident. I would not do it now. I have more sense of danger. In New York City the bike lanes have dedicated lights for bikes, designed to let you cross the junction when no-one's turning across your path. Jump those lights and they might be. Neither do I approve of what New York cyclists call 'salmoning' - going the wrong way up a street or bike lane like a salmon going upstream to spawn.

Here the main offenders, apart from Urban Cyclists, are the takeout delivery riders. These are a menace. Many ride electric bikes – not power-assisted pedelecs, which are legal in New York, but actual powered bikes, which were not until recently, but were widely tolerated. They weigh three times as much as an ordinary bike and are a lot faster. You do not want to meet them coming the wrong way. And yet I have a certain sympathy. The pizza delivery riders (a tribe Bike Snob doesn't talk of much) are at the bottom of the city anthill, striving to make a living in the cold and the heat, often born somewhere else, maybe undocumented, almost certainly uninsured.

One day I am riding north along the bike lane on First Avenue. It's a busy spring rush-hour and the lane is packed with Urban Cyclists, commuters on old road bikes, young women with full baskets and people like myself on CitiBikes. Ahead of me is a large young man on a very smart mountain-bike, dressed in the latest Lycra gear and brightly-coloured helmet. Suddenly a short, squat man of Asian appearance, with backward baseball cap and grimy anorak, appears around the corner ahead and charges towards us on an old mountain bike, not powered, the sort of old wreck the pizza guys use, with tape round its frame to guard against knocks. The two brake, feint to one side and another and nearly collide and then the large man blocks the Asian and screams at him "You're going the wrong way! You... Are... Going... The... Wrong... Way!" as if he were a drill sergeant and the Asian guy was a raw recruit who just shat the bed. I rode past. Dude, I thought, I hope you order in a pizza tonight and it comes late and cold, with a dead cockroach embedded in the cheese.

*

One tribe that Bike Snob does not discuss much is the Righteous Cyclist, who rides because it's a green thing to do, has a bike rescued from a dumpster and is convinced s/he is saving the world. Bike Snob does not seem to like them. He may be right. No-one loves the miasma of self-satisfaction that wafts around the righteous. And yet the fact is, they are on the right side of history.

British journalist Peter Walker's splendid 2017 book *Bike Nation: How Cycling Can Save the World* is an informative and readable guide to how bikes can do just that. Walker points out that the cyclist's emissions, for a start, are lower.

Of course cyclists do *have* emissions. Bikes are built of steel, or aluminium, or titanium, which takes energy to manufacture (unless you have a bamboo bike; still, that's not a big business just yet). And of course cyclists use extra energy, so consume more food, which takes up more land, and if they're on a healthy diet they're probably emitting quite a lot of methane as well. Still, Walker cites a 2011 study by the European Cyclists' Federation that factored in all of this (except perhaps the methane) and found that a cyclist emits 21g/Km of CO_2, against 101 per bus passenger and 271 per car passenger. Interestingly, e-bikes emitted only 1g/km more than bikes (though it's not clear how e-bikes are defined here). But Walker also quotes a US study that found e-bikes can be more efficient than rail.

And of course cycling is good for you.

"Along with lower weight, cycling brings astonishing improvements to cardiovascular health," says Walker, and reports a study in the north of England that found 32 regular cyclists had a "very significantly lower incidence of blocked arteries or other coronary obstructions." Mind you, this survey was from post-mortems, and some of those cyclists had perhaps been killed in traffic, as cyclists far too often are. Walker acknowledges the dangers but again, he marshals evidence; the health benefits outweigh the danger of cycling. This time he quotes a Utrecht University study that found the health benefits of cycling exceeded the danger of accidental death by nine to one. This was in the bike-friendly Netherlands, where bikes are often separated from other traffic. Even in more dangerous Britain, however, "the life-extending benefits were greater by a factor of seven." Walker does not say how the comparators were defined; after all, a non-cyclist need not be unfit. But it's true there's widespread evidence that the health benefits of regular cycling outweigh the dangers of accidents and pollution.

In fact, bikes can make you better. The exercise releases endorphins, gets your weight down, strengthens your heart and, maybe just as important, it makes you feel more optimistic about yourself. "In an age where there's a pill for everything, exercise is the billion dollar drug that never gets prescribed," says one cyclist, Phil Southerland, who took up cycling and found it greatly helped with Type 1 diabetes.

He's quoted in a rather nice book by Anna Hughes, called *Pedal Power: Inspirational Stories from the World of Cycling* (2017). Hughes teaches cycling, repairs bikes and writes for a living, and has cycled around the coast of Britain and down its length. She quotes a couple of stories like this – the most astonishing being that of Dr Nan Little, who turned to cycling as a treatment for Parkinson's and saw a very marked improvement in her condition. She took to bikes as part of a trial treatment programme run by a Dr Jay Alberts, who says that vigorous cycling increases brain function and this seems to ease the symptoms.

*

Of course, some of this is in your head. But it's no less real for that.

Cycling really *is* inspirational. As mentioned, Hughes's book tells us how bikes have made people better. But she has much else to tell, and this is a delightful book to dip into, or keep by your bed, or to read when the world seems dull. Hughes tells us (for example) of the Women's Rescue League of America, which at the end of the 19th century warned that cycling was unladylike and unchristian and could cause both infertility and sexual satisfaction (they thought the latter evil).

They had opposition. Hughes quotes one Ann Strong, writing in the *Minneapolis Tribune* in 1895: "Bicycles are just as good company as most husbands, and when they get shabby or old a woman can dispose of it and get a new one without shocking the whole community." Meanwhile in Britain two years earlier, a 16-year-old called Tessie Reynolds had ridden from Brighton to London and back in just eight and a half hours. Moreover she did it in pantaloons, to the horror of some. But the die was cast. The new safety bicycle was a liberation, and women did not intend to be left out.

Annie Kopchovsky wasn't, anyway. Hughes records that this mother-of-three set off from Boston in June 1894 to win a bet by cycling around the world. Rechristening herself Annie Londonderry, she left home, says Hughes, with a change of clothes and a pearl-handled revolver, riding a Columbia women's bike weighing a stonking 42lb, very nearly as much as a CitiBike.

She had a bit of a false start; the Columbia was too heavy and after riding it to Chicago, she swapped it for a 21lb Sterling and started back the other way. From then on she was in business. "Bold, charismatic and beautiful, she captured the imagination of the world's press," writes Hughes. "She was often dressed head to toe in ribbons advertising anything from milk to perfume." She won her bet.

Men have never had it their own way in the cycling world. Hughes talks too of Eileen Sheridan, who in 1954 smashed her way from Land's End to John o' Groats in just two days, 11 hours and seven minutes. It is 870 miles. Sheridan kept riding to make it the round 1,000 miles, which she did in three days and an hour. Hughes inspired me to find out more about Sheridan; now 97, she was just 4ft 1in and famous for the gusto with which she rode – pictures show her wearing a big, cheerful grin on her bike. The 1,000-mile record stood until 2002. Sheridan's London to Edinburgh record has, to this day, not been beaten. The 1,000-mile bike rests today in Coventry Transport Museum. One day I shall go there, and stand before it in awe.

There is much more to inspire in Hughes's likable book. Not least the story of Rob Holden, who decided to ride up Mont Ventoux on the London version of the CitiBike (it is, in fact, the same bike). Mont Ventoux is in the South of France; it is 6,000ft-plus (just under 2,000 metres) and has tortured many a rider on the Tour de France; indeed it killed at least one (the great British cyclist Tommy Simpson). Did Holden succeed? The answer's in Hughes's book.

*

This November morning I'm on much the same bike as Holden was, but my more modest journey is nearly over. I've made it down Seventh Avenue nearly to Times Square, and it's time for me to steer for the East Side. I swing into 46th Street, which crosses Park Avenue just where the latter vanishes under the buildings to make its bifurcated way past Grand Central Station. Today the junction's busy and I pause for a while; it's quite cold. Nowadays the cold affects my hands; even in mittens they become numb.

As a young man I had no fear of the cold. In 1985 I was a traffic broadcaster for the motoring organization, the RAC, and sometimes worked an early shift, with my first broadcast at 5.30 or so. The tube trains were not reliable enough at that hour, so I rode in the three or four miles from Stockwell on my bike. In summer this could be a wonderful journey, free of traffic, passing along the Lambeth Embankment and across Lambeth Bridge and seeing the Palace of Westminster mirrored perfectly in the Thames in the calm of the morning. But January 1985 was very bad. I borrowed bright-blue salopettes from my cousin and disinterred an old pair of high-heeled cowboy boots that had been fashionable some years before; I also wore a balaclava with a narrow space for the eyes. I looked like a Ruritanian paratrooper on his way to commit a burglary.

Here in New York I mostly find a leather jacket and jeans sufficient; only when it dips below 40 deg F will I need an outer coat. But sometimes when it is very cold, the ride has its rewards. One bitter evening in mid-December 2016 I was a little late leaving the office, and found myself the only person riding north through the darkness of Central Park. I breathed deeply as I struggled up the hill towards the reservoir. Then I came out on the long stretch past the Guggenheim; it was deserted, but a huge full moon had risen over the Upper East Side and was flooding the world with gold, and the frost on the surface, the snow and the ice glistened like jewels in the half-light.

*

When spring does come, I may ride both ways, using either of my two road bikes. One's a Fuji that is light and well-made but has somehow never charmed me. And there is my Panasonic.

Bike maintenance has its nice side; in a warm garage on a chilly night, for instance, adjusting things while listening to the radio and dreaming of rides in the spring to come; or making things work when they didn't before. Here in New York City, though, there's no garage and I must get the bikes up on the roof of our brownstone, where there's a hose to wash them. The Fuji's indexed gears need careful adjustment, with the bike on a chainstay stand, and I'll clean and oil the chain. (Not sure quite what to use for this, I once googled "chains and lubrication", but what I found had little to do with bikes.)

The Panasonic Villager, with its friction gearchange, is easier, and after 12 years I still find it a delight. It weighs in at 34lb – not bad for 1973, when it was built, but heavy now. But it always feels faster, with its smooth steel frame and good-tempered gears. The freewheel, oddly, is in the bottom bracket, not on the rear wheel, so that one stops pedalling and the chain continues to move. It was meant to make slow-speed gearchanges easier and it does, but it never caught on.

My first proper road bike was a Carlton Corsa that I got in the early 1970s when I was 15. That summer a friend and I rode across country from Banbury in the Midlands to the north-west tip of Wales. Snowdonia was steep and beautiful and yet it is not the mountains I remember, but a very long day's right across the Marches, that great long stretch of Shropshire and other counties that most English people barely know, yet has a quiet beauty and remoteness. We crossed a series of hills and valleys, following a tangled skein of narrow lanes through half-forgotten villages, past farmhouses where black-and-white collies lay in wait between the gateposts, seemingly asleep but springing up as we passed and barking and chasing off the wheeled invaders. It was a soft overcast day of deep greens and greys. Even now, nearly 50 years later, that day is somehow England in my mind.

But the ride of my life was somewhere else, far away. In 1992 I went to Bhutan, the small kingdom in the Eastern Himalayas. I was to work as a development volunteer. I stayed for two and a half years and was eventually very happy there, but the first few months were not so good; the other volunteers were clannish and withdrawn, the (English) head of the project did not seem pleased to see me there and the monsoon season was closing in, making me feel trapped in the narrow Thimphu Valley.

Most of all, I wanted a bike. I have never felt right without one. A fellow-volunteer down on the Indian border heard about this and got a friend to bring one from the nearest large Indian city, Siliguri. It was a Hero Hawk, a five-speed racing bike built in the Punjab, and it looked very smart in its red and white paintwork. It also weighed a ton and, although of good quality, had not been assembled properly. The handlebars moved around, the gear cable was too short and the pedals started to fall apart. Bit by bit I dealt with all this.

That year, the monsoon lasted a month longer than usual. Then at the end of October, it was as if a tap had been turned off. Suddenly it was warm and bright, and pleasantly cool at night. One day I decided to ride up the road that led to Dochula, the pass into Central Bhutan. I did not plan to reach the pass itself, which was some 20 miles away and was at over 10,000ft (3,000m), a climb of some 3,000ft from Thimphu. The road to the pass was the main East-West road that links the country together, but to an outsider it looked like a country lane; there was barely room for two cars to pass, and one of them would usually pull in. Yet the very presence of the lateral road, as it is called, was a triumph in such a landscape, rising and falling through immense elevations and clinging to steep, unstable terrain. It had been built by the Indian military. Until 1962 there had been no paved roads in Bhutan at all.

I began my climb slowly; there was little traffic; to my left the mountainside rose steeply, covered in pines and carpeted by pine-needles, and there was a fresh, heady scent. To my right the ground fell away increasingly suddenly as I climbed, until the isolated farmhouses in the valley below were dots in the variegated land-scape, surrounded by poplar-like trees and intricate terraces of rice paddies, the latter bare now although some would soon be planted to winter wheat. Bit by bit I climbed until I realised suddenly that I was not so very far from the pass, and after two hours or so I came out on the clear patch of land on the summit, beside a long prayer-wall, surrounded by prayer-flags. Ahead of me lay a sight such that I had never seen before, and shan't again; the whole of central Bhu-tan spread out before me in the clear afternoon sun, the Himalayas rising above it, and in the distance to the left the long line of snow-peaks that marked the border with Tibet. The eternal snows. A lit-tle nearer was a huge mountain with a strangely square shape; this was Masangang, at nearly 23,500ft (about 7,100m) one of the great peaks of the earth.

I stayed for two hours. Then it was getting dark. I had no lights that worked, and besides I should not have wanted to make the descent without daylight. Reluctantly I swung away back down towards Thimphu. I picked up speed as the light began to fade, pushing my luck on the sharp mountain bends, mindful of the weak pressed-steel brakes. A frantic journey brought me to the only decent straight stretch, some five miles from Thimphu; here I released the brakes and shot forward with the wind in my hair, and

I was laughing.

After that I was happy in Bhutan.

*

Now there are only the concrete canyons of Manhattan. I bump and rumble over the broken road, mindful of manhole covers that are not flush with the road (and are lethal when wet), construction barriers, potholes with savage little lips to them, opening car doors, sleepwalkers in the cross walk, dogs on long leads, the elderly, the distracted and the plain rude. A dog-leg down Lexington, past the great marble post office at Grand Central and left into 44th Street, then down to First Avenue and prepare to dock in the long CitiBike stand between Tudor City and the United Nations. The UN itself looms all large and dull glass, the flags outside it flapping in the wind; in the summer they hang dispirited in the still, muggy air. The sky over the East River is light grey, variegated, with fast-moving clouds.

I push the bike into one of the last empty stands; there is a click and a green LED tells me it is docked. Freedom, for now, is over. I will reclaim it in the evening, when I will put my key in the slot and sweep away up First Avenue.

If I have the energy. I am quite old now, and maybe tonight I will go by subway. Those rides across Shropshire, or up a Himalayan pass, are a dream; in a few years, perhaps, I shan't ride a bike at all. I don't know how I will deal with that. We all have things that make life worthwhile because we love them, in effect, more than we would care for life in itself. I suppose that for me, bikes have filled that role since that sense of wonder when I first realised, aged six, that I could stay upright.

I wonder what images will come to me in the last hours of my life. Drifting through Central Park on a spring morning, surrounded by flowers, or on a winter night bathed in moonlight. Flying through green lanes under a soft grey sky past farm gates with barking collies, or zipping through a shallow ford between high hedges under a bright blue sky with high white clouds, the water droplets from the wheels catching the morning sun. Looking for a last time towards the ramparts of Tibet before climbing back aboard a red-and-white bike and sweeping back down round curve after curve in the gathering twilight, hauling back on the brakes, laughing. Or a Kodachrome vision in primary colours, of a six-year-old boy in an Aertex shirt and leather sandals, tottering through the garden on a small blue bike on a bright green lawn, past lines of vivid roses.

Bibliography

Adenauer, K. (1966): *Memoirs 1945-1953* (Washington DC, USA: Regnery Publishing).

Aitkenhead, D. (2012): *JK Rowling: The worst that can happen is that everyone says, That's shockingly bad* (In: *The Guardian*, September 21 2012).

Allingham, M. (1923): *Blackkerchief Dick* (London, UK: Hodder and Stoughton).

Allingham, M. (1930): *Mystery Mile* (Norwich, UK: Jarrolds Publishing).

Allingham, M. (1929): *The Crime at Black Dudley* (Norwich, UK: Jarrolds Publishing).

Allingham, M. (1952): *The Tiger in the Smoke* (London, UK: Chatto & Windus).

Amis, K. (1986): *The Old Devils* (London, UK: Hutchinson).

Amis, K. (1991): *We Are All Guilty* (London, UK: Puffin Books).

Arendt, H. (1943, 2007): *Stefan Zweig: Jews in the World of Yesterday* (In: *Reflections on Literature and Culture*, pp58-68. Stanford: Stanford University Press).

Athill, D. (2016): *Alive, Alive Oh!* (London, UK: Granta Books).

Athill, D. (1963): *Instead of a Letter* (London: Chatto & Windus).

Athill, D. (1993): *Make Believe: A True Story* (London, UK: Sinclair-Stevenson).

Athill, D. (2008): *Somewhere Towards the End* (London, UK: Granta Books).

Athill, D. (2001): *Stet: An Editor's Life* (New York, USA: Grove Press).

Averroës (Ibn Rushd) (c. 1190): *On the Harmony of Religions and Philosophy* (London, UK: Dodo Press).

Baudrillard, J. (1994): *The Illusion of the End* (Redwood City, USA: Stanford University Press).

Bennett, A. (1968): *Forty Years On* (London, UK: Faber & Faber, 1985).

Bike Snob (2010): *Bike Snob: Systematically & Mercilessly Realigning the World of Cycling* (New York, USA: Chronicle Books).

Bloxham, D. Arnall (1958): *Who Was Ann Ockenden?* (London, UK: Neville Spearman).

Böll, H. (1957): *The Bread of Those Early Years* (London, UK: Arco Publications).

Carey, L. (2012): *The Escape Artist: The Death and Life of Stefan Zweig* (In: The New Yorker, August 20 2012).

Casson, S. (1937): *Progress and Catastrophe: An Anatomy of Human Adventure* (New York, USA: Harper & Brothers).

Chalmers, R. (2011): *Putting the world to rights: Trevor Griffiths on Olivier's dope-smoking, Marxist ranting and his 20-year purgatory* (In: *The Independent*, October 23 2011).

Chandler, R. (1944): *The Simple Art of Murder* (In: *The Atlantic Monthly*, December 1944).

Cheshire, L. (1943): *Bomber Pilot* (London, UK: Hutchinson).

Chisholm, A. (1998): *Rumer Godden: A Storyteller's Life* (London, UK: Macmillan).

Christie, A. (1977): *Agatha Christie: An Autobiography* (London, UK: Collins).

Christie, A. (1934): *Murder on the Orient Express* (London, UK: Collins Crime Club).

Christie, A. (1973): *Postern of Fate* (London, UK: Collins Crime Club).

Christie, A. (1920): *The Mysterious Affair at Styles* (New York, USA: John Lane).

Christie, A. (1922): *The Secret Adversary* (London, UK: The Bodley Head).

Cole, G.D.H. (1921): *Guild Socialism – A Plan for Economic Democracy* (New York, USA: Frederick A. Stokes Company).

Cole, G.D.H. (1932): *Some Essentials of Socialist Propaganda* (London, UK: The Fabian Society).

Collins, L. (2012): *Mail Supremacy: The Newspaper That Rules Britain* (In: *The New Yorker*, March 26 2012).

Collins, W. (1868): *The Moonstone* (London, UK: Tinsley Brothers).

Curie, È. (1943): *Journey Among Warriors* (New York, USA: Double-day, Doran and Co.).

Curie, È. (1937): *Madame Curie: A Biography* (New York, USA: Dou-bleday, Doran and Co.).

De Havilland, G. (1961): *Sky Fever: The Autobiography of Sir Geoffrey De Havilland* (London, UK: Hamish Hamilton).

Deedes, W. (2007): *The Real Scoop: Who was in Waugh's Cast List and Why* (In: *The Daily Telegraph*, May 28 2003).

Diamond, J. (2005): *Collapse: How Societies Choose to Fail or Succeed* (New York, USA: Viking Press).

Dimbleby, R. (1943): *The Frontiers are Green* (London, UK: Hodder & Stoughton).

Dimbleby, R. (1944): *The Waiting Year* (London, UK: Hodder & Stoughton).

Dobson, C, Miller, J. and R. Payne (1979): *The Cruellest Night* (London, UK: Hodder & Stoughton).

Donahue, A. (1942): *Tally-Ho! Yankee in a Spitfire* (London, UK: Macmillan).

Donahue, A. (1943): *Last Flight from Singapore* (London, UK: Mac-millan).

Drayton, J. (2008): *Ngaio Marsh: Her Life in Crime* (London, UK: HarperCollins).

Du Maurier, D. (1977) *Myself When Young* (New York, USA: Dou-bleday).

Eden, A. (1976): *Another World, 1897-1917* (London, UK: Double-day).

Eliot, T.S. (1942): *Little Gidding* (London, UK: Faber & Faber).

Eliot, T.S. (1925): *The Hollow Men* (In: *Poems: 1909-1925*, London, UK: Faber & Faber).

Farquharson, J. (1987): *'Emotional but Influential': Victor Gollancz, Richard Stokes and the British Zone of Germany, 1945-1949* (In: *Journal of Contemporary History* 22 (3), 501-519).

Farquharson, J. (1993): *The British Occupation of Germany 1945-6: A Badly Managed Disaster Area?* (In: *German History* 1993, 11:3).

Fisk, R. (1990): *Pity the Nation* (Oxford, UK: Oxford University

Press).

Frost, R. (1920): *Fire and Ice* (In: *Harper's Magazine* 142).

Forster, E.M. (1924): *A Passage to India* (London, UK: Edward Arnold).

Frank, M. (2006): *The New Morality – Victor Gollancz, Save Europe Now and the German Refugee Crisis, 1945-1946* (In: *Twentieth Century British History*, 17:2).

Gadol, T. (Ed.) (1982): *Rationality and Science: A Memorial Volume for Moritz Schlick in Celebration of the Centennial of His Birth* (Vienna, Austria: Springer Verlag).

Gibbons, S. (1932): *Cold Comfort Farm* (London, UK: Longmans).

Gibran, K. (1933) *Pity the Nation* (In: *The Garden of the Prophet*, New York, USA: Alfred A. Knopf).

Gibson, G. (1946): *Enemy Coast Ahead* (London, UK: Michael Joseph).

Godden, J. and Godden, R. (1966): *Two Under the Indian Sun* (New York, USA: Alfred Knopf).

Godden, R. (1989): *A House with Four Rooms* (London, UK: Macmillan).

Godden, R. (1987): *A Time to Dance, No Time to Weep* (London, UK: Macmillan).

Godden, R. (1939): *Black Narcissus* (London, UK: Peter Davies).

Godden, R. (1936): *Chinese Puzzle* (London, UK: Macmillan).

Godden, R. (1991): *Coromandel Sea Change* (London, UK: Macmillan).

Godden, R. (1997): *Cromartie vs. the God Shiva* (London, UK: Pan Macmillan).

Godden, R. (1969): *In This House of Brede* (London, UK: Macmillan).

Godden, R. (1953): *Kingfishers Catch Fire* (London, UK: Macmillan).

Godden, R. (1943): *Rungli-Rungliot* (London, UK: Peter Davies).

Godden, R. (1981): *The Dark Horse* (London, UK: Macmillan).

Godden, R. (1958): *The Greengage Summer* (London, UK: Macmillan).

Godden, R. (1937): *The Lady and the Unicorn* (London, UK: Peter Davies).

Godden, R. (1946): *The River* (London, UK: Michael Joseph).

Gollancz, V. (1947): *Germany Revisited* (London, UK: Victor Gollancz).

Gollancz, V. (1947): *In Darkest Germany* (London, UK: Victor Gollancz).

Gollancz, V. (1942): *Let My People Go: Some practical proposals for dealing with Hitler's massacre of the Jews and an appeal to the British public* (London, UK: Victor Gollancz).

Gollancz, V. (1945): *What Buchenwald Really Means* (London, UK: Victor Gollancz).

Goodyear, D. (2012): *Raw Deal* (In: *The New Yorker*, April 23 2012).

Gore, A. (2013): *The Future: Six Drivers of Global Change* (New York, USA: Random House)

Grass, G. (2003): *Crabwalk* (Boston, USA: Houghton Mifflin Harcourt).

Grass, G. (1961): *The Tin Drum* (New York, USA: Random House).

Gray, J. (2007): *Black Mass: Apocalyptic Religion and the Death of Utopia* (New York, USA: Farrar, Straus and Giroux).

Greene, G. (1938) *Brighton Rock* (London, UK: Williem Heinemann).

Greene, G. (1961): *In Search of a Character: Two African Journals* (London, UK: The Bodley Head).

Greene, G. (1932): *Stamboul Train* (London, UK: William Heinemann).

Harding, S. (1986): *The Science Question in Feminism* (Ithaca, USA: Cornell University Press).

Harris, M. (1986): *Sorry, You've Been Duped! The Truth Behind Classic Mysteries of the Paranormal* (London, UK: Weidenfeld & Nicolson).

Hastings, M. (2004): *A Very English Hypocrite* (In: *The Daily Telegraph*, May 9 2004).

Heller, J. (1961): *Catch-22* (New York, USA: Simon & Schuster).

Herrick, L. (2008): *The Mystery of the Crime Writer* (In: *The New Zealand Herald*, August 23 2008).

Hill, S. (1983): *The Woman in Black* (London, UK: Hamish Hamilton).

Hillary, R. (1942): *The Last Enemy* (London, UK: Macmillan).

Hiscock, E. (1977): *The Bells of Hell Go Ting-A-Ling-Ling: An Autobiographical Fragment Without Maps* (London, UK: Arlington Books).

Higgins, P. (2014): *Hidden History of Midcoast Maine* (Charleston, South Carolina, USA: The History Press).

Hofmann, M. (2010): *Vermicular Dither* (In: *London Review of Books*, January 28 2010).

Hofstadter, R. (1963): *Anti-Intellectualism in American Life* (New York, USA: Alfred A. Knopf).

Holden, A. (1971) *This Was Your Life* (In: *The Sunday Times Magazine*, May 2 1971).

Hollingworth, C. (1991): *Front Line* (London, UK: Jonathan Cape).

Horowitz, J. (2017): *In Italian Schools, Reading, Writing and Recognizing Fake News* (In: *The New York Times*, October 18 2017).

Hughes, A. (2017): *Pedal Power: Inspirational Stories from the World of Cycling* (Chichester, UK: Summersdale).

Iverson, J. (1977) *More Lives Than One? The Evidence of the Remarkable Bloxham Tapes* (London, UK: Pan Books).

Jack, I. (2017): *Waugh's Beast is back, still satirising those who make England so febrile* (In: *The Guardian*, July 29 2017).

James, P.D. (1980): *Innocent Blood* (London, UK: Faber & Faber).

James, P.D. (2013): *Who Killed the Golden Age of Crime?* (In: *The Spectator*, December 14 2013).

Jamkowski, M. (2005): *Ghost Ship Found* (In: *National Geographic*, February 2005).

Johnstone, D. (2012): *The Casual Vacancy, by JK Rowling* (In: *The Independent*, September 29 2012).

Jones, T. (2011): *The Great Fleet Street Novel* (In: *The New York Times*, July 28 2011).

Julian of Norwich (1373, 1670): *Revelations of Divine Love* (1901 edition, London: Methuen & Co.).

Kakutani, M. (2012): *Darkness and Death, No Magic to Help* (In: *The New York Times*, September 27 2012).

Kaye, M.M. (1978): *The Far Pavilions* (London, UK: Allen Lane).

Klein, D. (1919): *With the Chinks* (London, UK: John Lane).

Klein, J. (2018): *Michael Lewis Wonders Who's Really Running the Government* (In: *The New York Times,* October 8 2018).

Knowles, C. (2014): *Germany 1945-1949: a case study in post-conflict reconstruction* (In: *History and Policy,* January 29 2014).

Knowles, C. (2017): *Winning the Peace: The British in Occupied Germany, 1945-1948* (London, UK: Bloomsbury Academic).

Kuhn, T. (1962): *The Structure of Scientific Revolutions* (Chicago, USA: University of Chicago Press).

Lezard, N. (2009): *The World of Yesterday* by Stefan Zweig (In: *The Guardian,* December 4 2009).

Lewis, M. (2018): *The Fifth Risk* (New York, USA: W.W. Norton & Co.).

Lewis, N. (2003): *The Tomb in Seville: Crossing Spain on the Brink of Civil War* (London, UK: Jonathan Cape).

Lilla, M. (2016): *The Shipwrecked Mind: On Political Reaction* (New York, USA: New York Review Books).

Lodge, D. (2011) *Obituary: Sir Kingsley Amis* (In: *The Independent,* October 23 2011).

Lomborg, B. (2001) *The Skeptical Environmentalist* (Cambridge, UK: Cambridge University Press).

London, C. (1921): *The Book of Jack London* (two volumes) (New York, USA: The Century Co.).

London, J. (1908): *The Iron Heel* (New York, USA: Macmillan).

London, J. (1914): *The Mutiny of the Elsinore* (New York, USA: Macmillan).

London, J. (1904): *The Sea-Wolf* (New York, USA: Macmillan).

Lucas, C. (2015): *Honourable Friends?: Parliament and the Fight for Change* (London, UK: Portobello Books).

Maclean, F. (1978): *Take Nine Spies* (London, UK: Macmillan).

Mann, T. (1927): *The Magic Mountain* (New York, USA: Alfred A. Knopf).

Manning, F. (1930): *Her Privates We,* also published as *The Middle Parts of Fortune* (London, UK: Peter Davies).

Marley, D. (1933): *The Brown Book of the Hitler Terror and the Burning of the Reichstag* (London, UK: Victor Gollancz).

Marsh, N. (1934): *A Man Lay Dead* (London, UK: Geoffrey Bles).

Marsh, N. (1938): *Artists in Crime* (London, UK: Geoffrey Bles).

Marsh, N. (1965): *Black Beech and Honeydew* (London, UK: Collins; revised edition 1981, also by Collins).

Marsh, N. (1943): *Colour Scheme* (London, UK: Collins Crime Club).

Marsh, N. (1945): *Died in the Wool* (In: *Wagga Wagga Daily Advertiser*, Wagga Wagga, Australia, as a serial; first book edition in 1946 by Collins Crime Club, London, UK).

Marsh, N. (1982): *Light Thickens* (London, UK: Collins Crime Club).

Matuschek, O. (2013): *Three Lives: A Biography of Stefan Zweig* (London, UK: Pushkin Press).

Miller, H. (1934) *Tropic of Cancer* (Paris, France: Obelisk Press).

Moir, J. (2012): *Where's the magic in this tale of middle-class monsters? First review of J.K. Rowling's VERY grown-up novel* (In: *Daily Mail*, September 26 2012).

Monteil, C. (2016) *Ève Curie: L'autre fille de Pierre et Marie Curie* (Paris, France: Odile Jacob).

Moorhouse, R. (2018): *Ship of Fate* (London, UK: Sharpe Books).

Murdoch, I. (1966): *The Time of the Angels* (London, UK: Chatto & Windus).

Naipaul, V.S. (1975): *Guerillas* (London, UK: André Deutsch).

Newby, E. (1956): *The Last Grain Race* (London, UK: Secker & Warburg).

Nichols, T. (2017): *The Death of Expertise: The Campaign Against Established Knowledge and Why It Matters* (New York, USA: Oxford University Press USA).

O'Neill, M. (2014): *The Chinese Labour Corps* (Melbourne, Australia: Penguin).

Oreskes, N. (2004): *Science and public policy: what's proof got to do with it?* (In: *Environmental Science & Policy* 7: 369–383).

Orwell, G. (1947): *As I Please* (In: Tribune, January 17 1947).

Orwell, G. (1938): *Homage to Catalonia* (London, UK: Secker & Warburg).

Orwell, G. (1940): *Inside the Whale and Other Essays* (London, UK: Victor Gollancz).

Orwell, G. (1940): *Prophecies of Fascism* (In: *Tribune*, July 12 1940).

Orwell, G. (1949): *Reflections on Gandhi* (In: *Partisan Review*, January 1949).

Orwell, G. (1946): *The Decline of the English Murder* (In: *Tribune*, February 15 1946).

Pielke, R. (2004) When scientists politicize science: making sense of controversy over *The Skeptical Environmentalist* (In: *Environmental Science & Policy* 7: 405-417).

Pincher, C. (1965): *Not With a Bang* (New York, USA: Dutton).

Priestley, J.B. (1946): *Bright Day* (London, UK: William Heinemann).

Priestley, J.B. (1934): *English Journey* (London, UK: William Heinemann).

Priestley, J.B. (1962): *Margin Released* (London, UK: William Heinemann).

Priestley, J.B. (1933): *Wonder Hero* (London, UK: William Heinemann).

Prince, C. J. (2013): *Death in the Baltic* (New York, USA: St Martin's Press).

Prochnik, G. (2017): *When It's Too Late to Stop Fascism, According to Stefan Zweig* (In: *The New Yorker*, February 6 2017).

Ranfurly, H. (1994): *To War with Whitaker: The Wartime Diaries of the Countess of Ranfurly 1939–1945* (London, UK: William Heinemann).

Rivaz, R.C. (1943): *Tail Gunner* (Norwich, UK: Jarrolds).

Rivaz, R.C. (1945): *Tail Gunner Takes Over* (Norwich, UK: Jarrolds).

Roberts, Earl F. (1897): *Forty-One Years in India* (London, UK: R. Bentley).

Rowling, J.K. (2012): *The Casual Vacancy* (New York, USA: Little, Brown & Co.).

Russell, B. (1945): *A History of Western Philosophy* (New York, USA: Simon & Schuster).

Sayer, R. (1984): *Method in Social Science: A Realist* Approach (London, UK: Hutchinson).

Sayers, D. (1934): *The Nine Tailors* (London, UK: Victor Gollancz).

Sayers, D. (1928): *The Unpleasantness at the Bellona Club* (London,

UK: Ernest Benn).

Sayers, D. (1923): *Whose Body?* (London, UK: T. Fisher Unwin).

Schlick, M. (1925): *General Theory of Knowledge* (Vienna, Austria: Springer-Verlag).

Schwartz, A. (2016): *The Curious Case of Dorothy Sayers & the Jew Who Wasn't There* (In: *moment*, July-August 2016).

Scott, P. (1966): *The Jewel in the Crown* (London, UK: William Heinemann).

Sebald, W. G. (2003): *On the Natural History of Destruction* (London, UK: Hamish Hamilton).

Sellwood, A. and P. Haining (1964): *Devil Worship in Britain* (London, UK: Corgi).

Sellwood, A.V. (1973): *The Damned Don't Drown* (London, UK: Allan Wingate).

Semeonoff, A. (1933): *Brush Up Your Russian* (Philadelphia, USA: David McKay Publications).

Sokal, A. (1996): *Transgressing the Boundaries: Toward a Transformative Hermeneutics Of Quantum Gravity* (In: *Social Text* 46/47: 217-252).

Spengler, O. (1926): *The Decline of the West* (London, UK: Allen & Unwin).

Spiegel, R. (2019): *Renia's Diary: A Holocaust Journal* (New York, USA: St Martin's Press).

Starritt, A. (2017): *The Beast* (London, UK: Head of Zeus).

Steinbeck, J. (1942): *Bombs Away* (New York, USA: Viking Press).

Steinbeck, J. (1942): *The Moon is Down* (New York, USA: Viking Press).

Stevenson, J. (2006) *Queen of Crime* (In: *The Guardian*, August 19 2006).

Sullivan, M. B. (1979): *Thresholds of Peace* (London, UK: Hamish Hamilton).

Swain, J.F. (2001): *'His Own Privacy' – Frederic Manning: A Critical and Historical Analysis* (Glasgow, UK: PhD Dissertation submitted to the Dept. of English Literature, University of Glasgow).

Tainter, J. (1988): *The Collapse of Complex Societies* (Cambridge, UK: Cambridge University Press).

Toynbee, A. (1934-1961): *A Study of History* (12 volumes) (Oxford, UK: Oxford University Press).

Tuchman, M. (2010): *Remember: My Stories of Survival and Beyond* (Jerusalem, Israel: Yad Vashem).

Villiers, A. (1929): *Falmouth for Orders: The Story of the Last Clipper Ship Race Round Cape Horn* (New York, USA: Henry Holt & Co).

Villiers, A. (1965): *The Battle of Trafalgar* (New York, USA: Macmillan).

Wakefield, A. et al (1998): *Ileal-lymphoid-nodular hyperplasia, non-specific colitis, and pervasive developmental disorder in children* (In: *The Lancet* 351 no. 9103: 637–41; later retracted by journal).

Walker, P. (2017): *Bike Nation: How Cycling Can Save the World* (London, UK: Yellow Jersey).

Wall, D. (2014): *The World I Lost: A Memoir of Peace and War* (UK: Sortium Ltd.)

Watson, C. (2009) *Snobbery With Violence: English Crime Stories and Their Audience* (London, UK: Faber & Faber).

Waugh, E. (1938): *Scoop* (London, UK: Chapman & Hall).

West, Dame R. (1941): *Black Lamb and Grey Falcon: A Journey Through Yugoslavia* (London, UK: Macmillan).

West, Dame R. (1918): *The Return of the Soldier* (New York, USA: The Century Company).

West, E. (2015): *The Uber generation won't stand for the BBC – but it's still a national treasure* (In: *The Spectator*, November 12 2015).

Wilson, I. (1982): *Reincarnation?* (London, UK: Penguin Books).

Žižek, S. (2016): *Against the Double Blackmail: Refugees, Terror and Other Troubles with the Neighbours* (London, UK: Allen Lane).

Zweig, A. (1947): *The Axe of Wandsbeck* (New York, USA: Viking Press).

Zweig, S. (2016): *Messages from a Lost World: Europe on the Brink* (London, UK: Pushkin Press).

Zweig, S. (1913): *Burning Secret* (London, UK: George Allen & Unwin).

Zweig, S. (1943): *The World of Yesterday* (New York, USA: Viking Press).

www.ingramcontent.com/pod-product-compliance
Lightning Source LLC
Chambersburg PA
CBHW022004080426
42733CB00007B/472